All archaeological sites have been abandoned, but people abandoned sites in many different ways, and for different reasons. What they did when leaving a settlement, structure, or activity area had a direct effect on the kind and quality of the cultural remains entering the archaeological record – for example whether tools were removed, destroyed, or buried in the ground, and building structures dismantled or left standing.

The chapters, in this first volume to examine abandonment as a stage in the formation of an archaeological site, use ethnoarchaeological and archaeological data from many areas of the world: North and South America, Europe, Africa, and the Near East. They describe the many complex factors surrounding abandonment across entire regions and within settlement areas, and make an important theoretical and methodological contribution to this area of archaeological investigation.

Abandonment of settlements and regions

NEW DIRECTIONS IN ARCHAEOLOGY

Editors

Françoise Audouze
Centre de Recherches Archéologiques, Meudon, France

Richard Bradley
Department of Archaeology, University of Reading

Joan Gero
Department of Anthropology, University of South Carolina

Tim Murray
Department of Archaeology, La Trobe University, Victoria, Australia

Colin Renfrew
Department of Archaeology, University of Cambridge

Andrew Sherratt
Department of Antiquities, Ashmolean Museum, Oxford

Timothy Taylor
Department of Archaeology, University of Bradford

Norman Yoffee
Department of Anthropology, University of Arizona

Wendy Ashmore
Department of Anthropology, University of Pennsylvania

Abandonment of settlements and regions

Ethnoarchaeological and archaeological approaches

Edited by

CATHERINE M. CAMERON
and
STEVE A. TOMKA

CAMBRIDGE
UNIVERSITY PRESS

Published by the Press Syndicate of the University of
Cambridge
The Pitt Building, Trumpington Street, Cambridge CB2 1RP
40 West 20th Street, New York, NY 10011–4211, USA
10 Stamford Road, Oakleigh, Victoria 3166, Australia

First published 1993

Printed in Great Britain at the University Press, Cambridge

*A catalogue record for this book is available from the British
Library*

Library of Congress cataloguing in publication data

Abandonment of settlements and regions: ethnoarchaeological
and archaeological approaches / edited by Catherine
M. Cameron and Steve A. Tomka.
  p.   cm. – (New directions in archaeology)
ISBN 0 521 43333 9
1. Ethnoarchaeology. 2. Excavations (Archaeology) 3. Land
settlement – History. 4. Land settlement patterns, Prehistoric –
History. I. Cameron, Catherine M. II. Tomka, Steve A.
III. Series.
CC79.E85A23 1993
930.1 – dc20   92–23164   CIP

ISBN 0 521 43333 9 hardback

CE

Contents

Figures

Tables

Contributors

ROBERT BROOKS
State Archaeologist
Oklahoma Archaeological Survey
Norman, Oklahoma

CATHERINE M. CAMERON
School of American Research
Santa Fe, New Mexico

SUSAN DUBLIN
Department of Anthropology
City University of New York

PAUL R. FISH
Arizona State Museum
University of Arizona

SUSANNE K. FISH
Arizona State Museum
University of Arizona

T. J. FERGUSON
Department of Anthropology
University of New Mexico

MARTHA GRAHAM
Anthropology Department
American Museum of Natural History
New York

LEE HORNE
Editor *Expedition* and Research Associate
Museum Applied Science Center for
Archaeology
The University Museum
University of Pennsylvania

SISSEL JOHANNESSEN
Department of Anthropology
University of Minnesota

ARTHUR A. JOYCE
Department of Anthropology
American Museum of Natural History
New York

SUSAN KENT
Anthropology Program
Old Dominion University
Norfolk, Virginia

RICKY R. LIGHTFOOT
Crow Canyon Archaeological Center
Cortez, Colorado

KATINA T. LILLIOS
Department of Anthropology
Brandeis University

BARBARA J. MILLS
Department of Anthropology
University of Arizona

BARBARA MONTGOMERY
Department of Anthropology
University of Arizona

NAN A. ROTHSCHILD
Department of Anthropology
Bernard College
Columbia University

SARAH H. SCHLANGER
Museum of Indian Arts and
Culture Laboratory of Anthropology
Museum of New Mexico, Santa Fe

MARC G. STEVENSON
Department of Anthropology
University of Alberta
Edmonton

GLENN D. STONE
Department of Anthropology
Columbia University

STEVE A. TOMKA
Department of Anthropology
University of Texas, Austin

RICHARD WILSHUSEN
Advisory Council on Historic Preservation
Western Office of Project Review
Golden, Colorado

Acknowledgments

This volume began as a set of papers prepared for two symposia at the 1990 Society of American Archaeology meetings in Las Vegas, Nevada. Both of us independently conceived of the idea of developing an SAA symposium focusing on abandonment as an archaeological process. Michael Schiffer made us aware of our mutual interests and we joined forces. The resulting symposia were entitled: "Abandonment Processes: Structures and Sites," and "Abandonment Processes: Seasonal Variation and Regional Mobility." This division provided the organization for the present volume. Michael Schiffer and Richard Ahlstrom were enlisted as discussants for the first session and Paul Fish and Marc Stevenson were discussants for the second session. Each of them provided important insights on the papers that were presented and added his own wisdom to the consideration of archaeological abandonment.

The success of the SAA symposia encouraged us to seek publication for the resulting group of papers.

Several individuals offered advice and encouragement as we worked toward publication, most notably Carol Gifford, J. Jefferson Reid, and Norman Yoffee. Unfortunately, several of the participants in the SAA symposia were not able to contribute to this volume, but three additional papers (those by Fish and Fish, Joyce and Johannessen, and Lillios) were solicited, each of which fits well with the theme of the project. The editorial staff at Cambridge University Press, especially Jessica Kuper, helped us through the hurdles of the publication process.

The contributors to the volume have been a pleasure to work with. They read and commented on each others' papers, a procedure that we believe enhanced the coherence of the volume. They endured the lengthy review process with good humor and were timely with requested revisions. The successful completion of this volume is due to their efforts as well as to the assistance of those others who helped us along the way.

PART I

Introduction

1
Abandonment and archaeological interpretation

CATHERINE M. CAMERON

Abandonment conjures up images of catastrophe, mass migration, and environmental crisis. Archaeologists are not immune to the "disaster movie" mind set. Most archaeological studies of abandonment have focused on either the regional exodus (the abandonment of the Four Corners Region of the American Southwest at AD 1300) or spectacular cases of rapid abandonment (Pompeii). Since about 1970, abandonment has been increasingly recognized as a normal process of settlement, and, more importantly, identified as a key process in the formation of the archaeological record (e.g. Ascher 1968; Schiffer 1972, 1976, 1985; Stevenson 1982).

Papers in this volume address not simply the causes of abandonment, but the articulation between human behavior at the time of abandonment and resulting patterns in the archaeological record. Combining ethnographic, ethnoarchaeological, and archaeological data from a wide range of geographic areas and time periods, all contributions share the common theme of understanding the effect of abandonment on archaeological patterns. Several papers use data from the North American Southwest where abandonment has been of long-standing interest, while others break new ground in areas as diverse as modern Iran and Copper Age Portugal.

Abandonment can occur at the level of the activity area, structure, settlement, or entire region. All purely archaeological sites have been abandoned, but not all structures or settlements were abandoned in the same way. "Abandonment processes" – those activities that occur during abandonment – include behavior such as curation or caching of tools, dismantling of structures, and the interruption of normal disposal patterns (Schiffer

1987:89–98). The circumstances surrounding abandonment, such as speed, degree of preabandonment planning, or anticipation of return, determine the abandonment processes that occur. Abandonment processes condition the entry of cultural material into the archaeological record; they are the primary focus of this volume.

The importance of abandonment processes to archaeological interpretation can be illustrated by examining assumptions about artifact distributions. Should we assume that artifacts found on room floors were left exactly where they were used? Were they dumped there days or hours before abandonment when normal clean-up processes were relaxed? Were they, instead, cached for later use during an anticipated return? Do they represent trash tossed into an abandoned room years before the settlement was abandoned?

Archaeologists often assume the first, that artifacts found on living surfaces directly represent their original context of use (Schiffer 1985). Not only can serious misinterpretations result if the abandonment processes responsible for the deposition of cultural materials are not identified, but important information on settlement patterns, site use, and abandonment causes may be overlooked. Abandonment is an important stage in the formation of an archaeological site; in order to interpret sites accurately, archaeologists must understand abandonment processes.

Archaeological study of abandonment

Ascher (1968) was one of the first archaeologists to describe intra-site abandonment of structures and features as part of a normal process of settlement use and to explore its archaeological patterning. In the early 1970s, Schiffer (1972, 1976) differentiated abandonment processes from the normal use of activity areas. Deposition of artifacts through normal processes involves discard or loss; abandonment processes become operative as activity areas are being abandoned. Schiffer linked abandonment to the production of *de facto* refuse, which he defined as usable cultural material (tools, facilities, structures, etc.) left behind when settlements or activity areas are abandoned (1972:160; 1976:33–4; 1987:89). He recognized the effect of *curate behavior* (*sensu* Binford 1977, 1979), the removal of usable items from an abandoned activity area for use elsewhere, in depleting assemblages at abandoned activity areas and sites (Schiffer 1987:89–91).

During the 1970s, research on site formation processes intensified, often using ethnoarchaeological data to project archaeological patterns (e.g. Binford 1977, 1978;

DeBoer and Lathrap 1979; Gould 1980; Yellen 1977). Although a few ethnoarchaeological studies of the effects of abandonment on archaeological patterning appeared (Bonnichsen 1973; Lange and Rydberg 1972; Longacre and Ayres 1969; Robbins 1973), these were often simply cautionary tales in which the disparities between archaeological interpretations and systemic reality were demonstrated.

Baker's (1975) study of artifact caches at a lithic quarry was one of the few that explored the effects of a specific abandonment behavior on archaeological patterns. Murray (1980), in a cross-cultural study of mobile and sedentary societies, emphasized the differential effects of discard and abandonment behavior on artifact deposition.

Stevenson's (1982) study of gold rush sites in the Yukon was the first to explore processes of settlement abandonment systematically. He examined the effect of variables such as speed of abandonment and anticipation of return on patterns of artifacts and structures found at Yukon sites. He discovered that where abandonment was rapid, some structures were left while still under construction; where abandonment was planned and return was anticipated, artifacts might be cached or otherwise prepared for storage. Subsequent investigations of abandonment have further developed methods for examining abandonment processes. Deal (1985), in a study of pottery disposal in the Maya Highlands, suggested that archaeological assemblages are the result of an evolutionary sequence with three behavioral stages: preabandonment, abandonment, and postabandonment. Each stage has a different set of depositional modes. The model provides a framework for interpreting behaviors such as provisional discard, caching, and scavenging that can be used to identify these behaviors in the archaeological record.

Archaeologists in the American Southwest have had a long fascination with abandonment. Remarkable temporal control, detailed environmental reconstructions, a comprehensive understanding of prehistoric cultural developments, and an historically rooted interest in explaining abandonments ("lost cities") combine to make the Southwest ideal for the investigation of abandonment processes.

Interest in Southwestern abandonments began at the turn of the century when spectacular thirteenth-century cliff-dwellings were discovered in the Four Corners area. When first discovered, these sites looked as if they had been abandoned only days before, but they were obviously of great antiquity. A catastrophe seemed evident, but what sort? Southwestern archaeologists have offered many explanations over the decades, ranging from drought to raiding nomads. With the advent of the New Archaeology in the late 1960s, Southwestern abandonments began to be subject to more systematic examination. For example, Reid (1973) developed several innovative techniques for identifying the pattern of abandonment at Grasshopper Pueblo, a fourteenth-century site in east central Arizona. Since 1980, systematic exploration of Southwestern abandonments has increased.

Papers in this volume that focus on the Southwest have broader implications for archaeological interpretations throughout the world.

Scale of abandonment

Abandonment may occur on an increasingly inclusive scale from activity loci to large geographical areas. This continuum can be divided into two segments that are most important for understanding site formation processes. These are: (a) abandonment of settlements, which are often part of a regional system of settlement use, and (b) the abandonment of structures and activity areas within settlements (see also Cordell 1984:312–25). Recent studies of abandonment processes have begun to isolate variables that condition the character of the archaeological record at these two scales. The four Parts of the volume following this introductory chapter (Part I) contain papers using either ethnographic or archaeological data at each of the two scales, regional and intra-settlement.

The regional scale

Abandonment of regions, as addressed in this volume, is not primarily concerned with the depopulation of large territories. The regional approach taken here views abandonment as part of settlement systems that involve seasonal or periodic abandonment of settlements. Binford's (1973, 1977, 1978, 1979) work with hunter-gatherers provides much of the theoretical framework for such studies. Concepts he developed, such as "site furniture" and artifact curation, are the key to the identification of patterns associated with site abandonment in a regional system.

The abandonment of settlements is often a gradual process (e.g. Cameron 1991; Deal 1985:269; Schiffer 1987:91), although rapid, catastrophic abandonment obviously occurs (e.g. Rees 1979; Stevenson 1982). Where abandonment is planned and gradual, variables such as anticipated return to the site or distance to the next new settlement will affect abandonment behavior.

For example, where no return is anticipated, usable artifacts may be removed. If the distance to the new settlement is not great, even structures may be dismantled and building materials transported (Cameron 1991). Importantly, ritual may condition abandonment behavior, resulting in the deposition of unusual quantities or types of *de facto* refuse (Deal 1985:269; Kent 1984:139–41)

Settlement abandonment is "built into" the land-use patterns of many subsistence systems, including those of hunter-gatherers, pastoralists, swidden agriculturalists, and even some sedentary agriculturalists (cf. Kohler and Matthews 1988:559). Papers in Part II of this volume explore a variety of ethnographic settlement systems and show how the abandonment behaviors of each system may affect archaeological patterns.

Periodic settlement use by groups who rotate among a series of settlements throughout the year is examined in papers by Tomka and Graham: Tomka for transhumant agro-pastoralists in southwestern Bolivia; Graham for the agricultural Tarahumara of northern Mexico. These papers provide an interesting contrast in the types of artifacts left as site furniture and those curated and removed from temporarily abandoned sites.

Among agricultural villages in northeastern Iran, Horne recognizes continuity in the occupation or reoccupation of areas (locational stability) and discontinuity in activities at these areas (occupational instability). She suggests that cyclical or periodic changes in locational and occupational stability directly affect archaeological patterns in arid parts of the Middle East. Kent examines the effects of different mobility patterns among the Bushmen of Botswana on the assemblages of artifacts left at abandoned camps. At a broader scale, Stone defines two options for farmers faced with declining agricultural yields: intensification and abandonment. He examines "agricultural abandonment" as an adaptive response among Nigerian agriculturalists and seventeenth-century pioneers in the eastern United States.

Regional archaeological studies (Part III) seek methods for identifying the frequency and nature of abandonment of regions and link regional abandonment to larger environmental and social processes. Schlanger and Wilshusen examine abandonments of pit structures in the Four Corners region of the American Southwest between the seventh and tenth centuries AD. They associate climatic episodes with different types of structure abandonment. In the Tucson Basin of southern Arizona, Fish and Fish identify several periods of progressive abandonment during the Hohokam Classic period (twelfth to fourteenth centuries AD). Their

explanation of these regional abandonments has implications for the entire Southwest during the late prehistoric period. In lowland Portugal, Lillios examines widespread settlement abandonment at the end of the Copper Age (3500–2000 BC) using a center–periphery model. She suggests that the collapse of a regional settlement hierarchy led to the abandonment of many settlements and ultimately to the restructuring of the settlement system in the early Bronze Age.

Intra-site abandonment

Abandonment of structures or activity areas is a constant process in many settlements and has a direct effect on the entry of these features and the artifacts they contain into the archaeological record. The most important processes governing intra-site abandonment may be scavenging and reuse (Ascher 1968; Horne 1983; Lange and Rydberg 1972:422; Reid 1973:114–15; Schiffer 1976:34; 1987:25–46, 106–10). Although both scavenging and reuse can occur at abandoned settlements, these processes are especially pronounced in inhabited settlements where occupied and abandoned activity areas are in close proximity. Children's play is another process that affects abandoned portions of occupied settlements, as well as nearby abandoned sites (Deal 1985:273; see also Hayden and Cannon 1983:132–3).

Intra-site ethnographic studies presented in Part IV explore abandonment within continuously occupied settlements and in a recently abandoned settlement. Rothschild, Mills, Ferguson, and Dublin find that "abandoned" farming villages near the Southwestern pueblo of Zuni have simply changed function from full-time or seasonal residences to use for a variety of episodic purposes ranging from storage areas to sources of raw material. Different functions for structures in these villages affect the distribution of artifacts around structures. In a complementary study of an abandoned domestic compound in Oaxaca, Mexico, Joyce and Johannessen found that four structures at the site were subject to different abandonment processes reflecting their original function and plans for future use. They suggest that specialized structures may be less impacted by abandonment activities than non-specialized structures.

Archaeological intra-site case studies examined in Part V suggest innovative methods for identifying abandonment behavior in archaeological contexts and link such behavior to the causes and circumstances of abandonment – a first step in the archaeological identification of abandonment processes.

Montgomery uses a "room abandonment measure" to identify an unusual pattern of abandonment at the thirteenth century pueblo site of Chodistaas in east central Arizona. She found that ritual activities were involved in the abandonment of Chodistaas. Lightfoot recognizes three distinct types of abandonment for pit structures at the Duckfoot Site in southwestern Colorado by comparing ceramic assemblages for each pit structure with expected ceramic assemblages determined through a simulation study. His study offers methods of filtering out the effects of abandonment behavior on archaeological assemblages. Brooks has developed a series of measures, using both artifacts and architecture, for distinguishing planned from unplanned abandonment in a study of Native American groups on the Great Plains during the late prehistoric and historic periods. His study provides a set of procedures for determining the nature of abandonment processes operating at sites and for determining the integrity in spatial patterning of artifacts on house floors.

New directions

The investigation of abandonment as a site formation process is long overdue. Exploration of the complex interaction between abandonment processes and resultant archaeological patterns is approached systematically for the first time by the papers in this volume. At both the regional and intra-settlement scales of analysis, ethnoarchaeological and archaeological cases provide empirical patterns necessary for understanding abandonment behavior within the context of prehistoric cultural systems. These studies suggest new directions for the study of abandonment.

References

Ascher, Robert
    1968 Time's Arrow and the Archaeology of a Contemporary Community. In *Settlement Archaeology*, edited by K. C. Chang, pp. 43–52. National Press Books, Palo Alto.
Baker, Charles M.
    1975 Site Abandonment and the Archaeological Record: An Empirical Case for Anticipated Return. *Arkansas Academy of Science Proceedings* 29:10–11.
Binford, Lewis R.
    1973 Interassemblage Variability – The Mousterian and the "Functional Argument." In *The Explanation of Culture Change: Models in Prehistory*, edited by Colin Renfrew, pp. 227–53. Duckworth, London.

    1977 Forty-Seven Trips: A Case Study in the Character of Some Formation Processes of the Archaeological Record. In *Stone Tools as Cultural Markers*, edited by R. V. S. Wright, pp. 24–36. Australian Institute of Aboriginal Studies, Canberra.
    1978 Dimensional Analysis of Behavior and Site Structure: Learning from an Eskimo Hunting Stand. *American Antiquity* 43:330–61.
    1979 Organization and Formation Processes: Looking at Curated Technologies. *Journal of Anthropological Research* 35:255–73.
Bonnichsen, Robson
    1973 Millie's Camp: An Experiment in Archaeology. *World Archaeology* 4:277–91.
Cameron, Catherine M.
    1991 Structure Abandonment in Villages. In *Archaeological Method and Theory* Vol. III, edited by Michael B. Schiffer. University of Arizona Press, Tucson.
Cordell, Linda S.
    1984 *Prehistory of the Southwest*. Academic Press, Orlando.
Deal, Michael
    1985 Household Pottery Disposal in the Maya Highlands: An Ethnoarchaeological Interpretation. *Journal of Anthropological Archaeology* 4:243–91.
DeBoer, Warren R. and Donald W. Lathrap
    1979 The Making and Breaking of Shipibo-Conibo Ceramics. In *Ethnoarchaeology: Implications of Ethnography for Archaeology*, edited by Carol Kramer, pp. 102–38. Columbia University Press, New York.
Gould, Richard A.
    1980 *Living Archaeology*. Cambridge University Press, Cambridge.
Hayden, Brian and Aubrey Cannon
    1983 Where the Garbage Goes: Refuse Disposal in the Maya Highlands. *Journal of Anthropological Archaeology* 2:117–63.
Horne, Lee
    1983 Recycling in the Iranian Village: Ethnoarchaeology in Baghestan. *Archaeology* 36(4):16–21.
Kent, Susan
    1984 *Analyzing Activity Areas*. University of New Mexico Press, Albuquerque.
Kohler, Timothy and Meridith Matthews
    1988 Long-Term Anasazi Land Use and Forest Reduction: A Case Study from Southwest Colorado. *American Antiquity* 53:537–64.
Lange, Frederick W. and Charles R. Rydberg
    1972 Abandonment and Post-Abandonment Behavior at a Rural Central American House-Site. *American Antiquity* 37:419–32.

Longacre, William A. and James A. Ayres
　1968 Archaeological Lessons from an Apache Wickiup. In *New Perspectives in Archaeology*, edited by S. R. Binford and L. R. Binford, pp. 151–9. Aldine, Chicago.

Murray, Priscilla
　1980 Discard Location: The Ethnographic Data. *American Antiquity* 45:490–502.

Rees, John D.
　1979 Effects of the Eruption of Paricutin Volcano on Landforms, Vegetation, and Human Occupancy. In *Volcanic Activity and Human Ecology*, edited by Payson D. Sheets and Donald K. Grayson, pp. 249–92. Academic Press, New York.

Reid, J. Jefferson
　1973 *Growth and Response to Stress at Grasshopper Pueblo, Arizona*. University Microfilms, Ann Arbor.

Robbins, L. H.
　1973 Turkana Material Culture Viewed From an Archaeological Perspective. *World Archaeology* 5:209–14.

Schiffer, Michael B.
　1972 Archaeological Context and Systemic Context. *American Antiquity* 37:156–65.
　1976 *Behavioral Archaeology*. Academic Press, New York.
　1985 Is There a "Pompeii Premise" in Archaeology? *Journal of Anthropological Research* 41:18–41.
　1987 *Formation Processes of the Archaeological Record*. University of New Mexico, Albuquerque.

Stevenson, Marc G.
　1982 Toward an Understanding of Site Abandonment Behavior: Evidence from Historic Mining Camps in the Southwest Yukon. *Journal of Anthropological Archaeology* 1:237–65.

Yellen, John E.
　1977 *Archaeological Approaches to the Present: Models for Reconstructing the Past*. Academic Press, New York.

PART II

Regional abandonment processes: ethnoarchaeological cases

2

Site abandonment behavior among transhumant agro-pastoralists: the effects of delayed curation on assemblage composition

STEVE A. TOMKA

Introduction

In recent years studies by Binford (1979), Shott (1986, 1989), Torrence (1983, 1987), Bleed (1986), and others have significantly contributed to the understanding of the relationships between land-use patterns, technological organization, and assemblage composition. These studies focus primarily on the conditioning effects of subsistence organization. The effects of abandonment processes upon assemblage composition have received relatively less attention. In general, assemblage structure and content are seen as conditioned by artifact use life (Schiffer 1975; Shott 1989), various discard behaviors (Deal 1985; Schiffer 1987), and curation at the time of site abandonment (Binford 1973; Schiffer 1987). Abandonment studies have alerted us to another series of processes that condition the composition of archaeological assemblages (Joyce and Johannessen 1987; Lange and Rydberg 1972; Schiffer 1987; Stevenson 1982). Stevenson, working at nineteenth-century gold rush mining camps, was the first to consider systematically the effects of abandonment conditions on the proportion of curated and discarded artifacts. Based on the composition of abandoned assemblages and the presence of abandonment caches, Stevenson also suggested, among other things, that the anticipation of return may significantly affect abandonment behavior.

The gold rush camps distributed along Bullion Creek were abandoned relatively suddenly and in an unplanned manner because of flooding, poor working conditions, and the discovery of a rich strike some distance from Bullion Creek. The camps located on Mush Creek were abandoned under more normal conditions, and

without anticipation of return (Stevenson 1982:238–40). Although in anticipation of return to some of the Bullion Creek gold rush camps some artifacts were clustered in abandonment caches, the gold prospecting land-use pattern was not based on seasonal camp abandonment and reoccupation. In general, it is likely that the probability of return to these abandoned camps may have been quite low owing to the exploitation of a non-renewable resource (i.e. gold ore). It is clear that the organization of the overall system has significantly influenced the circumstances of site abandonment and, in turn, conditioned abandonment processes.

Although within some foraging (Fisher 1989) and most logistically organized (Binford 1978) resource acquisition systems the seasonal abandonment and reoccupation of sites is a central feature of the land-use pattern, few ethnoarchaeological studies document the nature of the abandonment processes operating under such conditions (Graham, this volume). While in logistically operating systems anticipated return underlies the planned seasonal abandonment of a site, its actual reoccupation may not always be feasible or desired. The probability of site reoccupation may be influenced by such factors as short and long-term fluctuations in climatic conditions, the structure and abundance of resources in the vicinity of existing sites, changes in household economic base, and changes in community and regional territorial boundaries. Little is known of the processes operating under circumstances when site abandonment is planned and return anticipated but subsequent reoccupation is delayed.

The fourteen-month ethnoarchaeological study of agro-pastoral transhumance, carried out between 1984 and 1988 in Estancia Copacabana, southwestern Bolivia, provided the opportunity to investigate the processes operating under conditions of extended site abandonment and anticipated, but delayed, reoccupation. The transhumant land-use system, described in more detail below, is based on the seasonal abandonment and reoccupation of distinct pastoral and agricultural residences. Owing to fluctuations in household economy and/or demographics, either of these may remain abandoned for extended periods (longer than the annual cycle) only to be reoccupied when feasible. The abandonment of either residence is not accompanied by regional abandonment; the area continues to be regularly criss-crossed by family members participating in intra and inter-regional reciprocity, barter, and market relationships. Consequently, these abandoned residences remain within the economically utilized regional sphere. The goal of this paper is to define one of the

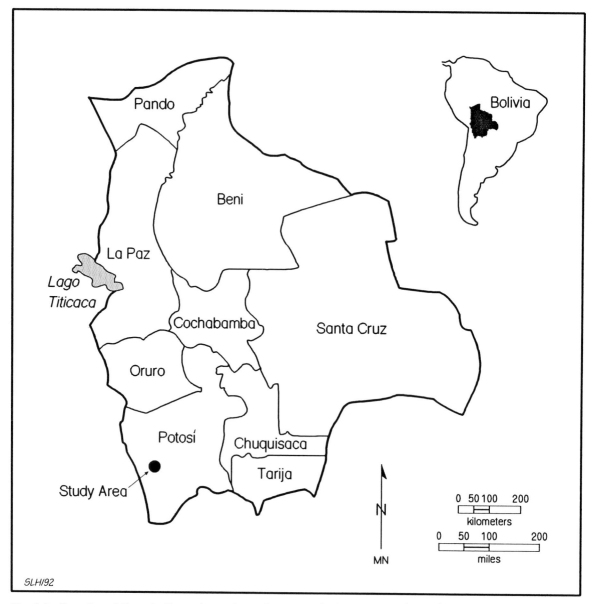

Fig. 2.1   Location of Estancia Copacabana, the study area, in the Department of Potosí, Bolivia.

abandonment processes operating under circumstances of anticipated but delayed site reoccupation, and monitor its effects on assemblage size and composition.

The transhumant agro-pastoral land-use system

Estancia Copacabana is located in the cold temperate montane desert lifezone (Holdridge 1967) of south-western Bolivia (Fig. 2.1). Mean annual rainfall is extremely low (100 mm), with over 90 percent falling between December and February, during the southern hemisphere summer (Johnson 1976:151). This inhospitable climate supports a vegetation of rosette perennials, cushion plants, and tussock grasses. The few glacial melt-water-fed rivers form veritable oases in the otherwise desert environment.

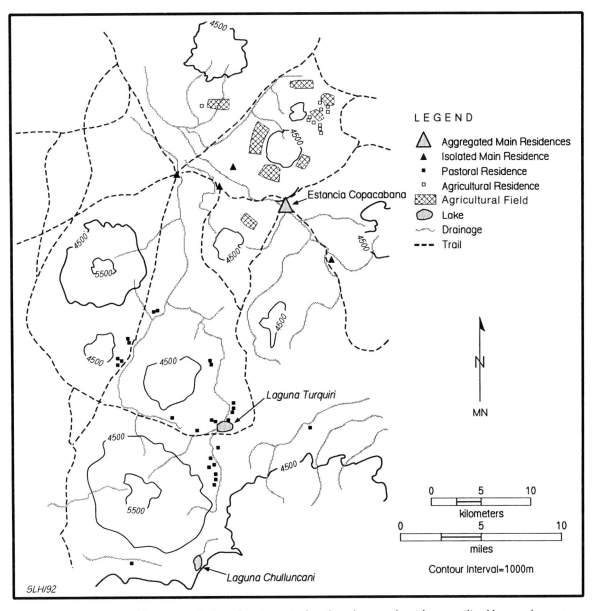

Fig. 2.2   *Distribution and locations of selected main, agricultural, and pastoral residences utilized by transhumant agro-pastoral households in Estancia Copacabana.*

The community members are subsistence agro-pastoralists. Most households rely on quinua (*Chenopodium quinua*) and tuber agriculture, and llama (*Lama glama*) and sheep herding. Two forms of agro-pastoral production are practiced: seasonally transhumant and semisedentary. Seasonally transhumant households utilize distinct pastoral, agricultural, and main residences. Semisedentary households occupy only main and agricultural residences.

Transhumant household main residences are centrally located between the lower agricultural and the higher pastoral residences (Fig. 2.2). The main and agricultural residences that belong to semisedentary households are located in the vicinity of those of transhumant households. The three residence types form the main, agricultural, and pastoral segments of the community.

Main residences are located at an elevation of about 3850 m. Some of the main residences are aggregated to form the political and religious center of the community. Others are isolated compounds located at some distance from the aggregated community. Main residences consist of a kitchen, a dormitory, one or more storage structures, and associated corrals. Main residences found in the aggregated community are walled. The structures found on isolated compounds are arranged in a linear or U-shaped pattern, with door openings facing away from the prevailing winter winds. The agricultural residences are built next to large rain-fed quinua fields located four to six hours' walk from the main segment of the community. These agricultural residences consist of either a single kitchen/dormitory/storage structure or a kitchen/dormitory and an associated storage structure. Sheep and llama corrals are associated with each of the agricultural residences. Households with multiple fields located in different parts of the community territory, and at some distance from their main residences, may own two agricultural residences used in alternate years. Agricultural fields found within an hour's walk of the main residences have no residential or storage structures. The facilities found at these fields may include windbreaks, hearths, and/or fieldhouses. Pastoral residences are isolated house compounds distributed along river courses and associated marshes found at an elevation of 4400 m, some six to eight hours from the main segment. These residences usually consist of a single kitchen/dormitory/storage structure. In a few instances, a separate but adjoined storage structure is built in addition to the kitchen/dormitory. Corrals are present at most of the pastoral residences studied.

Transhumant and semisedentary households use main and agricultural residences in similar ways. With the exception of short periods when family members are at the agricultural segments, the main residences are occupied throughout the year. The agricultural residences are occupied by entire families during field preparation (March), planting (October), and harvest (April–May). Depending on the size of the fields, these individual occupation episodes may total four to eight weeks. While crops mature and ripen (November–March), the agricultural fields are visited at least once every week for monitoring and maintenance. These visits are made by a single family member and require overnight stays at the agricultural residence.

The pastoral residences used by transhumant households are occupied between November and February.

Actual occupation dates depend on the timing and regularity of the rains. The number of occupants ranges from one to four individuals, but the majority are used by a single person. The pastoral residences are abandoned between March and October. Immediately prior to seasonal abandonment all site furniture (active gear) is cached at the residence. Abandonment caches are formed either in the single-room residence or the adjoining storage structure. Expedient tools (e.g. small anvil stones, round manos, sticks used to stir coals in the outdoor hearth) and stationary items (boulder-sized anvil stones) tend to be left in outdoor activity areas as *de facto* refuse. The site furniture remains in this passive state (Binford 1979:257) until the reoccupation of the residence.

Research methodology

Of the sixty-one families living in the community of Copacabana, nineteen (31 percent) were reported to be transhumant at the time of the study. The remaining forty-two (69 percent) were semisedentary agro-pastoralist households. Nine (47 percent) of the nineteen were actually engaged in seasonal transhumance during the 1986–7 field season. The other ten (53 percent) had not occupied the pastoral residence for an entire annual cycle or longer, but were planning to resume transhumance when circumstances permitted. These households retained ownership of all construction materials and the contents of the abandoned residences. This form of abandonment is referred to here as episodic abandonment. From discussions with the respective owners, it was established that three of these residences were abandoned for one year, and three others were abandoned for two years. Two of the remaining four were abandoned for three years and the remaining two were not used in four years. Of the forty-two semisedentary households, nine (21 percent) had been transhumant formerly. Their respective pastoral residences are permanently abandoned, that is, the former owners do not anticipate the reoccupation of these residences nor do they claim continued ownership rights to them. This study focuses on the abandonment of the nine seasonally, ten episodically, and nine permanently abandoned pastoral residences.

The nine seasonally abandoned pastoral residences were inventoried once during use and again following abandonment to document changes in assemblage composition between the active and passive states (Binford 1979:256–8). Because entire assemblages were cached at the time of seasonal abandonment the inventories were not different. The other nineteen abandoned pastoral residences were inventoried during various parts of the field season. The artifact assemblages represent complete inventories. The inventories include artifacts encountered in both outdoor (*de facto* refuse) and all indoor (abandonment caches) activity areas (Schiffer 1987). Primary and secondary refuse consisting of ceramic and glass sherds, bones, and small pieces of wire and cloth are not included in the inventories discussed here. All tools and tool fragments are included.

At the inception of the project it was assumed that two factors are relevant to how an item or tool is treated at the time of residence abandonment: (1) the condition (e.g. the degree of use-damage) of the item; and (2) the manner in which the tool or item is manufactured (manufacture type).

To gauge artifact condition, each item was classified as either good, worn, or broken. All tools and items lacking significant use-damage (e.g. dents, cracks) and/or signs of repairs, were classified as being in good condition. Repaired or use-damaged, but still functional, items were considered worn. Exhausted items (e.g. empty matchboxes) were also grouped into the worn. Broken, non-functional artifacts were assigned to the broken category.

To gauge manufacture type, each item was also classified as either expedient, improvised, craft, and/or industrial. Artifacts made with minimal or no alteration in the form and shape of locally available native raw materials were classified as expedient (e.g. basin metates, round manos, sticks used to stir coals). Locally manufactured or assembled specimens made of recycled articles of non-local origin (e.g. sardine can lids used as shearing knives) and/or secondary-use materials (e.g. large alcohol cans with wire handles used as buckets) were considered improvised. Locally manufactured items made of local native raw materials but involving moderate manufacture costs were classified as craft items (e.g. pottery vessels, slab manos, and metates). Finally, factory-made items and items made non-locally or non-local raw materials were classified as industrial manufacture (e.g. stoves, pots, plates, bottles, forks, buckets).

Analysis results

The total number of items recorded at the twenty-eight residences is shown in Fig. 2.3. The largest inventories ($\bar{x} = 91$) are found at the seasonally occupied pastoral residences. Inventories are smaller in the episodically ($\bar{x} = 44$) and permanently ($\bar{x} = 7$) abandoned pastoral residences. The steady decrease in assemblage size associated

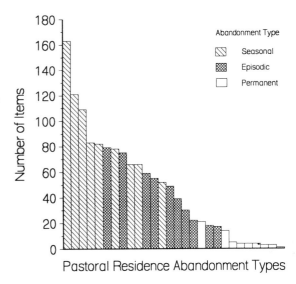

Fig. 2.3 The breakdown of inventory size by pastoral residence abandonment type (N = 28).

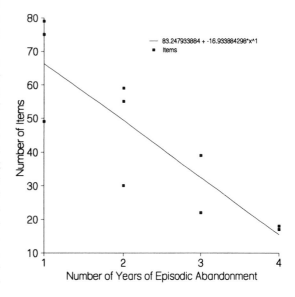

Fig. 2.4 The relationship between assemblage size and length of abandonment at ten episodically abandoned pastoral residences.

with increased abandonment length suggests that the mechanism responsible for the pattern operates while the residences are abandoned.

The relationship between assemblage size and length of episodic abandonment, illustrated in Fig. 2.4, strongly supports this suggestion. A moderately strong inverse relationship exists between length of abandonment and assemblage size ($r^2 = 0.74$; p < 0.001). As the number of years of episodic abandonment increases the number of items decreases.

Through time, artifact scavenging (Schiffer 1987), could generate the observed decreases in assemblage size. However, according to informants, scavenging tends to occur only after residences are permanently abandoned rather than while a family still claims ownership of the residential compound. The primary mechanism responsible for the pattern is delayed curation. Schiffer (1987:94) describes delayed curation as the curate behavior that occurs during several trips to a new site of location. As used in this paper, the term additionally incorporates the process by which cached site furniture and artifact assemblages are curated between the period of a site's late occupation and its subsequent reoccupation or its permanent abandonment. It operates in conjunction with, and in addition to, the normal curation of artifacts which occurs at the time of site abandonment (Binford 1973; Hayden 1976; Schiffer 1987).

At least during the early stages of abandonment, delayed curation does not usually involve the removal of the entire assemblage at one time. Rather, family members select individual items or groups of items for return to the main or agricultural residences. It is likely that the selection of these artifacts is not random but is subject to certain principles.

At the initiation of the study it was assumed that an item's condition plays an important role in its selection for delayed curation. It was not feasible, however, to gauge the condition of each item removed from the pastoral residences through delayed curation. Nonetheless, a comparison of artifacts left at the seasonally, episodically, and permanently abandoned residences should reflect the selection principles underlying delayed curation. Fig. 2.5 shows the mean percentage of the total inventory consisting of broken and worn items and specimens in good condition, at each of the three groups of pastoral residences. While the percentage of broken items steadily increases with length of abandonment, the most significant changes are noted between episodic and permanently abandoned residences. The percentage of worn items steadily decreases with increased length of abandonment. The percentage of items in good condition does not change between seasonally and episodically abandoned residences. However, it drops significantly at the permanently abandoned residences.

These patterns indicate that items in good condition

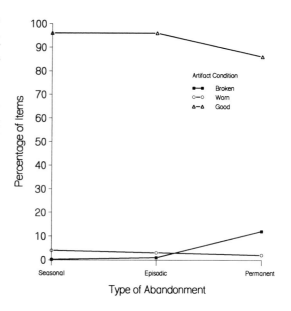

Fig. 2.5   The relationship between artifact condition and abandonment type in the combined artifact collections from seasonally (N=9), episodically (N=10), and permanently (N=9) abandoned pastoral residences.

are the primary targets of delayed curation. Although worn items are also targeted, curation is heavily skewed in favor of items in good condition. With the continued removal of good-condition and worn tools by their owners, the percentage of broken artifacts remaining in the assemblage rises by default. This pattern indicates that broken items are not selected for delayed curation.

It has been suggested above that delayed curation is responsible for the decrease in assemblage size noted at episodically and permanently abandoned residences. In addition, artifact condition appears to influence the selection of specific items targeted during delayed curation. Artifact manufacture type may also play a significant role in the selection of artifacts during delayed curation.

If manufacture type affects the selection of items returned to main and/or agricultural residences, then delayed curation should impact three aspects of assemblage composition: (1) the percentages of manufacture types within the overall assemblage; (2) the percentages of manufacture types within particular artifact categories; and, if manufacture type and artifact categories are related, (3) the percentage of specific artifact categories within the overall assemblage. More specifically, as abandonment length increases, the percentages of

Table 2.1. *Artifact category by manufacture type, seasonally abandoned residences (N = 9).*

Artifact category	Expedient		Improvised		Craft		Industrial		Total	
	No.	Row %	No.	Row %	No.	Row %	No.	Row %	No.	Column %
Cooking vessels	0	0	0	0	18	26	50	74	68	8
Serving vessels	0	0	5	8	0	0	58	92	63	8
Utensils	17	27	8	13	4	6	34	54	63	8
Containers	0	0	105	60	4	2	66	38	175	21
Ground/pecked stones	28	55	0	0	23	45	0	0	51	6
Kitchen accessories	17	30	35	61	0	0	5	9	57	7
Kitchen furniture	45	36	0	0	49	40	30	24	124	15
Weaving accessories	0	0	55	34	109	66	0	0	164	20
Agricultural tools	0	0	1	33	0	0	2	67	3	<1
Pastoral tools	0	0	17	100	0	0	0	0	17	2
Other tools	0	0	0	0	26	76	8	24	34	4
Total	107	13	226	28	233	28	253	31	819	100

improvised, craft, and industrial items should drop while the percentage of expedient items should rise in the overall assemblage. It should follow from these trends that the percentages of improvised, craft, and industrial items in any specific artifact category should drop while the percentage of expedient items should rise with increased abandonment length. Improvised, craft, and industrial items found in permanently abandoned assemblages should be dominated by worn (and/or exhausted) specimens. Finally, if manufacture type and artifact category are related, artifact categories composed primarily of improvised, craft, and industrial items should be under-represented while artifact categories composed primarily of expedient items should be over-represented in permanently abandoned assemblages.

To explore the relationship between manufacture type and delayed curation, all artifacts were classified into types (e.g. knives, spoons, pots, etc.). A total of seventy artifact types was defined in the inventory of the twenty-eight residences. To simplify the discussion, these types were grouped into a total of eleven broad functional categories (e.g., cooking vessels, serving vessels, kitchen accessories, etc.).

Table 2.1, 2.2, and 2.3 illustrate the numbers of percentages of expedient, improvised, craft, and industrially manufactured items in each of the eleven artifact categories at the three groups of pastoral residence. Since the proposed trends refer to the functional assemblage, broken items are not included in the inventories shown

in these tables. While industrially manufactured items constitute about a third of the seasonally (31 percent) and episodically (33 percent) abandoned assemblages, they represent only 17 percent of the permanently abandoned collections. Craft items constitute a slightly smaller percentage of the seasonally (28 percent) and episodically (26 percent) abandoned assemblages but they also drop in percentage (13 percent) in the permanently abandoned assemblages. Improvised items constitute about a fourth of the seasonally (28 percent) and episodically (24 percent) abandoned assemblages. Although they do decrease slightly in the permanently abandoned assemblages, improvised items remain a relatively significant portion (21 percent) of these assemblages. The occurrence of expediently manufactured items exhibits the opposite trend. The percentage of expediently manufactured items increases slightly in the episodically abandoned inventories and rises sharply to constitute almost half (48 percent) of the artifacts recorded at permanently abandoned residences. It is clear from these trends that manufacture type strongly conditions the selection of items for delayed curation.

Tables 2.1, 2.2 and 2.3 also show that the percentage of industrially manufactured items, within most artifact categories (i.e. cooking vessels, serving vessels, utensils, and agricultural tools), tends to decrease steadily with increased abandonment length (e.g. seasonal, episodic, and permanent). Even when the trend is not a steady decrease, the percentage of industrially manufactured items in a particular artifact category is lowest in the

Table 2.2. *Artifact category by manufacture type, episodically abandoned residences (N = 10).*

Artifact category	Expedient		Improvised		Craft		Industrial		Total	
	No.	Row %	No.	Row %	No.	Row %	No.	Row %	No.	Column %
Cooking vessels	0	0	0	0	12	34	23	66	35	8
Serving vessels	0	0	4	11	6	16	27	73	37	8
Utensils	13	42	6	19	3	10	9	29	31	7
Containers	0	0	60	54	2	2	49	44	111	25
Ground/pecked stones	16	33	0	0	33	67	0	0	49	11
Kitchen accessories	8	21	28	74	0	0	2	5	38	9
Kitchen furniture	38	38	0	0	30	30	31	31	99	23
Weaving accessories	0	0	0	0	26	100	0	0	26	6
Agricultural tools	0	0	0	0	0	0	0	0	0	0
Pastoral tools	0	0	8	100	0	0	0	0	8	2
Other tools	0	0	0	0	2	33	4	67	6	1
Total	75	17	106	24	114	26	145	33	440	100

Table 2.3. *Artifact category by manufacture type, permanently abandoned sites (N = 9).*

Artifact category	Expedient		Improvised		Craft		Industrial		Total	
	No.	Row %	No.	Row %	No.	Row %	No.	Row %	No.	Column %
Cooking vessels	0	0	0	0	0	0	0	0	0	0
Serving vessels	0	0	2	67	0	0	1	33	3	6
Utensils	2	100	0	0	0	0	0	0	2	4
Containers	0	0	4	100	0	0	0	0	4	8
Ground/pecked stones	4	67	0	0	2	33	0	0	6	12
Kitchen accessories	0	0	4	67	0	0	2	33	6	12
Kitchen furniture	19	63	0	0	5	17	6	20	30	58
Weaving accessories	0	0	0	0	0	0	0	0	0	0
Agricultural tools	0	0	0	0	0	0	0	0	0	0
Pastoral tools	0	0	1	100	0	0	0	0	1	2
Other tools	0	0	0	0	0	0	0	0	0	0
Total	25	48	11	21	7	13	9	17	52	100

permanently abandoned assemblages (i.e. containers, kitchen furniture, other tools). Kitchen accessories constitute the only artifact category that does not follow the proposed trend. The single industrially manufactured serving vessel found in the permanently abandoned assemblages is worn. The two industrially manufactured kitchen accessories are empty matchboxes, considered exhausted items. Finally, five of the six industrially manufactured kitchen furniture specimens found in two permanently abandoned assemblages were stored and forgotten while the remainder of the assemblage was moved to a newly constructed pastoral residence. In general, the percentage of craft items within each artifact category also decreases with increased abandonment length. The lowest percentages of craft items in all artifact categories are found in the permanently abandoned assemblages. The two craft-manufactured ground/pecked stone specimens, a slab mano and a slab metate, found in the permanently abandoned assemblage of a single residence, are not a functional pair. As such they

Table 2.4. *Artifact category by manufacture type, all pastoral residences (N = 28).*

Artifact category	Expedient		Improvised		Craft		Industrial		Total	
	No.	Row %	No.	Row %	No.	Row %	No.	Row %	No.	Column %
Cooking vessels	0	0	0	0	30	29	73	71	103	8
Serving vessels	0	0	11	11	6	6	86	83	103	8
Utensils	32	33	14	15	7	7	43	45	96	7
Containers	0	0	169	58	6	2	115	40	290	22
Ground/pecked stones	48	45	0	0	58	55	0	0	106	8
Kitchen accessories	25	25	67	66	0	0	9	9	101	8
Kitchen furniture	102	40	0	0	84	33	67	26	253	19
Weaving accessories	0	0	55	29	135	71	0	0	190	14
Agricultural tools	0	0	1	33	0	0	2	67	3	<1
Pastoral tools	0	0	26	100	0	0	0	0	26	2
Other tools	0	0	0	0	28	70	12	30	40	3
Total	207	16	343	26	354	27	407	31	1311	100

can be considered equivalent to exhausted or worn items. The five craft-manufactured kitchen furniture specimens are llama hide fragments. They are not considered broken because even as small fragments they may be employed as seat covers or sleeping platform linings. The percentages of improvised items decreased with increased abandonment length in three categories: utensils, weaving, and agricultural tools. However, the percentages of improvised serving vessels, containers, and kitchen accessories increased rather than decreasing in the permanently abandoned assemblages. The percentage of improvised items did not change with increased length of abandonment among pastoral tools. None of the improvised items found in the permanently abandoned assemblages was worn. The two cups grouped in the serving vessels category were two produce cans with lids fashioned into handles. Three of the four containers were recycled produce cans. The single pastoral tool was a shearing knife made of a reused sardine can lid. The percentages of expedient items increased steadily with increased length of abandonment among the utensils, ground/pecked stones, and kitchen furniture. However, the percentages of expedient kitchen accessories do not follow the proposed trend in that they appear to decrease with increased abandonment length.

With a few exceptions, found mainly among the improvised items and industrially manufactured kitchen accessories, the percentages of improvised, craft, and industrial items decreased in most artifact categories with increased abandonment length. A number of the industrial and craft manufacture items left at permanently abandoned pastoral residences were worn or exhausted. Some good-condition items were stored but forgotten. On the other hand, the percentage of expedient items increased with increased abandonment length in all artifact categories containing expedient items, except kitchen accessories.

To explore the relationship between artifact manufacture type and artifact category, the number and percentage of expedient, improvised, craft, and industrial manufacture items were calculated by artifact category in the combined inventory of the twenty-eight pastoral residences. Table 2.4 shows that a large percentage of the serving (83 percent) and cooking vessels (71 percent) and agricultural tools (66 percent) consist primarily of industrially manufactured items. Moderately high percentages of industrially manufactured items are also found among the utensils (45 percent). Craft items constitute a high percentage of the weaving accessories (71 percent), other tools category (70 percent), and ground/pecked stones (55 percent). Pastoral tools (100 percent), kitchen accessories (66 percent), and containers (58 percent) consist mainly of improvised items. Although four artifact categories contain expedient artifacts, only two, ground/pecked stone (45 percent) and kitchen furniture (40 percent), contain moderate percentages of expedient items.

Based on a number of patterns noted so far, it is likely that delayed curation can significantly affect assemblage composition with increased abandonment, particularly at permanently abandoned residences. In comparing the figures between seasonally (Table 2.1) and permanently (Table 2.3) abandoned residences, it is clear that of the four artifact categories with the highest percentages of industrially manufactured items (see Table 2.4), two (cooking vessels, agricultural tools) are entirely absent from the permanently abandoned assemblages. In addition, the percentages of utensils (4 percent) and serving vessels (6 percent) is the lowest in the permanently abandoned assemblages.

Since craft items constitute a relatively large percentage of the weaving accessories, other tools, and ground/pecked stones (Table 2.4), it is expected that these artifact categories will constitute a small percentage of the permanently abandoned assemblages. Table 2.3 indicates that other tools and weaving accessories are entirely absent from the assemblage. As mentioned above, the craft-manufactured slab mano and slab metate should be considered non-functional since they are not a pair. The increasing percentage of ground/pecked stones in the permanently abandoned assemblages is due to the presence of expediently made ground stone tools.

Given that improvised items constitute a significant proportion of the pastoral tools, kitchen accessories, and containers (Table 2.4), it is expected that these artifact categories will decrease somewhat in the permanently abandoned assemblages. While the percentage of containers steadily decreased and was at its lowest in the permanently abandoned assemblages, the percentage of pastoral tools is the same (2 percent) in all three abandoned inventories. The percentage of kitchen accessories actually increased compared to the seasonally abandoned assemblages. None of the improvised items or tools is worn.

Because the highest percentages of expedient items are found in the ground/pecked stones and kitchen furniture categories (Table 2.4), it is expected that these artifact categories will constitute a large percentage of the permanently abandoned assemblages. As proposed, the kitchen furniture category constitutes the higher percentage of the permanently abandoned assemblages. The ground/pecked stone category constitutes the second highest percentage of these assemblages.

Adjusted standardized residuals offer a way to identify more accurately the under or over-representation of particular artifact categories in a contingency table (Everitt 1977; Haberman 1973). Table 2.5 shows the adjusted standardized residuals calculated for each of the artifact categories (minus the broken items) encountered at the three groups of pastoral residences. Although only a few of the adjusted standardized residuals duals are

Table 2.5. *Adjusted standardized residuals by artifact category.*

Artifact categories	Seasonal	Episodic	Permanent
Cooking vessels	0.77	−0.09	−2.15
Serving vessels	−0.29	0.53	−0.57
Utensils	0.66	−0.27	0.98
Containers	−0.85	1.93	−2.56
Ground/pecked stones	−3.18	2.88	0.93
Kitchen accessories	−1.30	0.9	1.06
Kitchen furniture	−4.92	2.09	7.16
Weaving accessories	7.34	−6.28	−3.03
Agricultural tools	1.33	−1.23	−0.35
Pastoral tools	0.31	−0.30	−0.03
Other tools	2.99	−2.52	−1.31

Table 2.6. *Adjusted standardized residuals by raw material type.*

Material type	Seasonal	Episodic	Permanent
Metal	−0.89	1.78	−2.09
Wood	−2.32	0.43	4.72
Ceramic	−1.52	2.06	−1.2
Grass	0.11	0.28	−0.96
Stone	−1.12	0.84	0.75
Glass	1.13	−0.72	−1.05
Plastic	0.85	−0.49	−0.94
Leather	0.65	−1.27	1.47
Textile/wool	5.22	−4.41	−2.27
Metal/wood	−0.82	1.11	−0.65
Wood/ceramic	1.74	−1.59	−0.46
Other	0.36	−0.49	−0.29

statistically significant at the 0.05 level of significance (5 percent standard normal deviate = 1.96; Everitt 1977:47), some strong tendencies are evident in the data.

Ground/pecked stone artifacts and kitchen furniture are under-represented at seasonally abandoned pastoral residences. On the other hand, weaving accessories and other tools are over-represented. As residences are abandoned for extended periods (e.g. episodic), and especially once they are permanently abandoned, cooking vessels, containers, and weaving accessories become under-represented. Only the kitchen furniture category is over-represented at permanently abandoned residences.

The raw material types represented at the three groups of pastoral residences may further clarify the principles conditioning the selection of artifact categories for delayed curation. Table 2.6 presents the adjusted standardized residuals by raw material and pastoral site abandonment. Composite tools made of two or more raw materials are shown as combined material types.

As in the previous table, while only a handful of the adjusted standardized residuals are significant at the 0.05 level of significance, some consistent patterns are evident among the values. Artifacts made of wood are over-represented in permanently abandoned assemblages. On the other hand, artifacts made of metal and textile/wool are under-represented in these assemblages. All wood, except for milled lumber, used in the manufacture of tools and items, is considered a locally available native raw material. On the other hand, metal, glass, and plastics are obtained non-locally by direct purchase (e.g. kerosene lanterns), or are brought to the community as riders with other consumer goods (e.g. cans obtained from the purchase of alcohol, produce cans). Once the consumer goods make their way into the community, the riders are locally available but are here viewed as having a non-local origin. While in the past ceramics were manufactured locally, presently no potters work in the community. Given the lack of local sources, the replacement of clay wares would have to occur from non-local sources.

Discussion and conclusions

Scavenging (Schiffer 1987:106–14), various postdepositional processes (Gifford 1978), and curation at the time of site abandonment (Binford 1977:34, 1978:452), are the most commonly mentioned factors affecting the composition of abandoned artifact assemblages. Stevenson (1982) suggested that anticipation of return is an additional factor conditioning the curation and caching of artifacts at the time of abandonment. This ethnoarchaeological example shows that within a highly logistically organized system, such as the transhumant agro-pastoral land-use pattern described here, and under circumstances of delayed residence reoccupation and permanent abandonment, delayed curation is an additional process (Schiffer 1987:94) affecting the composition of artifact assemblages cached at abandoned sites.

To understand the meaning of delayed curation, as used here, it is necessary to view land-use as a dynamic system and abandonment as a continuous process. The

seasonal abandonment and reoccupation of residences is one of the central features of the transhumant agro-pastoral land-use system discussed here. In anticipation of the subsequent season's reoccupation, the entire site furniture (Binford 1978:339–40) is cached prior to seasonal abandonment. However, because of the ebb and flow in the dynamics of the household economy some of these seasonally occupied residences remain abandoned for extended periods. This residential abandonment is not followed by regional abandonment, rather the area continues to be criss-crossed by community members as part of intra and inter-regional exchange, barter, or market relations. As long as the potential to reoccupy episodically abandoned residences remains a distinct probability, the cached assemblage or a portion of it is left at these residences. Delayed curation is the mechanism by which elements of these cached assemblages are slowly withdrawn from these residences as the length of episodic abandonment increases and the probability of future reoccupation diminishes and finally becomes unlikely. Delayed curation takes place not in the context of seasonal abandonment and reoccupation, but during intermittent visits embedded in the trips criss-crossing the region. Since the numerous forms of scavenging involve the removal of artifacts discarded as *de facto* or secondary refuse at permanently abandoned sites (Schiffer 1987:106–14), delayed curation should be considered a distinct process. Delayed curation operates between a site's last occupation and its permanent abandonment. It impacts the entire formerly active assemblage cached at these sites rather than only artifacts discarded as *de facto* or secondary refuse.

It has been demonstrated above that delayed curation significantly alters cached assemblages. In addition to decreasing assemblage size, the selective curation of artifacts strongly skews the composition of the assemblage. Artifact condition and manufacture type (e.g. the manner of manufacture) appear to be the proximate factors conditioning this selection.

In order for delayed curation to be a significant explanatory device it is necessary to present its broader technological and sociocultural context. What are the factors leading to the delayed curation of abandoned assemblages, and what role does the transhumant land-use pattern play in its operationalization?

Taking a broad technological perspective, it appears that raw material availability accounts for the patterns noted in Table 2.6 only as it relates to manufacture types, and more importantly, artifact replacement costs. As mentioned earlier, artifacts found in household inventories were either manufactured locally of native locally available (expedient and craft items) or recycled non-local origin materials (improvised items), or were industrially manufactured of non-local raw materials (industrial items).

Different artifact replacement costs are incurred depending on the place of manufacture. The replacement of locally manufactured items involves raw material replacement costs and manufacture or assembly costs. The replacement of industrially manufactured items or tools involves purchase costs.

In general, local native raw materials are the most readily available in Estancia Copacabana or its immediate surroundings, followed by recycled or re-used materials of non-local origin. Industrially manufactured raw materials, in the form of finished products, are the least available.

Although most readily available, the replacement of locally available native raw materials may be costly if the acquisition (e.g. transportation) and/or processing of the raw material is labor intensive. The replacement of recycled or reused raw materials of non-local origin is even more costly because of higher initial acquisition costs (e.g. purchase of consumer goods), combined with the lesser availability of these materials in the community.

It is assumed here that, independently of raw material replacement costs, manufacture or assembly costs vary depending on the number of components making up the artifact, and the amount of time and energy necessary to assemble the components. From this perspective, expediently manufactured items have the lowest manufacture costs. Manufacture and/or assembly costs are also low for improvised items, since often the recycled or reused items require little (e.g. opening and cutting the lid off a produce can) or no alterations (reusing a bottle as a container). The assembly or manufacture of some improvised items does, however, necessitate higher costs (e.g. making a dust pan out of sheet metal, wood, and nails). Nonetheless, in general, of the locally made items and tools, craft items have the highest manufacture and/or tool replacement costs, while improvised items, as a group, are considered to have manufacture and/or assembly costs falling between expedient and craft items.

How do these two factors, raw material replacement costs and manufacture and/or assembly costs, interact to affect the composition of the assemblage found at permanently abandoned pastoral residences? Furthermore, how does artifact condition (e.g. use-damage or wear) affect the manner in which these factors condition the delayed curation or items cached at pastoral residences? It is evident from the patterns documents in Table 2.1–2.4, and Fig. 2.5, that taken alone neither raw

material availability, artifact replacements cost, nor artifact condition can sufficiently account for the observed patterns. Rather, the delayed curation of specific artifacts is controlled by a complex inter-relationship between all of these factors. When raw material is the native locally available type and its acquisition and processing are low, and artifact manufacture costs are also low, the artifact has a low probability of being targeted for delayed curation (e.g. support sticks used to hang items on walls). Artifacts with low manufacture costs but high locally available native raw material replacement costs (e.g. high material acquisition and processing costs) tend to be targeted for delayed curation on a regular basis (e.g. grass brushes). Artifacts made of locally available native raw materials but involving high manufacture costs are also likely to be targets of delayed curation (e.g. slab manos and metates). Regardless of raw material availability, as manufacture costs increase artifact replacement costs also increase, as does the likelihood of delayed curation. The probability of delayed curation of low manufacture-cost artifacts made from materials of non-local origin tends to be higher than that of low manufacture-cost artifacts made of locally available native raw materials.

This perspective offers a fuller explanation of the principles underlying delayed curation. However, it is important to view delayed curation within an even broader context. Based on indications by informants and the patterns noted in the abandoned assemblages, the number and types of artifacts removed by delayed curation during the early states of abandonment are determined by a combination of immediate and anticipated artifact replacement needs at the other residences utilized by a household. As items break, wear out, or are lost at main and/or agricultural residences, they are replaced with items cached at the pastoral residences. In this case, delayed curation responds to relatively immediate tool replacement needs at the other residences of the settlement system. Although it was not systematically documented, some of the items returned to the main residences were not introduced immediately into the active assemblage. Rather, they were stored in anticipation of future needs. These items may have been primarily artifacts with high overall replacement costs. These aspects indicate that the passive assemblage cached at the pastoral residences functions as a resource area. The use of pastoral residence artifact caches as sources of replacement tools may be preferred over the alternative of having to manufacture new ones; especially if either raw material replacement or manufacture costs are expected to be high. The delayed curation of items cached at abandoned pastoral residences would only require transportation costs, this being relatively low given the burros and llamas owned by each household. Artifact caches are also more readily accessible than the regional market, from both logistical and economic perspectives. Motorized transportation is not readily available and the acquisition of goods at the nearest urban market center (approximately 180 km or 8 hours by truck) is limited by the low purchasing power of most community members.

At an even broader level, the delayed curation of cached assemblages occurs because of two factors. First, most of the activities performed at the pastoral residences are also performed at the main residences. As a result, all of the tools cached at the pastoral residences can be used at the main residences. Second, although in case of episodic and permanent abandonment the pastoral residence is eliminated from the land-use pattern, herding remains a substantial part of the activities carried out at other residences. This means that most of the complete and still functional artifacts (e.g. pastoral tools) remain potentially usable at other residences. In addition, the few items and tools that may have been diagnostic of site function (e.g. the role of the site in the overall land-use pattern) are removed from these abandoned residences to be utilized elsewhere. Although this is a discouraging prospect for archaeologists, the situation is not as hopeless as it appears. The analysis suggests that artifacts diagnostic of site function, as well as those diagnostic of site use (e.g. food preparation, tool manufacture), may be left at permanently abandoned sites if they have low overall replacement costs (e.g. artifacts that have low raw material replacement and manufacture costs) or are worn (exhausted) or broken non-functional items.

An additional factor, the role of the particular land-use pattern, needs to be emphasized to account fully for the patterns of delayed curation described here. It was noted earlier that the episodic abandonment of the pastoral residences is not accompanied by regional abandonment nor the termination of herding activities. Relatively regular visits continue to be made to the vicinity of the episodically abandoned residences, in the context of intra and inter-regional exchange trips. These visits not only permit the continued monitoring of the abandoned residences but also facilitate the embedded delayed curation of artifacts.

Different abandonment processes (e.g. different forms of curation) may be expected under land-use patterns in which the distinct site types are located further apart or in regions not accessible in the context of inter and

intra-regional travels. In addition, it is possible that changes in land-use that result in the termination of an entire element of the subsistence pattern (e.g. subsistence agro-pastoralism to specialized agriculture) will result in different abandonment processes as well. Under such circumstances, the entire active assemblage used at the pastoral residences may be abandoned without its subsequent delayed curation. This land-use context may result in abandonment processes which mimic, in some respects, catastrophic abandonment. On the other hand, it is possible that the entire assemblage would be curated at the time of seasonal site abandonment since site reoccupation is not anticipated. The broad technological factors and socio-cultural contexts that condition the variation in caching behavior need to be better understood before systematic expectations can be developed.

The case study described here illustrates an example of site abandonment within the context of fluctuations in the role of the component elements of household economy, specifically the pastoral subsystem. The abandonment of the pastoral residences is followed by the delayed curation of cached assemblages. The delayed curation of passive artifact assemblages cached at seasonally occupied sites may have played a significant role in circumstances where sites were relatively easily accessible from each other and delayed curation costs were less than raw material replacement and manufacture costs, or other forms of tool replacement.

Acknowledgments
I wish to thank several people who have read earlier versions of this paper and provided useful comments that unquestionably improved the presentation. M. B. Schiffer read two papers that are combined here and provided useful comments and terminological guidance. Britt Bousman, Marybeth S. F. Tomka, and Linda Nance provided useful and much appreciated editorial help. A conversation with Ray Mauldin at the 1988 Annual Meeting of the Society for American Archaeology provided the seeds of these ideas. Britt Bousman has been a helpful sounding board and a catalyst for stimulating discussions. Prewitt and Associates Inc. provided the stimulating environment to think these ideas through, and Sandra Hannum patiently taught me the mysteries of computer graphics and drafted the two maps. A great deal of thanks go to all. Of course, any shortcomings are due to personal oversights. Last, but not least, special thanks to the Wenner-Gren Foundation for providing the funding for the fieldwork.

References

Binford, L. R.
1973 Interassemblage Variability – The Mousterian and the "functional argument." In *Explanation of Culture Change: Models in Prehistory*, edited by C. Renfrew, pp. 227–54. Duckworth, London.
1977 Forty-Seven Trips: A Case Study in the Character of Archaeological Formation Processes. In *Stone Tools as Cultural Markers: Change, Evolution and Complexity*, edited by R. V. S. Wright, pp. 24–36. Australian Institute for Aboriginal Studies, Canberra.
1978 *Nunamiut Ethnoarchaeology*. Academic Press, New York.
1979 Organizational and Formation Processes: Looking at Curated Technologies. *Journal of Anthropological Research* 35:255–73.

Bleed, P.
1986 The Optimal Design of Hunting Weapons: Maintainability of Reliability? *American Antiquity* 51:736–47.

Deal, M.
1985 Household Pottery Disposal in the Maya Highlands: An Ethnoarchaeological Interpretation. *Journal of Anthropological Archaeology* 4:243–91.

Everitt, B. S.
1977 *The Analysis of Contingency Tables*. London: Chapman and Hall.

Fisher, J. W.
1989 Links in the Lives of Hunter-Gatherers: Archaeological Implications among Efe Pygmies. Paper presented at the annual meeting of the Society of American Archaeology, Atlanta.

Gifford, D. P.
1978 Ethnoarchaeological Observations of Natural Processes Affecting Cultural Materials. In *Explorations in Ethnoarchaeology*, edited by R. A. Gould, pp. 77–101. University of New Mexico Press, Albuquerque.

Haberman, S. J.
1973 The Analysis of Residuals in Cross-Classified Tables. *Biometrics* 29:205–20.

Hayden, B.
1976 Curation: Old and New. In *Primitive Art and Technology*, edited by J. S. Raymond, B. Loveseth, C. Arnold, and G. Reardon, pp. 47–59. The University of Calgary, Alberta.

Holdridge, L. R.
1967 *Life Zone Ecology*. Revised Edition. Tropical Science Center, San Jose.

Johnson, A. M.
1976 The Climate of Peru, Bolivia and Ecuador. In *Climates of Central and South America*, edited by W. Schwerdfeger, pp. 147–217. Elsevier Scientific Publishing Company, Amsterdam.

Joyce, A. A. and S. Johannessen
1987 Formation Processes of House Sites: The Ethnoarchaeology of La Concha, Oaxaca, Mexico. Paper presented at the annual meeting of the Society for American Archaeology, Toronto.

Lange, F. W. and C. R. Rydberg
1972 Abandonment and Post-Abandonment Behavior at a Rural Central American House Site. *American Antiquity* 37: 419–32.

Schiffer, M. B.
1975 The Effects of Occupation Span on Site Content. In *The Cache River Archeological Project: An Experiment in Contract Archeology*, edited by M. B. Schiffer and J. H. House, pp. 265–9. Research Series No. 8, Publications in Archeology, Fayetteville: Arkansas Archeological Survey.
1987 *Formation Processes of the Archaeological Record*. University of New Mexico Press, Albuquerque.

Shott, M. J.
1986 Technological Organization and Settlement Mobility: An Ethnographic Examination. *Journal of Anthropological Research* 42:15–51.
1989 Diversity, Organization, and Behavior in the Material Record. *Current Anthropology* 30:283–315.

Stevenson, M. G.
1982 Toward an Understanding of Site Abandonment Behavior: Evidence from Historic Mining Camps in the Southwest Yukon. *Journal of Anthropological Archaeology* 1:237–65.

Torrence, R.
1983 Time Budgeting and Hunter-Gatherer Technology. In *Hunter-Gatherer Economy in Prehistory: A European Perspective*, edited by G. Bailey, pp. 11–22. Cambridge University Press, Cambridge.
1987 Re-tooling: Towards a Behavioral Theory of Stone Tools. In *Time, Energy and Stone Tools*, edited by R. Torrence, pp. 57–66. Cambridge University Press, Cambridge.

3
Settlement organization and residential variability among the Rarámuri

MARTHA GRAHAM

Introduction

Our assumptions about what we expect to see in the archaeological record influence our interpretations of that record and of the cultural adaptations we strive to understand. Understanding abandonment is a case in point. As the papers in this volume show, the term "abandonment" includes a variety of meanings and physical manifestations. Interpreting abandonment of habitations through the archaeological materials left at a site has implications at the level of the residential sites and in terms of regional settlement patterns. If we assume a single kind of abandonment in archaeological contexts, then the variations in assemblages must be interpreted along other lines – for example population, wealth, or social status. If we consider that the archaeological record may represent several different contexts for abandonment, then we can address the problem of how to distinguish between them.

Punctuated abandonment is the regular, planned movement of a household from one residence to another. The term "punctuated abandonment" implies both planned departure from and anticipated return to a residence. When regular intervals of abandonment and reoccupation are an integral part of a subsistence-settlement system, they strongly influence the kinds of goods and the organization and use of space at contemporary habitations. An ethnoarchaeological study of the Rarámuri (Tarahumara) of northern Mexico provides an example of punctuated abandonment and the resulting material assemblages expected at residences. This discussion considers how formal and distributional aspects of materials at habitations are indicative of the

general settlement system of punctuated abandonment.

Can archaeologists distinguish between variability associated with mobility strategies and that resulting from other aspects of cultural organization? The Rarámuri data suggest currently we cannot. The Rarámuri, as mobile agro-pastoralists, challenge many expectations archaeologists generate about agriculturalists' settlement organization, and what we expect to see in archaeological assemblages. A system of punctuated abandonment results in distinctive contemporary material assemblages at the different types of residences. Comparing the material assemblages of residences from different abandonment contexts underscores the range of assemblage variation archaeologists must anticipate in developing their models and their methods of data recovery and interpretation. While assemblages from permanently abandoned sites might be more what we *think* we expect in the archaeological record, we cannot assume this to be the case.

This paper describes a system of punctuated abandonment and the material record of residences within that system. The contemporary material assemblages discussed in this paper are not viewed as archaeological assemblages. Archaeological assemblages are the product of materials that have gone not only through use, discard, abandonment, and other processes as part of a living system, but subsequently through postdepositional processes. But, an understanding of the material record in the context of the system that creates it is critical to understanding and interpreting the archaeological record. This paper articulates how mobility and abandonment, as integral parts of a settlement system, affect the distribution of activities and materials at sites. It then offers several ideas archaeologists might use to identify important variability in the archaeological record and more accurately interpret this variability. The findings are critical to the creation of models of residential mobility and to generating expectations of the archaeological record under these conditions.

Rarámuri subsistence-settlement system

The Rarámuri are subsistence agro-pastoralists living in the rugged country of the Sierra Madres of southwestern Chihuahua, Mexico (Fig. 3.1). The information discussed in this paper comes from the Rarámuri community of Rejogochi (see Graham 1989; Merrill 1981, 1988). Rejogochi is a dispersed community of thirty-two households. The various residences and fields are scattered for about 5 km along a broad valley bottom and on the low benches and mountain slopes above it. Rejogochi lies in

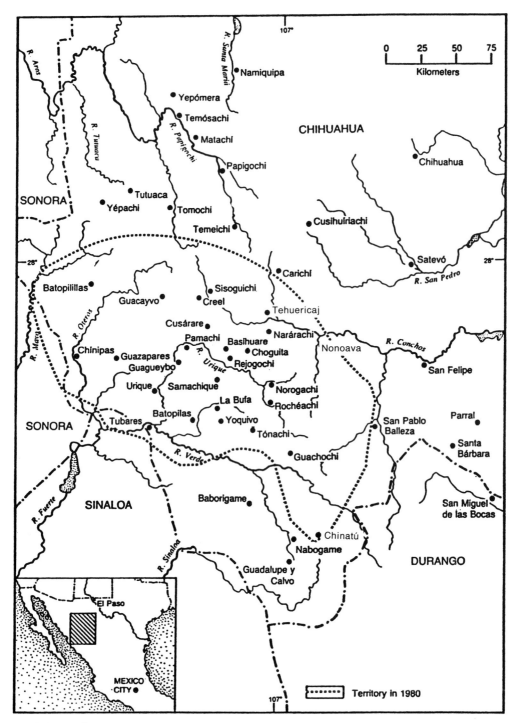

Fig. 3.1   Rarámuri homeland (from Merrill 1988:Figure 1).

Fig. 3.2   Main residence, August 1987. The dwelling has two connected structures, both made of logs and hand-lumbered boards. The small structure at the left is an animal pen. The garden in the foreground contains corn and squash, and has been planted in the residence's refuse area.

the transition zone between the canyons and the uplands in the Sierra Madres (Sierra Tarahumara). In this region, farmers cultivate corn fields and gardens in the relatively wide valley floors, and plant swidden bean fields on the slopes.

Residences in Rejogochi today typically consist of one or two dwellings, a storage structure, and various outbuildings. The dwellings enclose between 15 and 20 sq m of space. Many Rarámuri occupy two, three, or more residences during the year. First, the *main residence* is a warm-weather habitation in the community where the household spends most of the year (Fig. 3.2). The household usually locates this residence near some or all of its fields in the main community. The entire household spends perhaps six or more months of a year at this residence, with episodes of abandonment while they occupy another residence. Secondly, the household also may occupy a separate *winter residence*. This habitation is protected from inclement weather by being located above the valley floor, or made secure against drafts and precipitation. Often winter residences are located in rockshelters (Fig. 3.3). Occupation of these residences is during the coldest three to four months of the year, generally between December and March. Finally, many households own and tend agricultural fields in other communities. Households generally have habitations, termed *agricultural residences*, in these communities as well. The household periodically occupies agricultural residences while tending its fields and participating in co-operative work parties and communal social and religious events. Periods of habitation may be for several days or several weeks at a time, three or four times during the year.

Fig. 3.3   Winter residence, February 1987. One dwelling at this residence is near the center of the photograph. The roof is used for storage. The wood pile and group of hens feeding are downslope and to the right of the structure. One wall of the second dwelling is seen at the left edge. A new wooden plow sits at the center of the photograph. The woman at the bottom left is weaving.

Both the main and the agricultural residences lie on the valley floor. Rockshelters and other locations on the mountain sides offer protection from the wind and weather and good sun exposure during the winter. Most main and agricultural residences are currently constructed of wood. If the residence is a rockshelter, the rockface is incorporated into the shelter as walls and ceiling, supplemented by stone and log walls and brush.

The main and agricultural residences are not different functional types of residences; these residences are occupied during the same time of year and the same kinds of activities occur in both. Agricultural residences differ from main residences only in the total number of days the residence is occupied and the duration of each episode. The main residence is that habitation occupied for the greatest number of days during the year. The agricultural residence is left unoccupied during most of the year. A habitation occupied as the main residence one year may become an agricultural residence the next.

Winter residences in Rejogochi are typically 15–30 minutes' walk from the main community and fields. Frequently, they lack storage structures; households store food for this occupation at the main residence, bringing it to the winter dwelling as needed. In parts of the Sierra, winter residences are at a greater distance from the main community than is usually the case around Rejogochi. In these cases, households sometimes plant fields near their cold-weather homes to provide stores during the winter (Champion 1962). On the other hand, the winter dwelling may be closer to the agricultural

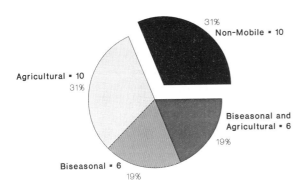
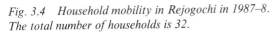

Fig. 3.4　Household mobility in Rejogochi in 1987–8. The total number of households is 32.

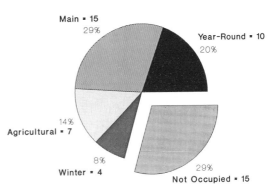

Fig. 3.5　Residence types in Rejogochi 1987–8. The total number of residences is 51.

residence than to the main one. In this case, stored foods may be brought to the cold-weather residence from this nearer habitation.

When the household is a nuclear family, the entire household will make its residential moves as a unit throughout the year. Households made up of extended families also move together, but some household members (for example a young married couple or the grandparents) may have land or obligations not shared by the rest of the household and will join with another household for part of its annual round.

During 1987–8, thirty-two households lived in Rejogochi (Fig. 3.4). Twenty-two (69 percent) of these households made residential moves during that time. Twelve households made moves from warm to cold-weather dwellings (main residence to winter residence), and sixteen made moves during the agricultural cycle (main residence to agricultural residence). Six households moved both biseasonally and during the agricultural cycle, each occupying at least three different habitations during the year

The community of Rejogochi consists not only of households, but also of residences. Considering the latter gives us a slightly different picture of the community. Of the fifty-one habitable residences in Rejogochi in 1987–8, households occupied thirty-six for some portion of the year (Fig. 3.5). Of these, ten were the exclusive, year-round residence of a household and fifteen were the main residences of households. Four habitations were winter dwellings, and seven were inhabited only during the growing season by households whose main residences were in other communities. Thus, in 1987–8, only 71 percent of the residences in Rejogochi were inhabited. Only 20 percent of the habitable residences were not abandoned during some

part of the year while the household occupied another habitation.

Households move not only *within* Rejogochi, but *beyond* it. Rejogochi is part of a larger system; that is, households move *through* the community, residing here for part of the time, but also occupying residences in other communities. For example, twelve households made biseasonal moves in 1987–8, but only four residences in Rejogochi were identified as winter residences; some households moved to winter residences in other communities. In the same way, sixteen households made agricultural moves, but only seven of Rejogochi's residences were inhabited exclusively during the agricultural cycle.

The relationship between number of residences occupied and number of habitable residences present suggests the ease with which archaeologists might overestimate population in the valley and in the region. Archaeologists have long been aware of the problem of estimating population from archaeological material (for example, Powell 1988:168–91 discusses the methods, assumptions, and problems in reconstructing Anasazi demography). Archaeologists endeavor to limit the potential for error by identifying meaningful correlates of population in the material remains at archaeological sites. In the Southwestern United States, these correlates have ranged from measuring floor area (e.g. Naroll 1962; LeBlanc 1971; Schiffer 1972) to room counts (e.g. Hill 1970; Longacre 1976) to artifactual debris (e.g. Cook 1972).

Southwestern archaeologists continue to adjust their revised understanding of agricultural adaptations and archaeological processes when measuring population. This is done by focusing on methods that distinguish between population size, population aggregation, site size, and occupation duration in the archaeological record (e.g. Crown 1991; Schlanger 1988; Wills and Windes 1989). Archaeologists also recognize the need to accommodate biseasonal or pueblo-to-fieldhouse residential moves in their population estimates (cf. Orcutt 1991; Wills and Windes 1989), although the means to do so are not always explicitly addressed.

The distinctions observed by Gilman (1987) and Powell (1983) in settlement variability depended on seasonal and architectural differences between residences. While Rarámuri biseasonal mobility results in differential placement of habitation sites, residential mobility during the growing season is not indicated by distinctive changes in residence location or activities. The Rarámuri case is not presented here merely as a cautionary tale. Nor do I advocate that archaeologists indiscriminately adopt a Rarámuri settlement model for prehistoric agriculturalists in the Southwest. The Rarámuri system is significant as a way in which archaeologists can approach understanding mobility in agricultural settings and interpreting archaeological settlement patterns.

Access to stored resources, increased intensification of labor, and access to knowledge and/or limited goods are offered as explanations for increased sedentariness (e.g. Cordell 1984; Dean 1988; Rindos 1984; Wills 1988). Mobility during the agricultural cycle allows Rarámuri households to tend fields in other communities. Living and working in these communities allows them to maintain social ties through the labor networks they have in the region (Merrill and Graham 1990; Kennedy 1978 provides a lengthy discussion of these networks). Crops in these other communities provide an important supplemental food source, especially when fields in the main community do not yield sufficient harvest to last the year (Hard and Merrill 1992).

In some sense, the Rarámuri are mobile for the same reasons offered to explain sedentariness. Stored resources are distributed across the landscape at the household's various agricultural residences. The labor networks in which households participate crosscut communities. A household will be part of a network that extends through its main community and other communities where it has agricultural fields. Their network may include communities where they have social ties but no agricultural land. These networks also provide a context for the exchange of goods and information between households and communities.

Hunter-gatherers move in order to monitor the landscape, and in response to resource availability (seasonal or after depletion through use: e.g. Wills 1988). When living year-round on stored resources supplemented by seasonal plant foods and game, these explanations for residential mobility seem inappropriate. Recognizing this unsuitability, archaeologists are unable adequately to model agriculturalist mobility in the context of an annual round.

Agricultural models typically explain population movements in terms of risk reduction, environmental degradation or improvement, and arguments of carrying capacity (e.g. Gumerman 1988). Population movements modeled on these factors tend to be at a larger scale than that of a single settlement system in an annual or multiple-year cycle (Powell 1990; Schlanger 1990). Because the distribution of sites across a landscape is influenced by mobility patterns at both scales we must develop means for understanding and approaching the archaeological record at various levels (Nelson 1990; Powell 1990; Schlanger and Wilshusen this volume).

The Rarámuri case shows some very different dynamics from those typically modeled for the distribution of agriculturalists' residences across a landscape. If these reasons are not unique to Rejogochi, archaeologists must address the questions of how to increase our understanding of agricultural settlement systems, under what conditions we can expect agriculturalists to be mobile, and what the archaeological consequences of such systems might be. What aspects of the settlement patterns indicate a less than year-round occupation of sites? What other evidence exists for the distribution of agriculturalists' multiple residences that will enable us to extrapolate population?

Of equal or greater importance to estimating population accurately through the distribution of archaeological materials, perhaps, are the implications for discussions of social and political organization (e.g. Cohen 1984; Gumerman 1988; Powell 1988). Evidence for aggregations during Basketmaker III times in the Southwest, particularly at Shabik'eschee Village in Chaco Canyon, New Mexico, has provided a forum for archaeologists to discuss the possible social and political factors resulting in this regional settlement pattern. In 1982 Lightfoot and Feinman proposed a big-man system of social and political organization for Mogollon pithouse villages. At the risk of over-simplifying their arguments, Lightfoot and Feinman interpreted differences in early village size, presence and amount of trade goods in villages, and variations in house and storage facility sizes as indicative of inter-regional exchange networks requiring a level of organization beyond that of the household (see Cordell 1984:226–7; Powell 1988:187–8; and Wills and Windes 1989:363–4 for more complete discussions of this argument). Lightfoot and

Feinman were not able to control for contemporaneity of structures at the village sites, nor of trade goods with pithouse occupations, and their arguments are not widely accepted (Schiffer 1983).

More recently, Wills and Windes (1989) reviewed this and other interpretations of Shabik'eschee Village and reported on the results of recent survey and excavation at that site. Their conclusions relative to Lightfoot and Feinman's big-man model affirm that the lack of temporal control at the site means the model cannot be verified. Their own interpretation emphasizes a more mobile population with a mixed subsistence economy of both produced and collected foods. While occasional aggregations at Shabik'eschee Village occurred in order to collect locally available wild resources, such gatherings were not common. The social and political leadership in such situations would more closely resemble those seen among hunter-gatherers than of a big-man system (pp. 364–5).

It is important to note that additional survey and excavation was required at Shabik'eschee Village in order to assess Lightfoot and Feinman's (and others', e.g. Steward 1937; Schelberg 1982) interpretation of the data. Wills and Windes' own interpretation reflects the current move to distinguish between sedentariness, dependence on agriculture, and a continued use of wild foods. In addition to developing models that include mobility in agriculturalist systems, this example indicates the need for data collection that will allow us accurately to identify and interpret variability in the archaeological record.

Currently, archaeologists cannot always offer criteria that distinguish unambiguously between significantly different interpretations of the archaeological record. This inability stems from an inadequate understanding of agriculturalists' settlement organization and the resulting assemblages. A closer look at the nature and distribution of materials at Rarámuri habitations provides the basis for better understanding the relationship between the settlement system and assemblage composition.

Punctuated abandonment and reoccupation at residential sites

Within their annual round, the Rarámuri regularly anticipate the causes and circumstances of residential abandonment. Toward the beginning of cold weather, a household will make plans to occupy their winter residence. They will review what items are already at the residence, anticipating what they will need to bring to the habitation and what can remain at the main residence. Returning to occupy the main residence after the winter, the household then restores the items brought from it to the winter dwelling. In the same way, a household preparing to occupy an agricultural residence will consider the requirements of that occupation. They will assess the adequacy of the goods stored there for the anticipated residency. Knowing the range of activities and length and season of occupation at each residence, the Rarámuri can plan in detail what must be taken to or left at a habitation.

The abandonment assemblage

The materials remaining at the residence while the household is absent from the site comprise what I call the abandonment assemblage. Among agriculturalists who live year-round on stored foods, many processing and preparation activities performed at the residence remain the same, regardless of season (Fig. 3.6). Other activities, such as tool manufacture, and many leisure activities are also performed year-round at Rarámuri residences. One result of this redundancy in on-site activities is that, despite the time of year or length of occupation, the same basic abandonment assemblage is left at each site type (Graham, field notes 1987–8). Because the abandonment assemblage remains at the residence in anticipation of reoccupation, the contents of the assemblage have more to do with the expected return to the habitation than with the process of abandoning the particular residence or residence type.

Site furniture

Site furniture is any item left at a site, belonging *to the site itself*, rather than to the occupants of the site (Binford 1977, 1978). Fig. 3.7 shows the two major classes of site furniture on Rarámuri sites – structural facilities and equipment needed for food preparation.

Structures The structures at the residence – for example, the dwelling(s), animal pens, corrals, and storage structures – and other movable facilities like boards for bedding or shelving and branched poles, are important elements left at the residence in anticipation of return. With these facilities left in place, re-establishment of the active residence is possible within a few minutes even after months of abandonment. Structural elements may be borrowed from the site on occasion, and are all highly movable (the Rarámuri themselves are their main mode of transport). But they are recognized as belonging to a certain residence, and generally remain at that place throughout the course of a given year.

Fig. 3.6   Rarámuri woman grinding corn, April 1988. The corn is first parched, then ground on the metate. The second metate is then used to render the consistency of the corn meal finer.

Food processing and preparation   Because most food processing and preparation activities remain the same year-round for the Rarámuri, the household leaves duplicate processing and preparation assemblages at each residence. This equipment includes the series of manos and metates used in most of the food processing activities (Fig. 3.6), basic cookware, utensils, and other housewares (for example, baskets, bowls, and cups). Planned social events like co-operative work parties also influence the equipment used during an occupation and subsequently left during abandonment. These items include one or more large metal cooking pots (tambo), tesguino ollas (large ceramic pots that hold the fermented corn beer drunk on these occasions), and perhaps a couple of medium to large ollas (ceramic cooking pots) for beans or meat stew.

Storage   The ability to protect site furniture remaining at a residence during abandonment requires adequate storage facilities. In residences occupied during the warm part of that year, and in roofed (secure) winter residences, the dwellings themselves serve as storage facilities during abandonment phases. Items left in

passive storage (Binford 1978, 1979) in and around the main residence during occupation are more formally stored during periods of abandonment. Fig. 3.8 shows the interior of the dwelling at a household's main residence, mapped while the household was living in its cold-weather residence. Structure A is completely walled and roofed. Structure B has a roof, but its walls (approximately 1.5 m high) do not extend to the roof, allowing plenty of light into this activity space. The assemblage of site furniture – metates, cookware, beds, and so on – is all present. In addition, the enclosed room (Structure A) has an assortment of foodstuffs, ollas, utensils, and personal gear stored in areas used as activity space when the household is in residence.

The presence or absence of food storage facilities is dependent on the nature and length of occupation at a residence. When a household has fields and a dwelling beyond the main community, they store the harvest at that habitation (the agricultural residence) rather than transporting it to the main residence. The household consumes this food when living at the agricultural residence. These stored foods are a factor allowing households to extend their occupation of these residences at

MOVABLE FACILITIES

Shelter

Dwelling(s)
Storage Structure
Animal Pens/Corrals

Boards (Sleeping, etc.)

Shelving

FOOD PREPARATION

Metate(s)

Mano(s)

Ceramic Assemblage

Cookware for Work Parties
Tambo
Large Ollas
Tesguino Ollas

Basic Utensils

Fig. 3.7 Site furniture: items left in anticipation of reoccupation at a residence.

intervals during the growing season (Merrill and Graham 1990). The subsistence activities during these occupations and at harvest are identical with those performed at the main residence.

On Rarámuri residences, bulk food storage facilities are separate from the dwelling. Few winter residences have the storage structure commonly found at the main and agricultural residences. When the winter dwelling is a rockshelter, it is generally only partially roofed. These dwellings are less secure against intruders than other types of dwellings the Rarámuri occupy. Without adequate storage facilities at winter residences in Rejogochi, few items beyond the most basic site furniture remain at the abandoned site. Instead, items may be cached at or near the residence and retrieved as time permits or as necessity dictates.

The introduced assemblage at reoccupation
Personal gear
A household also introduces a number of items to a residence it is reoccupying after a period of abandonment. These items are termed "personal gear" (Binford 1979). The critical difference between personal gear and site furniture is that personal gear remains *with personnel of the household* throughout the sequential occupations and abandonments of their residences. Site furniture remains at a specific location.

Personal gear includes items necessary in the daily activities of the residence and possessions belonging to individual household members. Examples of the former include knives, bedclothes, axe, and *molino* (a mechanical grinder used in some food processing tasks). Personal gear belonging to individuals includes clothing and personal ornaments. Personal gear can be expensive – either in terms of the time invested in its manufacture or as items purchased by cash or through bartering. It is frequently unique in the household and so must be transported from residence to residence, and carefully monitored to prevent theft or loss. The store-bought foods brought to a residence at the time of reoccupation are grouped here with personal gear.

Variable items
Many household tools fall somewhere between personal gear and site furniture. How a household decides whether or not to keep these items or leave them at a residence depends on the item's frequency of use, the degree of security at a residence during abandonment, and the relative wealth of the household. Looms, weaving tools, and ceramic manufacturing goods are examples of these items. Households that do much weaving will set up a loom at both the winter and the main residence. They will move the loom back and forth between these habitations. Because the loom is moved

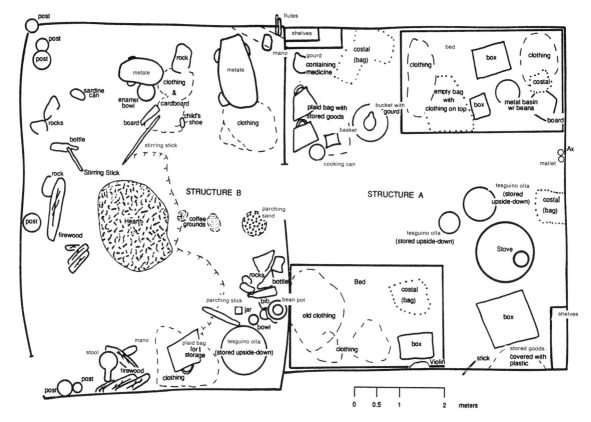

Fig. 3.8 Interior of main residence during winter abandonment, December 1988. Structure A is a tightly chinked log dwelling; the walls of Structure B extend up only about 1.5 m, allowing for more light in the structure. Activity space in Structure A (on the beds and in front of the stove) is being used for storage during this episode of abandonment. The tesguino ollas are turned upside-down for long-term storage.

from residence to residence, it can be considered personal gear. If the winter residence is secure and consistently occupied by the same household, then the household may construct a second loom, keeping one at the main residence and the other at its winter habitation. The same situation is also possible with the agricultural residence. In this case, personal gear for one household is site furniture at another's residences. The molino also could be considered variable gear; because it plays an essential role in food preparation and therefore occurs at any occupied site, it is conceivable that a wealthy household could keep one at each residence. These grinders are quite expensive, however, and, like the axe, households cannot afford to leave a molino at an abandoned residence and risk its theft.

Cookware for large work parties is another example of variable gear. If the main and winter residences are near each other some of these items may be transported back and forth between the residences. Here, site furniture may become personal gear. (The distance may be too great to transport these pots between either of these habitations and the agricultural residence, in which case duplicate cookware probably would be part of that residence's site furniture.) Generally, variable items will be more common between the main and winter residences than between the main and agricultural residences.

Discussion

Punctuated abandonment is an integral part of the Rarámuri subsistence-settlement system. The regularly anticipated movement of agriculturalists between several established residences results in contemporary assemblages indicative of this type of mobility. Differences among material assemblages at the three kinds of Rarámuri residences are determined less by variability in the activities and functions occurring at the habitations than

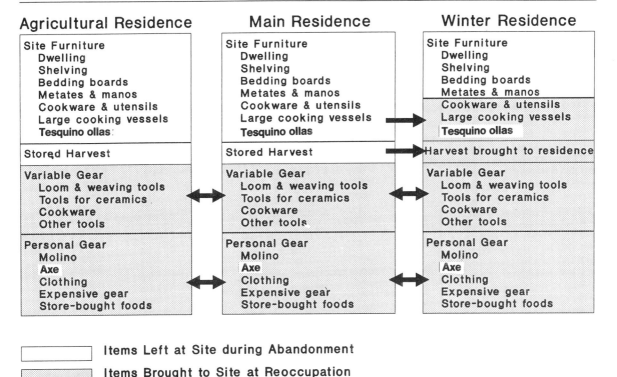

Fig. 3.9   Material assemblages at Rarámuri residence types.

by how households equip their residences within the system of punctuated abandonment and reoccupation. Fig. 3.9 illustrates the composition of the assemblages at residences during both occupation and abandonment. Personal gear is the most dynamic part of each assemblage, representing important items traveling with the household as the occupants move between residences.

The main and the agricultural residences differ primarily in the length and periodicity of their occupations. The assemblages of the main and agricultural residences are more similar to each other than is either to that of the winter residence. Several factors ensure the similarity of assemblages at the main and agricultural habitations in contrast to the winter residence. These include the distance between the main and the agricultural residences, their occupation during warm weather, the duplication of the range of activities performed there, and the need to store annual harvests at both residences. Moreover, the occupation emphasis of the main and agricultural residences frequently alternates, making differences between them less obvious through time. The winter

residence has the most variability in material assemblages during periods of both abandonment and occupation. As storage facilities are infrequent at this habitation, and because it is near the main residence, goods are easily carried between the two. The household uses the main residence to store necessary items, and retrieves them as required in their frequent trips to the valley floor.

Permanent abandonment at residential sites

In contrast to punctuated abandonment, permanent abandonment of a residence occurs when a household leaves the site and has no expectations of returning to it. When a Rarámuri household permanently abandons a habitation, it moves everything of value or use, including structures, from that residence to a new location. The material assemblage at permanently abandoned habitation sites is quite different from those discussed previously.

The Rarámuri have many reasons why they permanently abandon a residence. Dreaming of the dead is a frequently given response. In other cases, when a

Fig. 3.10   Permanently abandoned residence, February 1988. The dwelling and other elements of the habitation were removed in August 1987. Two logs from the dwelling walls and a canoa *(a trough-like log used to form the roof) and some foundation stones remain where the dwelling stood. In the foreground is the edge of the household's field. The dwelling was surrounded by a maintained activity area, seen as the hard-packed surface between the dwelling and field. At the left side of the photograph is a stump fashioned into a stool; this piece of site furniture was not taken to the new residence. In the background behind this residence is another dwelling, currently used as a goat barn.*

household member inherits a dwelling (or other out-buildings) they will move the structure to a place of their own choosing; many houses in Rejogochi have been in use for more than a generation, but rarely have they stayed in the same place for all that time. While people do not cite insect infestation as a reason to move their houses, it may be a factor in the permanent abandonment of some residential sites. Sometimes a household will establish its residence at the location of a permanently abandoned site.

During the 1987–8 field season, three main residences in Rejogochi were abandoned permanently. In August 1987 an extended family who had lived at two separate main residences joined them into a single main residence at a third location. Fig. 3.10 illustrates the remains of one of these abandoned residences. In February 1988 another household sold the dwelling at an uninhabited residence to a household that relocated the dwelling and established its own habitation.

The material assemblage at permanently abandoned residences

The material assemblages at residences during episodes of punctuated abandonment are left in anticipation of a return to the residence, with the knowledge of at what time of the year reoccupation will occur and the kinds of activities that will be performed at the time of occupancy. When a household permanently abandons a residence, the most important factor influencing the assemblage left at the site is that the household anticipates establishing a new residence elsewhere.

With few exceptions, all objects that were in use while the residence was occupied are taken to the new location. What remains at the permanently abandoned site are discarded objects, accumulated trash, and a few items that were overlooked or left in long-term passive storage. *Discard* behavior is very much a part of the process of abandoning one habitation permanently to establish a new one elsewhere. *Storage* behavior plays a major role in the establishment of the material assemblage left in anticipation of reoccupation at residences during punctuated abandonment.

Site furniture

The household takes away most of the residence's site furniture when it abandons a site. The structural site furniture – dwellings, bedding, and storage structures – form the physical core of the residence. The food processing and preparation elements of site furniture are the basis for many day-to-day activities occurring at the residence. These elements are some of the first removed from a permanently abandoned residence.

Some site structural elements do remain at the abandoned site. Old roof beams, logs used in wall construction, and other construction components used at the residence are left behind when they are rotten or infested by insects (Fig. 3.10). Low investment facilities like windbreaks and turkey and chicken pens (often simple structures of piled stone or wood) are abandoned, especially if the materials to construct new facilities are readily at hand in the new location. Ground stone, especially manos, may be left behind at the abandoned residence. Heavy facilities, for example simple stone feeding troughs used for animals, are not worth the effort of carrying to a new location.

Other gear

The household also takes with them most of the personal gear and variable items discussed above at the time of abandonment. Implements for craft production are carefully curated, as are food processing implements. As with the site structural elements, however, the household may take the opportunity to discard worn or broken tools.

Functional cookware is rarely found at permanently

abandoned residences. While ceramics make up the largest single class of artifacts (24 percent, or 216 of 918) at the one permanently abandoned residence inventoried, this figure only represents a large number of small sherds. Some cans and a flattened pail (used as a *comal*, for cooking tortillas) were present at the inventoried site. Because the actual abandonment of the residence was not observed, however, it is impossible to say whether these items were left at the time of abandonment or discarded prior to relocating the habitation.

Expensive items are also removed from the permanently abandoned residence. Most *refuse* at any Rarámuri residence consists of items that would be identified here as personal gear. Since this category includes purchased goods whose packaging remains long after the goods themselves have been used or consumed, these items are highly visible, and highly durable, trash.

In summary, the material assemblage at permanently abandoned residences has few items of functional site furniture or the gear that is used daily and/or for essential activities by the inhabitants. The assemblage at residences during punctuated abandonments is distinct from the refuse of everyday life. In contrast, that at the permanently abandoned habitation is the final episode of discard, typically at an object's locus of use or storage, in combination with the accumulated refuse of the occupation.

The Rarámuri settlement system from an archaeological perspective

The archaeological record at a residential site derives in part from the materials brought to the site during its use, from the use and maintenance of these materials, and from the locations of their use and their discard. Tomka (this volume) shows that the nature and distribution of archaeological materials is a function of the activities occurring not only at that site, but within the general subsistence-settlement system. Post-depositional processes ultimately transform the materials at areas occupied or used in the context of a cultural system into the archaeological record. This paper focuses on cultural processes influencing the material assemblages at residences, with the caveat that taphonomic factors play an important role in the formation of the archaeological record.

This paper is the first step in identifying the types of material assemblages present in a cultural system practicing punctuated residential abandonment. While it is by no means expected that the distribution and nature of materials covered here will appear in their entirety in the archaeological record, several implications of these findings are important to archaeologists. First, there is a qualitative difference between assemblages from residences during a phase of punctuated abandonment and those that are permanently abandoned. Secondly, not only assemblage composition but also its distribution throughout the site are indicative of the type of abandonment in which a residence was left. A third important implication is the clear need for a better understanding of subsistence-settlement systems and more appropriate models to apply to the archaeological record. Such models would enable us to evaluate assemblage variability as resulting from (in this case) different types of abandonment behaviors rather than from any other factors.

Site structure

The Rarámuri system as one of mobile agro-pastoralists challenges archaeologists by underscoring the inadequacies of our models for anticipating mobility, particularly among people who are *not* hunter-gatherers. Investment in permanent architecture, use of ceramics, and high dependence on agricultural production have traditionally indicated decreased mobility and increased sedentariness. The Rarámuri case demonstrates these are not adequate measures of sedentary year-round occupations.

Subsistence-settlement systems influence not only the materials brought to and taken from a location, but also the *placement* of materials at that location. The organization and use of a place is called site structure (Binford 1978; 1983:144–92). For the Rarámuri, the relatively low occupation intensity at residences (because they are not occupied continuously for long periods of time) influences the way households organize their activity space. Mobile agriculturalists like the Rarámuri have a more flexible organization and use of space than do more permanently settled agriculturalists. Among more sedentary groups there is a change in residential site structure. As intensity of occupation increases – either through increased length or duration of occupation, or through increased number of inhabitants at the site – the placement of activities and the nature of maintenance becomes more formalized (Graham 1989). This change in site structure occurs while the subsistence base and most of the activities carried out at the residence remain the same.

The nature of facilities at residences is an example of the flexibility in Rarámuri site structure. Many items identified as site furniture above are the foci for various activities. On Rarámuri residences, a metate is the locus of many food processing activities and sleeping boards also serve as work surfaces during the day. The *placement* of facilities and features is variable, however, and many facilities themselves remain highly movable. Thus, Rarámuri women will set up their metates virtually anywhere at the residence. Establishing the metate's placement depends on weather, lighting conditions, and factors such as the need for privacy or the opportunity to socialize. Sleeping boards, too, are moved in response to changes in weather, household size, or other demands. Beds may be made from the boards of dismantled storage structures. If necessary they may be used to construct temporary structures such as animal shelters. While some features, like the hearth, are not movable, multiple occurrences of these features provide the same kind of flexibility in use of space. The important aspect of the flexible placement of features and facilities is not so much in the relative ease with which they are moved or made. Rather, it is the availability of *generalized activity space* that can be modified into places where specific activities are performed (Graham 1989).

Among more permanently settled agriculturalists, many of these facilities become permanent fixtures in *activity-specific* and *activity-exclusive* areas (Arnold 1991; Dodd 1989). For example, the hearth is replaced or supplemented by a built stove or fire box. Mealing facilities become constructed features, and food processing and preparation activities are relegated to a specific structure (e.g. a "kitchen"). Sleeping areas are also separated from other kinds of activity space. Thus, much of the "site furniture" among groups whose settlement organization includes some degree of mobility become permanent fixtures, or built facilities, among more settled groups (Graham 1989).

Settlement systems with various forms of residential mobility need to be modeled so archaeologists can modify their data collection and analysis strategies to identify this important variability in the archaeological record. Without these models, archaeologists have an inadequate framework in which to look at artifacts and their distribution in space. In conjunction with developing appropriate models, this paper suggests that learning to identify the abandonment behaviors associated with different types of settlement systems (here, punctuated abandonment) can inform us about those settlement systems.

Archaeological patterns of punctuated abandonment

A system of punctuated abandonment creates several types of assemblages as residential sites across the landscape. The nature of the differences in assemblages is a function not so much of different activities occurring at the sites as of the anticipated abandonment and reoccupation of the sites. Seasonal variation of occupation does play a role in assemblage differences among the Rarámuri; the abandonment assemblage at winter residences is not as extensive as at the other types of habitation because of its proximity to the main residence. To identify this type of settlement system, archaeologists must have data from a sufficient number of sites to recognize the variations as part of the pattern. They must further work within a framework that allows the potential for different kinds of abandonment – e.g. permanent and punctuated – that may result in meaningful assemblage variability.

Archaeologists can begin developing recognition criteria for assemblages from residences in a period of punctuated abandonment. Among the Rarámuri, site furniture is a consistent element of periodically occupied residential sites. Learning to recognize site furniture (and the variable items described above) is not always an easy task. It includes identifying the essential elements necessary to site function and determining the ease and need to transport these items from one place to another. At residential sites, *facilities* very often represent a significant portion of the site furniture. The use of site furniture implies investment in the site as a resource itself (cf. Graham and Roberts 1986), to be returned to and used later.

Other gear that plays a crucial role in the successful occupation of a site may never be left at a residence during an episode of punctuated abandonment. Valuable and expensive tools accompany a household through its settlement round. These items will be invisible archaeologically until they are sufficiently worn and then discarded, or if they are lost. In the Rarámuri example, these artifacts often are associated with common household activities (for example, cooking and chopping wood). Others frequently relate to manufacturing household goods (for example, textiles and ceramics).

Archaeologists can use the spatial distribution of materials at residences to monitor types of abandonment. When a residence is in use, the household will keep activity areas clear of objects that impede the flow of activities or occupy usable space. During a period of punctuated abandment, the household uses interior activity space for active storage of site furniture (Fig. 3.8). The distribution of artifacts is different again under conditions of permanent abandonment, when objects are discarded with little thought about where they are in relation to activity space and features – since those areas are defunct on the abandoned site.

Under the conditions of punctuated abandonment, the household plans its move and assumes it will reoccupy the residence at a later date. This paper discusses the nature of the material assemblages found during occupations and punctuated abandonment episodes at the three types of inhabited Rarámuri residences and contrasts them with that from permanently abandoned sites. Identifying the nature and distribution of the material correlates of a subsistence-settlement system is only a part of the process of interpreting the archaeological record. With the information on organizational strategies and the resulting material assemblages presented here, archaeologists also need to develop a greater understanding of the formation of the archaeological record from the material record (cf. Todd 1990, especially 338–9), and better general theory about agriculturalists' systems, and the role of mobility in them. Without work on these three areas, archaeologists have no framework for identifying, much less interpreting, critical assemblage variability in the archaeological record.

Conclusions

As this volume illustrates, the term abandonment covers many different processes, and has no single archaeological consequence. Archaeologists frequently deal with permanently abandoned sites, but we cannot assume this is always the case. On some level, while archaeologists acknowledge that most of the archaeological record is trash, we must approach the record in such a way as to try to distinguish between different contexts of discard. Relative to this discussion, there are meaningful distinctions between materials disposed of as a consequence of site maintenance and those left at a site with the knowledge of whether the habitation will ever be reoccupied. At permanently abandoned residential sites, not only is the bulk of site furniture missing from the site, but the spatial arrangement of objects has more to do with the process of dismantling the site than with the use of its activity areas. During episodes of punctuated abandonment, an abandonment assemblage of site furniture consisting of facilities and other tools commonly used at the residence remains at the site. Some tools are *not* expected to be seen in contexts of abandonment. Among the Rarámuri these tend to be personal items and costly objects (in terms of labor or money) that are often unique in the household's gear. Patterning in the material record that relates to abandonment requires detailed attention to the distribution of artifacts at the site in conjunction with the identification of activity areas. At sites during episodes of punctuated abandonment, activity space is used to store the abandonment assemblage. When a site is permanently abandoned, the site structure of the residence as it is perceived by its occupants breaks down, and objects are discarded (abandoned) irrespective of activity areas, sheltered space, or trash areas.

The Rarámuri case offers an opportunity to identify some of the consequences of abandonment at residential sites. Perhaps the most important point to emphasize is that abandonment encompasses more than a single behavior or material consequence. If we assume we know what the archaeological record will look like – for example, the permanently abandoned sites described here – then assemblage variability will be explained in terms of other factors. The resulting interpretations might include discussions of permanent residences, inflated population estimates, and elaborate social organization. We must have appropriate models of settlement organization, and design our data collection strategies so that we can recover relevant information in the record in order to interpret variations in archaeological assemblages accurately.

Acknowledgments
Funding for my fieldwork among the Rarámuri comes from Sigma Xi, the Tinker Foundation of the University of New Mexico Latin American Institute, and a Dissertation Improvement Grant from NSF (BSN-8611525). A Graduate Student Fellowship and a Pre-Doctoral Fellowship at the Smithsonian were both critical to the success of my research. I very much appreciate the opportunity Cathy Cameron and Steve Tomka have provided in asking me to participate in this volume. The paper has greatly benefited from discussions with or comments by Bill Barnett, Jaymie Brauer, Cathy Cameron, Bill Latady, Nan Rothschild, Chuck Spencer, Michael Schiffer, Larry Todd, Steve Tomka, and three anonymous reviewers. Larry offered the term "punctuated abandonment" as a more interesting and accurate one than periodic or temporary abandonment. Any errors are my own.

References

Arnold, P. J., III
1991 *Domestic Ceramic Production and Spatial Organization: A Mexican Case Study in Ethnoarchaeology.* Cambridge University Press, Cambridge.
Binford, L. R.
1977 Forty-Seven Trips: A Case Study in the Character of Some Formation Processes. In *Stone Tools as Cultural Markers*, edited by R. V. S. Wright, pp. 24–36. Australian Institute of Aboriginal Studies, Canberra.
1978 Dimensional Analysis of Behavior and Site Structure: Learning from an Eskimo Hunting Stand. *American Antiquity* 43:330–61.
1979 Organization and Formation Processes: Looking at Curated Technologies. *Journal of Anthropological Research* 35:255–73.
1983 *In Pursuit of the Past.* Thames and Hudson, London.
Champion, J. R.
1962 Study in Culture Persistence: The Tarahumaras of Northwestern Mexico. Unpublished PhD dissertation, Department of Anthropology, Columbia University, New York.
Cohen, M. N.
1984 *The Food Crisis in Prehistory: Overpopulation and the Origins of Agriculture.* Yale University Press, New Haven.
Cook, S. F.
1972 *Prehistoric Demography.* Addison-Wesley Module in Anthropology 16, Reading.
Cordell, L. S.
1984 *Prehistory of the Southwest.* Academic Press, New York.
Crown, P. L.
1991 Evaluating the Construction Sequence and Population of Pot Creek Pueblo, Northern New Mexico. *American Antiquity* 56:291–314.
Dean, J. S.
1988 A Model of Anasazi Behavioral Adaptation. In *The Anasazi in a Changing Environment*, edited by G. J. Gumerman, pp. 25–44. Cambridge University Press, Cambridge.
Dodd, W.
1989 Organizational Aspects of Spatial Structure in Guarijío Sites. Draft of PhD dissertation, Department of Anthropology, University of Utah, Salt Lake City. Ms in possession of author.
Gilman, P. A.
1987 Architecture as Artifact. *American Antiquity* 52:538–64.
Graham, M.
1987–88 Fieldnotes, Rarámuri Residential Site Structure Ethnoarchaeological Project. Notes on file with author.
1989 Rarámuri Residential Site Structure: An Ethnoarchaeological Approach to Settlement Organization. Unpublished dissertation, Department of

Anthropology, University of New Mexico, Albuquerque.

Graham, M. and A. Roberts
1986 Residentially Constrained Mobility: A Preliminary Investigation of Variability in Settlement Organization. *Haliksa'i: UNM Contributions to Anthropology* 5:104–15.

Gumerman, G. J. (ed.)
1988 *The Anasazi in a Changing Environment.* Cambridge University Press, Cambridge.

Hard, R. J. and W. L. Merrill
1992 Mobile Agriculturalists and the Emergence of Sedentism: Perspectives from Northern Mexico. *American Anthropologist* 94:601–20.

Hill, J. N.
1970 *Broken K Pueblo: Prehistoric Social Organization in the American Southwest.* Anthropological Papers of the University of Arizona no. 18. University of Arizona Press, Tucson.

Kennedy, J. G.
1978 *Tarahumara of the Sierra Madre: Beer, Ecology, and Social Organization.* AHM Publishing Corporation, Arlington Heights.

LeBlanc, S. A.
1971 An Addition to Naroll's Suggested Floor Area and Settlement Population Relationship. *American Antiquity* 36:210–11.

Lightfoot, K. G. and G. M. Feinman
1982 Social Differentiation and Leadership in Early Pithouse Villages in the Mogollon Region of the American Southwest. *American Antiquity* 47:64–86.

Longacre, W. A.
1976 Population Dynamics at Grasshopper Pueblo. In *Demographic Anthropology: Quantitative Approaches*, edited by Ezra Zubrow, pp. 169–84. University of Texas Press, Austin.

Merrill, W. L.
1981 The Concept of Soul Among the Rarámuri of Chihuahua, Mexico: A Study in World View. Unpublished PhD dissertation, Department of Anthropology, University of Michigan, Ann Arbor.
1988 *Rarámuri Souls: Knowledge and Social Process in Northern Mexico.* Washington, DC, Smithsonian Institution Press.

Merrill, W. L. and M. Graham
1990 Tarahumara Residential Moves: Mobility Strategies among Subsistence Agriculturalists. Paper delivered at the 55th Annual Meeting of the Society for American Archaeology, Las Vegas.

Naroll, R.
1962 Floor Area and Settlement Population. *American Antiquity* 27:587–9.

Nelson, M. C.
1990 Comments: Sedentism, Mobility, and Regional Assemblages: Problems Posed in the Analysis of Southwestern Prehistory. In *Perspectives on Southwestern Prehistory*, edited by P. E. Minnis and C. L. Redman, pp. 150–6. Westview Press, Boulder.

Orcutt, J. D.
1991 Environmental Variability and Settlement Changes on the Pajarito Plateau, New Mexico. *American Antiquity* 56:315–32.

Powell, S.
1983 *Mobility and Adaptation: The Anasazi of Black Mesa, Arizona.* Southern Illinois University Press, Carbondale.
1988 Anasazi Demographic Patterns and Organizational Responses: Assumptions and Interpretive Difficulties. In *The Anasazi in a Changing Environment*, edited by G. J. Gumerman, pp. 168–91. Cambridge University Press, Cambridge.
1990 Sedentism or Mobility: What Do the Data Say? In *Perspectives on Southwestern Prehistory*, edited by P. E. Minnis and C. L. Redman, pp. 92–102. Westview Press, Boulder.

Rindos, D.
1984 *The Origins of Agriculture: An Evolutionary Perspective.* Academic Press, New York.

Schelberg, J. D.
1982 The Development of Social Complexity in Chaco Canyon. *Newsletter of the New Mexico Archaeological Council* 4:15–20.

Schiffer, M. B.
1972 Cultural Laws and the Reconstruction of Past Lifeways. *The Kiva* 37:148–57.
1983 Toward the Identification of Formation Processes. *American Antiquity* 48:675–706.

Schlanger, S. H.
1988 Patterns of Population Movement and Long-Term Population Growth in Southwestern Colorado. *American Antiquity* 53:773–93.
1990 Artifact Assemblage Composition and Site Occupation. In *Perspectives on Southwestern Prehistory*, edited by P. E. Minnis and C. L. Redman, pp. 103–21. Westview Press, Boulder.

Steward, J. H.
1937 Ecological Aspects of Southwestern Society. *Anthropos* 32:87–104.

Todd, L. C.
  1990 Review of *The Anatomy and Biology of the Human Skeleton, The Archaeology of Animals,* and *Teeth. Journal of Field Archaeology* 17:337–40.
Wills, W. H.
  1988 *Early Prehistoric Agriculture in the American Southwest*. School of American Research Press, Santa Fe.
Wills, W. H. and T. C. Windes
  1989 Evidence for Population Aggregation and Dispersal during the Basketmaker III Period in Chaco Canyon, New Mexico. *American Antiquity* 54:347–69.

4
Occupational and locational instability in arid land settlement

LEE HORNE

Introduction

Khar o Tauran[1] is a present-day village district in northeastern Iran (see Fig. 4.1). On the map and in the minds of its inhabitants, the area is settled. But settlement everywhere is a dynamic rather than a static phenomenon. Its fluidity in Khar o Tauran is well attested from present-day evidence as well as from archaeological remains that show shifting locations and varying sizes of occupation across time.[2] Some of this instability is inherent in the technology of settlement, part of an intentional production strategy typical of arid land occupations; some of it is visited upon the residents by factors outside their control.

The degree of settlement stability in Khar o Tauran varies with settlement type, size, and location relative to social and environmental resources. This variation has implications not only for an understanding of settlements as elements in the local strategies of production, but also for the archaeological reconstruction of population and land use.

Settlement stability (or instability) may be viewed in two ways, locational and occupational.[3] I use the term locational stability as a *spatial* concept referring to the degree to which settlements are continuously or repeatedly located in the same places. Examples of locationally stable settlements might be seasonal pastoral stations that rely on patchy resources such as springs, to which the residents return year after year.

Occupational stability, on the other hand, is a *temporal* concept referring to how long an occupation continues without interruption at a given location. An occupationally unstable area may present a shifting scene of people and activities against a background of continuity of location. The same pastoral settlements mentioned above, for example, may be used for only a few months out of each year, and thus exhibit relatively low occupational stability.

Stability of settlement in Khar o Tauran

Khar o Tauran is relatively isolated.[4] Agricultural mechanization and motorized transportation have begun to appear, but neither piped water nor electricity, tube wells, nor mechanized ploughing are present. The local economy is based primarily on irrigated agriculture combined with a strong pastoral component (for greater detail see Martin 1982; Horne 1988). The whole area covers about 3300 sq km with a population density of only 0.8 persons per sq km. The 120 sq km of the central plain is the most densely occupied part of the district, with about 10 persons per sq km and nearest neighbors 1.8 km apart on average. There are three main types of residential settlement in the area: permanent year-round villages of mud brick where both agricultural and pastoral activities take place, summer stations for tending sheep and goats and for processing milk products, and winter stations for pasturing animals in the "off" season. Summer and winter stations vary greatly in their distance from a home village; a few are within 100 m, most are a half day's walk or more. Summer and winter stations may also merge as year-round stations, although the specialized structures and spaces of the two seasons' use are visibly and spatially distinct.

Fig. 4.1 Map of Iran showing the study area.

43

Winter stations

In both the locational and the occupational sense, winter stations are the least stable of all settlement types in Khar o Tauran. In the first place, they are seasonal, used from October through April by male shepherds rather than entire households. Second, until the recent introduction of chemical pesticides, they were especially short lived on account of their periodic infestation with vermin and consequent burning and relocation. Third, their relatively uniform distribution reflects the fact that pasture and building materials are uniformly dispersed. Water sources for winter stations are not uniformly distributed, but it is not necessary (or desirable) to have one nearby: the animals drink only every other day in the winter, and the few domestic activities that take place do not require much water. Thus, winter stations are not tied to localized resources in the way that summer stations and villages are.

Active winter stations are located 6 km apart on average (based on data from Brian Spooner, pers. comm., and Hamlin 1976). A winter survey undertaken by Project team members (Hamlin 1976) showed that less than 50 percent of the winter stations they located were in use that year, largely because of frequent relocations. Not only is a particular station used for only about half the year, upon reoccupation the next winter it is frequently moved elsewhere if it needs much restoration; that is, it will be built anew rather than rebuilt. The move is not usually very far and the new station is frequently, but not necessarily, within view of the previous site.

Summer stations

Like winter stations, summer stations are seasonal, usually occupied from May to August, depending on the condition of the range. The occupants include women and children, however, as well as men, and may represent all or parts of several households. In the winter the women and children return to their home villages; the men may accompany them for the winter or may move to winter stations in the following months. While the main activities at winter stations revolve around tending the animals, those at summer stations are more fully domestic. Herding, milking and milk processing dominate the daily round (Martin 1980).

Locationally, summer stations are more stable than winter stations. Like villages and unlike winter stations, they are heavily dependent upon water sources, both

natural springs and artificial wells or *qanats* (see below). Their occupational stability, however, appears to be low, although it was difficult to collect systematic histories on them and only a few were mapped. Like small villages in the outlying areas, they appear to be less stable than the larger villages on the central plain.

Villages

Villages, the third major type of settlement, are occupied year-round by most of their inhabitants; in most villages only a few households have winter or summer stations. A full complement of activities takes place within them and in their immediate environs, including those that take place at winter and summer stations. Over the long term, the locational stability of villages and agricultural fields in Khar o Tauran appears to be high relative to other kinds of settlement. Sherd scatters at some of the villages suggest an initial occupation 2000 years ago or more. Nevertheless, tells, or mounds, are not characteristic of this area. Among the reasons for their absence is a lower continuity of occupation than is apparently found in other parts of the arid Near East. (For other factors in mound formation or the lack thereof, see Horne 1988.)

In fact, although their locations are relatively permanent, villages are not necessarily continuously occupied even over the short term. In surveys taken at ten-year intervals, between five and twelve sites out of all village sites were abandoned (field data and Iran 1969, 1973). In terms of occupation rates, this means that out of forty-three modern village site locations, 28 percent were unoccupied in 1956, 12 percent in 1966, and 26 percent in 1976. These were not always the same sites, moreover. A grand total of eighteen sites (42 percent) were either abandoned or reoccupied or both during that period of time.

Villages also vary in their degree of stability, according to location and size (which are themselves correlated). Smaller villages in the peripheral areas are much less stable than those on the central plain. Fig. 4.2 sums up occupational stability for villages in two different parts of the area over the same twenty-year period referred to above. The central group of villages have a mean size of about twenty-one households. In 1956 only one of these fifteen village sites (about 7 percent) was unoccupied. In contrast, the twenty-five outliers are much smaller, with a mean size of about seven households. In 1956 ten of the twenty-five outlier locations (40 percent) were unoccupied. Similarly, in 1966 none of the central villages but 20 percent of the outliers were unoccupied, in 1973 13 percent of the central villages and 16 percent

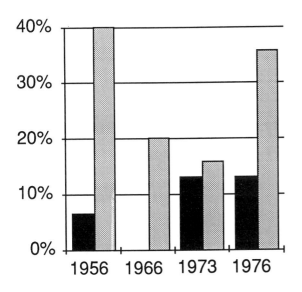

Khar o Tauran
Sites Unoccupied 1956-1976

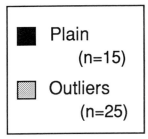

■ Plain
  (n=15)

▨ Outliers
  (n=25)

Fig. 4.2 Percentage of village sites unoccupied in Khar o Tauran between 1956 and 1976. Small outliers are less stable in occupation than are the larger sites on the Plain. The small number of sites on the Plain makes the full occupation of 1966 appear unusual; in fact in 1956 only one site was unoccupied, and in 1973 and 1976 only two sites were unoccupied.

of the outliers were unoccupied, and in 1976 13 percent of the central villages and 36 percent of the outliers were unoccupied.

Archaeological recognition and recovery

The dynamic nature of settlement and variation in stability according to settlement function(s) carries a number

of implications for archaeologists. Short-term locational instability may give the impression of a greater number of sites than were ever actually occupied during a given period of time. As archaeological data, they would be "double-counted" or worse unless a correction is made to account for their instability. Variation in the stability of different types of settlement means that the archaeological record will show a disproportionate accumulation of some compared to others. As Dewar (1986:80) points out, "the relative frequency of site types ... may bear little or no relation to the relative numbers of places in use at any point in the past." Occupational instability means that population and carrying capacity figures may be over-estimated. It is important not only to recognize that some sites are occupied only seasonally, but also to consider whether their occupants are the same ones who occupy year-round villages, or whether these come in from outside the region. Such is the case in Khar o Tauran, for example, where Sangsari transhumants from the mountains to the northwest increasingly bring their flocks down to winter on these lower plains (Martin 1982). Pastoral stations should here, therefore, be given full weight for production estimates but not for resident population estimates.

Given differential degrees of instability, the most immediate question should be whether it is possible to distinguish among settlement types when they are occupied, when they are unoccupied and, more to the point here, when they are abandoned. While occupied, settlements differ decidedly in terms of how they look and what they contain, which are in turn products of the location, seasonality, functions, and personnel of the settlement. It is not that all settlements within a type are exactly alike. There is, in fact, something of a continuum on account of a tendency to reuse one kind of site for a different purpose (the archaeological consequences of reuse at different types of sites are discussed more fully in Horne 1988). Most, however, do have a distinctive appearance that conforms to the local idea of what each type of settlement should look like.

The structures of a winter station are semi-subterranean; the roof is substantial – more so than a summer station which is used in the dry season – and waterproofed with dung plaster (Fig. 4.3). Because the animals are penned, their stables and the surrounding areas are quickly altered by the intense use of the flocks as they move in and out to food and water. A visibly degraded area extends between 1 and 1.5 km beyond pastoral stations (winter or summer) with a central circle 500 m in radius of heavily altered surface (Nyerges 1982).

Fig. 4.3   A winter pastoral station photographed during the summer. Winter stations typically consist of a central hut for the shepherds and flanking shelters for the flocks. Both types are semisubterranean and are built of stone or slabs of packed dung with roofs of brush, dirt, and dung supported by wooden poles.

The nature of the structures and the way the surroundings are altered by the activities of the animals make the location of a winter station obvious long after its abandonment. An unoccupied winter station appears much as it does when occupied, except that the people, animals and portable objects and equipment are gone. Only broken and discarded items are left. For example, the dwelling of one station visited in the summer following its winter use contained only half an oil drum, one small rusted oil can, an empty food tin and a broken kettle. Nor are items like these likely to accumulate within, since they will be removed and discarded outside the following year.

Like winter stations, summer stations tend to contain perishable storage equipment (skins, cloth, woven sacks) rather than pottery. At season's end, portable items are removed and only the trash is left. The structures are not secure enough to risk leaving anything of value, and in any case most people cannot afford duplicates of their belongings. The structures themselves are not dis-

mantled in the usual course of things. To do so would effectively require complete rebuilding upon return the following season.

Summer stations are less substantially built than are winter stations; they are neither as waterproof nor as windproof (Fig. 4.4). They do not include animal stables, since the animals are not in need of shelter during the summer, but they do include series of large hearths and other equipment used in the preparation of milk products (Martin 1980). An unoccupied summer station, even one used the previous year, is not necessarily easy to recognize (Fig. 4.5), especially when residents make use of natural features such as the rock outcrops in their hut construction, as they have in this illustration. Moreover, in this case, uncertainty about returning meant that the roof was removed so that the poles could be used elsewhere if necessary. Ordinarily, however, the structures are not altered when people move back to their village for the winter.

Fig. 4.4 The kitchen hut of an occupied summer milking station. Summer stations are more variable in layout and in number of occupants than are winter stations, but usually hold one to three households. They differ in appearance from either winter stations or year-round villages. Lacking animal shelters, they also lack the packed dung of which winter stations are frequently constructed.

Seasonally absent residence from pastoral stations is of course intentional, as is, for the most part, the intent to return the following year. The mudbrick-walled and domed structures of year-round villages (Fig. 4.6), built to accommodate a full range of activities, personnel, and seasonal conditions, are not purposely intended to go unoccupied at any time. All three types can become abandoned for good, but abandonment at summer stations and villages is always almost a gradual process rather than an abrupt action, whether intended or not. Future archaeological recognition of site type in Khar o Tauran would be complicated by the recycling of settlement both upwards and downwards. That is, while individual structures are recycled in one direction only (for example, from dwelling to storeroom to animal house: see Horne 1983; 1988:189–97), whole sites may be recycled in either direction. These reuses in fact are part of the flexible nature of settlement (Fig. 4.7) in this arid region.

Do settlement types differ in how they are treated or appear when they are seen as abandoned, whether temporarily or permanently? Natural taphonomic processes, of course, operate differently upon the different materials and in the microclimatically different locations of these functionally distinct types. Human agency probably has greater effect at pastoral stations than at mudbrick villages. For example, the wooden poles that hold up the structures of both summer and winter stations may be pulled out and used for building elsewhere or for fuel along with the brush used for roofing and fencing. Elsewhere in Iran (and the Near East in general) rural houses are built with flat, wooden pole-supported roofs and ceilings. On the Iranian Plateau, however, roofs are typically mudbrick vaults or domes, constructed without using any wood at all. Although they collapse from lack of upkeep (replastering, for example, is essential), they are not subject to scavenging

Fig. 4.5   An "abandoned" summer station. The brush and pole roofs of the three visible structures have been removed because the occupants did not think they would return. In fact, the station was used again the following summer by the same households.

for the value of their wood as happens elsewhere (for example, Kramer 1982:94–5). Otherwise, an abandoned site is not particularly subject to removal of materials or other alteration that would set it apart from the normal processes of material cycling in an ongoing settlement.

The gradual nature of abandonment here and these complexities of reuse underscore the necessity for a wide repertoire of ethnographic examples when developing archaeological reconstructions of settlement processes. In particular, this Iranian case should encourage the construction of alternative explanations for the distributions and relative counts of morphologically and locationally distinct types of sites wherever they are found.

Qanat irrigation technology and settlement stability

Settlement in these rural areas is not just a matter of where people live while they work, but is itself part of the strategy of production. All three types are intimately connected with a particularly arid land form of irrigation technology. This traditional technology, which has supported permanent settlement on the Iranian Plateau for the past three millennia, is also a factor in cycles of occupation and in settlement abandonment. The very nature of the technology explains a large part of the variation in settlement stability, at least in areas of marginal productivity such as Khar o Tauran.

Qanats are artificial subterranean galleries whose gravity flow systems take advantage of the special hydrological conditions of endoreic basins, or playas (for a discussion of traditional irrigation in Iran, see Spooner 1983). Constructing and maintaining a *qanat* is expensive. Without continuous maintenance, both the land and the water systems deteriorate. Leaks and blockages are frequent; earthquakes and acts of destruction are infrequent but devastating (Melville 1984). Ideally, *qanats* should be given routine maintenance yearly and

Fig. 4.6   Villages have more permanent architecture than do pastoral stations, but they also have structures for pastoral activities. Here, slabs of dung and earth dug up from the floor of a village stable to be spread as fertilizer on village fields. At winter stations, the same slabs are used in building construction.

major maintenance every ten years or so (Holmes 1975; Hartl 1979). Barring acts of God or war, prompt and continuous reinvestment in a *qanat* system could keep it running almost indefinitely.

On the one hand, the effects over the years of leveling, terracing, and silting within agricultural fields in the course of intentional and unintentional improvements to the irrigation system make an older site more attractive than an unimproved or newly established one. On the other hand, the failure of the irrigation system on which the field system depends is a frequent cause of abandonment, and the reasons are social as much as or more than they are technological or environmental.

A case study from a set of *qanat*-irrigated villages in the mountains near Bakshahr to the north of Khar o Tauran (Holmes 1975) illustrates well the social context of technological failure as well as the cyclical nature of prosperity and decline in these systems. In Holmes' model, the cycle begins when a new *qanat* is built or an existing one purchased by an urban entrepreneur. Local agricultural workers are brought in to sharecrop for him;

he himself remains in the city as an absentee landlord. Over the next generation or two the system remains the same size, but the number of shares increase as they are divided among the heirs of the original investor. Each share, of course, becomes smaller as the number of share holders increases. At the same time, the need for maintenance remains constant or increases. The more people with an interest in the system and the lower their income, the more difficult it is to organize the cost of undertaking repairs; if one of the owners defaults or delays, the *qanat* flow continues to decline and with it the productivity of the land and the income from the shares. As the quantity and value of land and water continue to decrease, the land no longer provides a profit. There are then two possibilities. Either another entrepreneur buys out the remaining shares and restores the *qanat* to working order, thus starting the cycle anew, or the site is abandoned, at least temporarily. After five years or so, the site may deteriorate so badly that it can no longer attract a new investor and so becomes permanently abandoned. According to Holmes, a typical cycle of investment,

Fig. 4.7   Since failure of the water source on account of flooding, this settlement is no longer occupied as a village but continues to support a summer station for those who once lived there year-round.

decline, and reinvestment lasts twenty-five to forty-five years – perhaps thirty to thirty-five years on average (that is, within the lifetime of the original purchaser's grandchildren). If *qanats* were not periodically renewed, the average life-span of villages would be very short indeed.

Bakshahr, although it appears to be typical of much of Iran at that time, differs in some important ways from Khar o Tauran. In Khar o Tauran, land and water shares are owned and farmed by local village residents, rather than by absentee landowners and their share-croppers. Difficult as it may be for local villagers to organize and pay for maintenance and repairs, it is greatly to their advantage to do so, for their living depends directly upon their own efforts. Unfortunately, no new *qanats* have been built in Khar o Tauran within recent memory, and we could not collect reliable *qanat* histories.

Indirect evidence suggests that the present-day organi-

zation of fields and labor is relatively new, and introduces still another variant on the organization of *qanat* irrigation. In other parts of Iran, large landholders or *khans* had either the wealth or the "clout" to build large *qanat* systems and see that they were maintained properly and rebuilt when disaster struck (Spooner 1974). There is evidence that "big-men" of this sort controlled settlement and land in Khar o Tauran in the recent past if not even further back (Martin 1982). These men depended for their power on the absence of a central authority and the general lawlessness in the area until well into the 1950s. Certainly the size and quality of architectural ruins on the plain (Fig. 4.8) suggest greater social stratification and wealth in the past than in the present (Horne 1991).

The abandonment of *qal'as*, the residential forts from which these powerful men oversaw their water and flocks, also demonstrates how across-the-board kinds of abandonment occur with social or economic change

Fig. 4.8   A "qal'a" (fortified residence) on the Tauran Plain abandoned fifty years ago. A year after the photograph was taken, the ruins were turned into a pastoral station for a neighboring village. The new structures were built against the interior walls and finished with mud and dung.

rather than as part of a cyclical process inherent in, for example, a kind of water management practice. It seems safe to say that *qal'as* have dropped out of the cycle as a settlement type, and are not likely to be revived.

General comments

Factors such as investment in water systems and the presence of local big men are part of a larger political and economic scene. They tend to affect settlements in concert rather than individually. Thus, settlements that may have little relationship to each other otherwise may nevertheless share a common historical trajectory that permits generalizations from one to the other. Most of the causes of occupational instability in the area are probably characteristic of large areas in the more arid parts of the Middle East. There are, for example, the normal vicissitudes of climate and pasture, and the

concomitant switching back and forth between sedentary agriculture and more mobile forms of pastoralism. Individual settlements in the area have for the most part always been small, and the usual random fluctuations in demography have their greatest effect on very small settlements, making them inherently less stable than larger ones. There will also be major crises, such as the forced relocation of settlement of pastoral nomads for political reasons – Khorasan has repeatedly been the destination of centrally ordered tribal relocations from the west and south. Some of these factors are of a cyclical nature; *qanat* irrigation and seasonality of occupation are two examples. Others, such as the deterioration of pastureland in the Middle East and processes of desertification, are long-term, directional trends that are not easily reversed.

One way that local populations in Khar o Tauran cope with these cyclical and directional changes is by maintaining flexibility in the structures and functions of their settlements. More pastoral stations available than actually in use means places to move into when flocks increase. Maintaining a summer station at a dwindling water source means fields for melons to help make up for a failed tobacco crop at home. Thus, settlement instability, whether a conscious strategy or not, can also be viewed more positively as a means of adjusting to an inherently unstable social or physical environment. Abandonment is not just a perturbing factor in the reconstruction of the "real" state of an archaeological site, but an informative aid to understanding local adaptations and long-term, processes of settlement.

Notes

1 The fieldwork on which this paper is based was carried out in the late 1970s under the aegis of the Iranian Department of the Environment. It was funded in part by the UNESCO Secretariat in Paris as a component of MAP Project 11: Integrated Ecological Studies on Human Settlements and was part of the "The Turan Programme of Ecological Research in and around the Iranian Deserts," directed by Dr Brian Spooner. I am especially grateful to Dr Spooner and to Mary Martin for the ideas and data they have made available to me. A detailed description and analysis of spatial organization and settlement in Khar o Tauran may be found in Horne 1988.

2 Historians have neglected the rural areas of the Middle East in favor of its cities. Aside from a few nominal mentions by medieval geographers at the time when Khar o Tauran serviced a minor caravan route across the north of Iran (Aubin 1971) and British travelers of the eighteenth and nineteenth centuries (Forster 1970; Vaughan 1893), its past has gone largely unrecorded. No systematic settlement data of any sort are available until the 1956 Census of Iran. This study therefore draws heavily upon that and subsequent censuses, local oral history, the physical remains of previous settlements, and ethnographic data collected in the late 1970s by myself and other members of the Turan Programme. It is necessarily restricted to little more than 100 years in scope.

3 Dewar (1986) uses similar concepts, which he calls "temporal continuity" and "spatial congruence." I am grateful to Luann Wandsnider for drawing Dewar's work to my attention while this paper was being revised.

4 For reasons of convenience I use the present tense

throughout this paper, although most of the data were collected before 1978. There have undoubtedly been changes since then, but I can only speculate on what they might be.

References

Aubin, Jean
1971 Réseau pastoral et réseau caravanier: les grand'routes du Khurassan a l'époque mongole. *Le Monde Iranien et l'Islam* 1:105–30.

Dewar, Robert E.
1986 Discovering Settlement Systems of the Past in New England Site Distributions. *Man in the Northeast* 31:77–88.

Forster, George
[1808] 1970 *A Journey from Bengal to England.* 2 Vols. Languages Department Vol. I and II, Punjab.

Hamlin, Christopher L.
1976 Tape transcript on file, Turan Programme (Dr Brian Spooner, Dir.), Department of Anthropology, University of Pennsylvania.

Hartl, Martin
1979 *Das Najafabadtal: Geographische Untersuchung einer Kanatlandschaft im Zagrosgebirge, Iran.* Regensburger Geographische Schriften 12. Institut für Geographie an der Universität Regensburg, Regensburg.

Holmes, Judith E.
1975 A Study of Social Organization in Certain Villages in West Khurasan, Iran, with Special Reference to Kinship and Agricultural Activities. PhD Thesis, University of Durham (by permission of the author).

Horne, Lee
1983 Recycling in an Iranian Village: Ethnoarchaeology in Baghestan. *Archaeology* 35(4):16–21.
1988 *The Spatial Organization of Rural Settlement in Khar o Tauran, Iran: An Ethnoarchaeological Case Study*, PhD Dissertation, University of Pennsylvania.
1991 Reading Village Plans: Architecture and Social Change in Northeastern Iran. *Expedition* 33(1):44–51.

Iran, Government of
1969 *Village Gazetteer*, Vol. VII. Plan Organization, Statistical Centre of Iran, Tehran.
1973 *Agricultural Census.* Plan Organization, Statistical Centre of Iran, Tehran. (Unpublished study.)

Kramer, Carol
  1982 *Village Ethnoarchaeology: Rural Iran in Archaeological Perspective*. Academic Press, New York.
Martin, Mary A.
  1980 Pastoral Production: Milk and Firewood in the Ecology of Turan. *Expedition* 22(4):24–8.
  1982 Conservation at the Local Level: Individual Perceptions and Group Mechanisms. In *Desertification and Development: Dryland Ecology in Social Perspective*, edited by Brian Spooner and H. S. Mann, pp. 145–69. Academic Press, London.
Melville, Charles
  1984 Meteorological Hazards and Disasters in Iran: A Preliminary Survey to 1950. *Iran* 22:113–50.
Nyerges, A. Endre
  1982 Pastoralists, Flocks and Vegetation: Processes of Co-adaptation. In *Desertification and Development:*

Dryland Ecology in Social Perspective, edited by Brian Spooner and H. S. Mann, pp. 217–47. Academic Press, London.
Spooner, Brian
  1974 Irrigation and Society: The Iranian Plateau. In *Irrigation's Impact on Society*, edited by Theodore E. Downing and McGuire Gibson, pp. 43–57. Anthropological Papers 25, University of Arizona Press, Tucson.
  1983 Abyari, "Irrigation" in Iran. *Encyclopaedia Iranica*, Vol. I, Fasc. 4, edited by Ehsan Yarshater, pp. 405–11. Routledge and Kegan Paul, London.
Spooner, Brian and H. S. Mann, eds.
  1982 *Desertification and Development: Dryland Ecology in Social Perspective*. Academic Press, London.
Vaughan, Lt H. B.
  1893 A Journey through Persia (1887–1888). *Royal Geographical Society Supplementary Papers* 3:89–115.

5
Models of abandonment and material culture frequencies

S U S A N   K E N T

Introduction

What is the relationship between camp abandonment, mobility (actual and planned), material culture, and the archaeological record? Archaeologists have used artifact frequencies as one indicator of length of occupation and mode of abandonment. However, in order to understand the relationship between mobility, abandonment, and artifact frequencies, it is necessary to examine the factors influencing the accumulation of material culture at camps that have been occupied for various periods of time. The following explores variables traditionally considered important in abandonment studies.

This chapter is based primarily on quantitative data collected in 1987 at a community located just outside the Khutse Game Reserve in the Kalahari Desert of Botswana, although research has been conducted at the community periodically from 1987 to 1992 (Fig. 5.1). The settlement is inhabited by Basarwa ("Bushmen," San) and Bakgalagadi (Bantu-speakers). It is comprised of a number of scattered camps that are occupied by one to twenty-four people (Fig. 5.2). Camps consist of huts, ash areas where ashes from hearths are dumped, storage platforms, roasting pits, hearths, windbreaks, and informal storage loci such as trees. Some camps also contain goat kraals and pens. Formal middens are not used at Kutse (the alternative spelling for the community to distinguish it from the game reserve). Trash is routinely deposited at ash areas. Since length of camp occupation at Kutse is variable, it is possible to test time-dependent hypotheses. Some camps are inhabited for up to three or four years; however, it is more common for camps to be occupied for one or two years. After that

period of time, people relocate their camp within the dispersed Kutse community (Fig. 5.2). Reoccupation of sites does not commonly occur at Kutse, even for those sites only inhabited for six months or less. People simply do not typically reuse abandoned camps.

At Kutse, wage work is not available and most people can be considered to be primarily, though not exclusively, foragers (Kent 1992a, n.d.b). Some individuals also own a small herd of goats and a few occasionally plant a garden, although only in 1988 did any gardens yield a bountiful harvest. Approximately 90–95 percent of all meat consumed comes from wild animals obtained with traditional weapons (i.e. not with guns, horses, or motorized vehicles). An average of 91 percent (range is 81 to 100 percent) of subsistence time is spent foraging (Kent, 1992a).

The Kutse community provides an unique opportunity to test hypotheses concerning artifact accumulation. Because everyone has equal access to the exotic trash

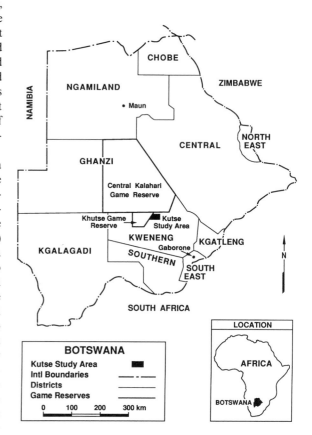

Fig. 5.1 Map of the study area.

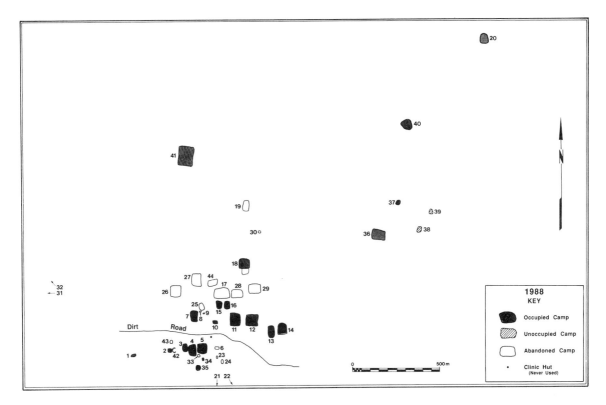

Fig. 5.2   Map of the Kutse community.

deposited by tourists and/or game scouts, located near the community's only water supply, wealth is not a factor in object accumulation. As a consequence, wealth, as measured by the number of objects alone can be held constant in this analysis. There is no store at Kutse from which to purchase objects, even if wage work were locally available. Later inventories (post-1987), including ownership and acquisition histories of all objects, indicate that whereas there is much sharing of tools between those camps participating in a sharing network, it does not appear to be differential in that some individuals within those networks consistently lend out possessions more than others. Therefore, the artifact inventory conducted in 1987, upon which this study is based, is not differentially affected by sharing in terms of the questions being asked here (though this is the case for artifacts, I suggest below, that the sharing of meat is differential between camps, which influences the distribution of faunal remains). Furthermore, all abandoned and occupied camps have been intensively inventoried, revealing that the storage of artifacts at abandoned camps is not common, and the rare times it does occur

the number of objects is very small and the types of objects are not unique (i.e. most people do not cache artifacts either at abandoned camps at Kutse or at camps in different communities). Therefore, there is no evidence to suggest that pre-existing wealth differences occur among residents that might generate differential use or ownership in the number of items inventoried at camps.[1]

This chapter suggests that mobility strategies influence abandonment processes primarily in two ways: (1) people who plan to stay at a camp for a short period of time will have a smaller artifact inventory than those who anticipate a long occupation; and (2) groups who plan a short occupation also invest less effort in site construction and perform fewer camp maintenance activities than those who anticipate a long occupation. Both of these factors will influence archaeological visibility and interpretations of abandonment behavior.

There are basically two levels of mobility patterns – one on the inter-group or cross-cultural level and one on the intra-group level. Various kinds of nomadism and sedentism refer to cross-cultural or inter-group mobility patterns, such as short-term sedentism (Kent 1992b). Within each cross-cultural category of nomadism or sedentism, there is another influential dimension of intra-group mobility patterning which I have called "anticipated mobility" and "actual mobility" (Kent and Vierich 1989). This level of mobility patterning can be divided into categories of short, medium, or long occupations. An illustration of the range that exists within anticipated and actual mobility strategies is the nomadic !Kung pattern wherein groups traditionally spend two to four months at a pan during one season and eight to ten months in a number of camps scattered across the landscape (referred to as "tethered nomadism," Kent and Lee 1992; Binford 1980; Taylor 1964). Within a nomadic society, people can have anticipated longer and shorter occupations and still be categorized as nomadic. However, even their longer occupations are relatively short compared to those of sedentary groups. Thus, we should expect mobility and, concomitantly, site diversity, on two separate but related levels – the intergroup level where such general terms as "nomadic" and "sedentary" are applicable (the latter referring to year-round occupation and permanence) and the intra-group level where such terms as anticipated "short," "medium," or "long" occupation are applicable (termed "duration" by some, e.g. Ames 1991). As will be shown below, mobility affects abandonment processes and archaeological visibility.

The influence of mobility on the amount of possessions people have and on site structure can be evaluated by comparing groups with a similar culture who use different mobility strategies. Although there is much diversity between Basarwa groups, by knowing what differences exist between them and why, comparisons are possible, if the variability is taken into account (see Kent 1992a). For instance, and as would be predicted by the model presented below, nomadic Basarwa artifact inventories collected twenty to forty years ago are very different in number, although not necessarily in kind (with the exception of Western artifacts), from the semi-sedentary and sedentary Basarwa inventories I have recorded at Kutse located south and east of the !Kung and G/wi areas (e.g. Lee 1979; Silberbauer 1981; Yellen 1977). These and other studies indicate that nomadic camps, where inhabitants planned a brief (less than three months) occupation, have fewer possessions, less architectural permanence, fewer formal storage facilities, and smaller sites than those at which inhabitants plan a longer occupation (Kent 1991, 1992b; Kent and Vierich 1989). The following is an extension of the afore-cited

research that was based on data collected by Vierich at Ngware on the eastern margin of the Kalahari. The results of those studies suggest that the anticipated length of occupation is a significant and stronger predictor of various facets of site structure than are the actual camp duration as defined below, season of occupation, number or ethnicity of inhabitants, and subsistence orientation, such as primarily hunting-gathering, agro-pastoralism, employment, or a mixture including wage work.

Models of the variables influencing the camp feature inventories

For this study, six variables were analyzed to determine their significance in influencing (1) number of faunal remains and (2) total number of objects, including faunal remains, at site features (Table 5.1). The analysis, based on data recorded in 1987 from forty-six sites includes 4787 objects located in features. Of these objects, 594 were faunal remains. The appendix lists the objects located in windbreaks[2] at two camps. Each site was classified according to the variables listed in Table 5.1. These were as follows:

1. Type. The variable type refers to whether the site was occupied (Type 1, an ethnographic site) or was abandoned (Type 2, an archaeological site) at the time of my 1987 investigations. The length of time between abandonment and my observations varied among the Type 2 sites from several months to four years (as noted above, people do not generally reoccupy camps).[3]

2. Distance. Distance measures proximity to the village core or the highest concentration of camps (Fig. 5.2). Camps within a ten-minute walk of the village nucleus are classified as Distance 1. Those camps located beyond a ten-minute walk of the village center are classified as Distance 2 and include camps located a thirty to forty-five-minute brisk walk away. Camps classified as Distance 1 are quite close to other camps and there often is much interaction between them. Those classified as Distance 2 generally do not have other sites located near them.

3. Ethnicity. Camps are identified as inhabited by Basarwa ("Bushmen" or Ethnic 1), Bakgalagadi (Bantu-speakers or Ethnic 2), or mixed Basarwa-Bakgalagadi. The latter category represents camps at which families or friends of both ethnic groups reside (Ethnic 3).

4. Population. The site population includes both adults and children. The number of site occupants varies from one to twenty-four individuals, excluding short-term visitors. Population is grouped into three categories:

Table 5.1. *The original variables monitored in the models.*

Variable	Number of camps	Percentage of camps	Mean artifacts	Mean bones
Type 1	24	52.2%	120.25	2.83
Type 2	22	47.8%	90.32	23.91
(1 = occupied; 2 = abandoned)				
Distance 1	34	73.9%	111.06	14.18
Distance 2	12	26.1%	91.42	9.33
(1 = in village core; 2 = not in core)				
Ethnicity 1	24	52.2%	94.12	7.17
Ethnicity 2	5	10.9%	107.60	7.80
Ethnicity 3	17	37.0%	122.01	22.53
(1 = Basarwa; 2 = Bakgalagadi; 3 = mixed)				
Population 1	16	34.8%	113.38	16.06
Population 2	27	58.7%	105.82	11.74
Population 3	3	6.5%	67.33	6.67
(1 = less than 4 residents; 2 = 5–9; 3 = over 9)				
Anticipated Mobility 1	3	6.5%	34.00	1.00
Anticipated Mobility 2	8	17.4%	56.86	4.14
Anticipated Mobility 3	36	78.3%	121.47	15.61
(1 = short; 2 = medium; 3 = long)				
Actual Mobility 1	9	19.6%	67.56	3.44
Actual Mobility 2	13	26.1%	82.77	4.31
Actual Mobility 3	24	54.3%	132.88	21.13
(1 = short; 2 = medium; 3 = long)				

Population Group 1 consists of camps with one to four individuals; Population Group 2 with five to nine individuals; and Population Group 3, more than nine individuals.

5. Anticipated Mobility. The length of time residents plan to occupy a camp, as determined from interviews, is called Anticipated Mobility. The anticipated length of stay is categorized as short, i.e. occupations that are under three months (Anticipated Mobility 1), medium, i.e. occupations of three to six months (Anticipated Mobility 2), and long, i.e. over six months (Anticipated Mobility 3).

6. Actual Mobility. The length of occupation at the time of observation is coded as Actual Mobility. As with Anticipated Mobility, this variable is categorized into short occupations of under three months' duration (Actual Mobility 1), medium occupations of three to six months (Actual Mobility 2), and long occupations of over six months and often over several years (Actual Mobility 3). This variable refers to the actual length of time spent at a camp at the time of my observations and/or its abandonment. When archaeologists discuss

duration, they usually implicitly mean actual rather than planned. As described in more detail elsewhere (Kent 1992b), there is an assumed incremental growth in site size, number of objects, and other variables the longer a site is inhabited. If actual mobility is an influential variable, it should impact the dependent variable(s) being monitored at whatever point the measurement is made. In other words, occupied camps where inhabitants had just moved should have a similar pattern to abandoned ones of similar lengths of occupation, unless other factors, such as anticipated length of stay or specific abandonment processes, are also influencing the dependent variables.

A time-dependent increase in the number of objects at features that is a direct function of elapsed time must be, by definition, visible if one visits a camp after one week, six months, or two years of occupation. To hold preservation, abandonment, and visibility constant, I recorded camps that were still occupied or, at most, only very recently abandoned. I reasoned that if the dependent variables are directly influenced by the length of time a site is occupied, then it should not matter whether or not a site is still inhabited at the time of determining its actual length of occupation. Uncontrolled variation can occur if only abandoned camps are examined when investigating occupation duration and the dependent variables. The result is an inability to control for variation resulting from different lengths of abandonment, mode of abandonment, postabandonment scavenging, curation, etc. (e.g. Schiffer 1987, and elsewhere; also Tomka, this volume). The variable, Actual Mobility, is my attempt to try to hold these factors constant.

The data and their collection

All objects located on the surface of features were inventoried at the forty-six camps. As mentioned above, features included ash areas, hearths, roasting pits, storage platforms, windbreaks, huts, kraals, and goat pens. Both obvious trash and material still in use at occupied camps were recorded (see Appendix). Everything visible was noted, from unidentifiable splinters of bone, ostrich egg shell fragments, and tin cans to plastic threads from a mealie meal bag. In this data set collected in 1987, interior assemblages of occupied huts were not inventoried, although objects located outside on the hut were (such as items located on the roof or stuck in the walls). However, all objects were recorded, beginning in 1988. The later data do not appear to contradict the findings here. Residents were questioned about the length of occupation they anticipated at a camp both at the establishment of the camp and at the time of the interview. Actual mobility was determined by the actual length of time a camp had been inhabited at the time of recording objects.

Each object was coded by attributes (e.g. bone, cloth fragment, anvil), by feature, and by camp, among other variables. Earlier ethnoarchaeological studies among very different groups suggested that bones have a distinct depositional history which differs from that of artifacts because bones are affected by the activities of dogs (Kent 1981). As a consequence, faunal remains were analyzed separately below to determine if they are, in fact, impacted by different factors than are artifacts.

Hypotheses underlying the models

It was hypothesized that, with the exception of ethnicity, each of the variables discussed above significantly affects the frequency of faunal remains and number of objects at features. It was hypothesized that ethnicity is not a significant variable (see Hypothesis 3 below). The hypotheses are as follows:

1. Archaeological or abandoned sites (Type 2) have a lower number of objects than currently occupied camps (Type 1) but a higher number of bones owing to a suspension of refuse maintenance activities.

2. Camps located beyond a ten-minute walk from the village core (Distance 2) contain more bones and a greater total number of artifacts than those located within the village nucleus (Distance 1). As a result of postabandonment scavenging by both human and canine neighbors, sites located in close proximity to other occupied camps (i.e. the village core) will have a depleted artifact inventory.

3. Because there are few subsistence or other behavioral differences between the Basarwa and the particular kind of Bakgalagadi at Kutse, the ethnicity of the inhabitants does not significantly affect the frequency of objects or bones. The variable needs to be included in the model to determine the validity of this proposition (i.e. p should be $>$ than 0.05 for the hypothesis to be valid).

4. Camps at which occupants plan a brief stay (under three months) will contain less material than those at which longer stays are anticipated. People who plan to move a great deal tend not to own as many possessions. In addition, people who plan to inhabit a particular location only briefly do not bring as many objects with them in comparison to those who anticipate a long occupation. As mentioned earlier, wealth does not influence the accumulation of possessions at Kutse because many durable, bulky objects, such as tin cans and glass containers, can be salvaged by anyone, rich or poor, mobile or sedentary, from the refuse pit at the nearby game reserve camp where tourists dump their imported refuse. So even if poor people happen to be the more mobile ones in the Kalahari, they can acquire objects from the trash pit as easily as can sedentary people. This situation allows us to see the influence of mobility on the material assemblage unaffected by wealth differences that could create discrepancies in camp artifact inventories.

5. The actual length of occupation at the time of observation impacts the number of bones and the total number of objects located in features; that is, the longer a habitation, the more bones and objects will accumulate.

6. The number of camp residents influences the number of bones and artifacts at a camp so that the larger the population, the larger the number of bones and artifacts at features.

Assumptions, limitations of the database, and caveats

Only objects at features were recorded in the inventories conducted in 1987 during the first field season of a multiyear project. Analysis of all faunal remains located on the surface of camps recorded in 1990 suggests that 20–21 percent of the total bone assemblage at a camp is located at a feature. Despite the selective nature of the data (i.e. only features were examined), the data can be used to test models concerning abandonment. Given that many archaeologists do not recover even 20–21 percent of the entire faunal remains assemblage at a site and because many tend to focus their excavations on features, the data here are not inconsistent with those from most archaeological contexts. In 1987 storage bags and pieces of plastic bags were recorded but their contents not listed; however, later research indicates that this did not significantly influence relative object counts.

Multicolinearity (highly intercorrelated variables, Blalock 1979:485) is not a problem with this data set. Tolerances are generally high and inflation factors or VIFs are generally low (e.g. VIFs are 5 or less; see Table 5.3; also Blalock 1979). These levels indicate that anticipated mobility is not, for example, highly correlated with actual mobility. Non-significant variables were entered into models composed of various combinations of significant and non-significant variables from the bivariate tests to determine whether some variables become significant in combination with other variables. Since none did, non-significant variables were not included in the final models, although they were present in the initial ones.

Results of the evaluation of assumptions led to a logarithmic transformation of the number of objects in order to improve homoscedasticity (i.e. to equalize the variances) and normality (Dowdy and Wearden 1991: 503–11). For two of the six independent variables – Population and Distance – the dependent variable, number of bones, required transformation. Population was regressed against the log number of bones and Distance was regressed against the squared number of bones. Because a few camps had no bones, a constant of 0.01 was added to each observation before the logarithmic transformation and the regression of Population (Neter, Wasserman, and Kutner 1990:149).[4]

A small sample size, as in this study (n = 46 camps) can be problematic for the use of multivariate statistics, even if basic assumptions[5] have been met. Although the precise number of cases needed per independent variable is not agreed upon by all statisticians, a bare minimum is usually to have at least five more cases than independent variables (Tabachnick and Fidell 1989).[6] This minimum was met in all models tested. Even so, because statistical significance is more difficult to establish with small sample sizes,[7] particularly when standard deviations are large as most were here, a bivariate regression was run

on each independent variable to ensure that the lack of significance is not merely an artifact of the number of cases to independent variables ratio. It is not uncommon for a non-significant variable in a bivariate correlation to gain significance or a significant variable to lose its significance in a multivariate model (as occurred in this analysis) because of unique and shared variation. Both non-significant and significant variables were first tested together, as can be seen in models 1 and 2 below (interaction effects were tested in separate models because of the sample size and the number of potential interaction terms). After all variables were tested together, a model containing those variables with a $p > 0.06$ and a model containing those with a $p < 0.06$ were tested separately.

Since the order in which variables enter the model can influence the rise in R^2 in hierarchical regression as that used here (Tabachnick and Fidell 1989), variables were entered in different combinations. The order of variables was found not greatly to impact the statistics or alter interpretations.

Testing the models

The two models were formulated thus:

Model 1: Number of Objects = Type + Distance + Ethnicity + Anticipated Mobility + Actual Mobility + Population.

Model 2: Number of Faunal Remains = Type + Distance + Ethnicity + Anticipated Mobility + Actual Mobility + Population.

Model 1 was significant (F = 3.002; $p = 0.0078$; $R^2 = 0.46177$). Model 2 was not significant (F = 1.276; $p = 0.2810$). Elsewhere I have pointed out that the meaning ascribed to the magnitude of R^2 values varies between types of data, particularly between human behavior and physical data, such as attributes of ceramic sherds (Kent 1992b). An R^2 of 0.98 might be considered to be too small to be used in physics, whereas an R^2 of 0.20 to 0.30 might be considered high or at least acceptable for explanation in the social sciences, which deal with more widely varying human behavior (Achen 1982; SAS 1990:15; Kent 1992b). Therefore, the size of R^2 must be viewed within the context of the study, the analysis, and the data. Unless one is interested in developing non-theoretical predictions, achieving the highest R^2 possible is neither the purpose behind statistics nor the purpose behind the testing of models (Achen 1982; Lewis-Beck 1990). Instead, in theory testing, one is interested in determining the validity of hypotheses and which independent variables best explain the dependent variable. In theory testing, as done here, both significance

Table 5.2. *Bivariate regression (categorical variables were converted into dummy variables; $N = 46$).*

Dependent variable[a] = Log of total objects at features	F value	Prob > F	R^2
*Type	11.28	0.0016	0.2040
*Anticipated Mobility (short, medium, long)	7.56	0.0015	0.2601
*Actual Mobility (short, medium, long)	3.09	0.0557	0.1257
Distance	0.93	0.3407	0.0207
Ethnicity	0.67	0.5183	0.0950
Population	0.51	0.6046	0.0231
Adults	2.26	0.1171	0.0949
Females	2.22	0.1212	0.0935
Males	0.48	0.4903	0.0109
Dependent variable[b] = Just faunal remains at features	F value	Prob > F	R^2
*Type	6.32	0.0157	0.1255
Males	4.03	0.0509	0.0839
Adults	2.68	0.0801	0.1108
Females	1.43	0.2502	0.0624
Actual Mobility	2.43	0.1004	0.1014
Anticipated Mobility	0.82	0.8195	0.0367
Distance	0.47	0.4969	0.0106
Ethnicity	1.74	0.1885	0.0747
Population	0.22	0.8000	0.0103

[a] Because of the presence of heteroscedasticity, the dependent variables were transformed to stabilize the variance. Transformation was accomplished by taking the log of the dependent variable.
[b] In order to meet basic assumptions, the variable Population was regressed against the log number of faunal remains and Distance was regressed against the square of the number of faunal remains. Before the log transformation, a constant of 0.01 was added to each observation because a few camps had no bones (this is true only for the variable population and number of faunal remains; see Neter, Wasserman, and Kutner 1990:149).

and R^2 must be taken into account, along with the kind of data (cultural versus physical behavior or attributes), and the purpose of the analysis.

Because I did not anticipate the lack of significance between the dependent variables and Population, I broke the variable down into different components in order to investigate possible relationships further. I thought the number of children at a camp may have masked a potential relationship between the number of adults and the number of objects and/or the number of faunal remains at a camp. It is possible that including children in the population count was responsible for the small amount of variance explained by the number of camp inhabitants. I further reasoned that the frequency of faunal remains at sites might be gender linked; therefore camps with more men (the primary hunters in the society) would have more faunal remains. The test results show that the number of adults – that is, males and females together – or the number of adult males or the number of adult females separately are not significantly correlated with the number of objects at a location, either in a bivariate (Table 5.2) or multivariate model. In contrast, for the number of faunal remains at features, the variable Males is only barely non-significant in a bivariate model ($p = 0.0509$; $R^2 = 0.0839$). However, Adults and Females are not correlated with faunal remains abundance at all (they have high p-values and low R^2; Table 5.2).

For faunal remains, only Type, referring to whether a camp is occupied or abandoned, explains a significant amount of variation in both the bivariate and multivariate models. Whereas the variable Males is barely non-

Table 5.3. *Model of variables from the bivariate relationships with a p<0.06 (N = 46) – interaction effects were tested and were not found to be significant.*

Dependent variable[a] = Log of the number of total objects at features

	F value	Prob > F	R^2			
Full model	6.11	0.0003	0.4329			
	T value		Prob > T	VIF	Standardized estimates	Parameter estimate[b]
Type	3.41		0.0015	1.04	0.4208	0.7642
Anticipated Mobility 2	1.70		0.0974	3.57	0.3821	0.9623
Anticipated Mobility 3	1.27		0.0237	4.25	0.5776	1.2670
Actual Mobility 2	−0.05		0.9627	2.28	−0.0085	−0.0170
Actual Mobility 3	1.88		0.3071	2.76	−0.2047	0.3701

Contribution of variables to the model's R^2:

Variable	Incremental R^2	Model R^2	C_p	F	Prob > F
Type	0.2040	0.2040	14.147	11.277	0.0016
Anticipated Mobility 3	0.1483	0.3523	5.687	9.845	0.0031
Anticipated Mobility 2	0.0510	0.4033	4.092	3.587	0.0651
Actual Mobility 3	0.0296	0.4329	4.002	2.142	0.1509
Actual Mobility 2	0.0000	0.4329	4.002	0.002	0.9627

Dependent variable Dependent variable = Number of faunal remains at features

	F value	Prob > F	R^2			
Full model	4.533	0.0164	0.1741			
	T value		Prob > T	VIF	Standardized estimates	Parameter estimate
Type	2.17		0.0358	1.05	0.3072	16.6236
Males	1.59		0.9563	1.05	0.2254	8.2631

[a] Because of the presence of heteroscedasticity, the number of objects was transformed to stabilize the variance. Transformation was accomplished by taking the log of the dependent variable.
[b] Note that the parameter estimate is based on the log number of objects at features.

significant in a bivariate model, it is completely non-significant in the multivariate model because of shared variation with Type ($p=0.9563$; Tables 5.2 and 5.3). No other independent variables are statistically significant in the bivariate or multivariate models.

As one might expect, Type is also significant for the number of objects at features in both bivariate and multivariate models. In addition, Anticipated Mobility is significant in both bivariate and multivariate models (Tables 5.2 and 5.3). This latter relationship is consistent with my overall hypothesis concerning the influence of mobility on object abundance. Together, Type and

DEPENDENT VARIABLE = LOG OF THE TOTAL NUMBER OF OBJECTS

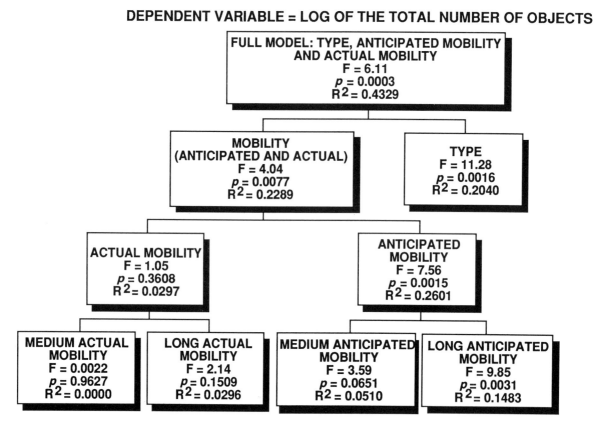

Fig. 5.3   Hierarchical regression of the log number of objects located at features.

Anticipated Mobility have an R^2 of 0.4033 (Table 5.3). Because of shared variation, Actual Mobility does not explain a significant amount of variation when in a multivariate model with Type and Anticipated Mobility (see standardized estimates for a rank order of the amount of variance explained by each variable in Table 5.3). Adding the variable Actual Mobility to the model only raises R^2 by 0.0296, an insignificant amount (see Table 5.3). This lack of significant contribution to the model is visible in the relatively small drop in Mallow's C_p statistic when Actual Mobility is added to the model (the statistic is a measure of model-fit; Dowdy and Wearden 1991:488).

A hierarchical regression was also conducted. Only main effects were included because, as mentioned above, interaction effects were insignificant and explained very little variance.[8] Hierarchical regression is useful in determining the significance of variables by themselves and in theoretically important groups or blocks. Hierarchical regression also examines the amount of unique and common variation explained by groups of independent variables and by each independent variable by itself, in addition to their contribution to the total R^2 (Tabachnick and Fidell 1989). The top level in Fig. 5.3 shows all variables in the model regressed as a block against the dependent variable, object abundance at features. The second level separates mobility from Type (Actual and Anticipated Mobility are together as one block). This level shows that both Type and mobility patterns are significant in the model. The third level separates Actual and Anticipated Mobility, with Type still in the model (Fig. 5.3). This level of the hierarchy shows that Actual Mobility is not significant by itself whereas Anticipated Mobility is when both are in the presence of the variable Type. The bottom level separates Anticipated and Actual Mobility into their individual categories with Type still in the model (medium and long categories are being compared to short which is not shown in Fig. 5.3).

Discussion and interpretations

It was not unexpected that Type would be significantly correlated with the number of objects and faunal remains at features. I also hypothesized that Anticipated Mobility would be a significant variable, but I did not expect the lack of significance of the variable, Actual Mobility. Instead, I originally hypothesized that the actual length of occupation would be a significant, although weaker, predictor of object and faunal remain abundance than anticipated length of occupation.

Type

I was not surprised that the single variable that explained more unique variance than any other is whether or not a site is occupied at the time of the inventory (Type). If for no other reason, I expected people to leave refuse around a camp more often just before it was abandoned, as long as abandonment was anticipated (i.e. a relaxation of site maintenance activities prior to a planned abandonment, Hypothesis 1). Conversely, I expected fewer bones in a camp if inhabitants had no intention of leaving. Bones at abandoned camps, I reasoned, should have had less destruction or displacement from dogs. Although perhaps more vulnerable to disturbance from occasional wild scavengers, such as hyenas, bones at abandoned camps are not subjected to the day-to-day scavenging by the three to six dogs which commonly reside at an occupied camp. In fact, the analysis indicates that the difference between the means at abandoned and occupied sites is significant, with more faunal remains at abandoned camps (mean = 2.8 bones for occupied camps; mean = 23.9 bones for abandoned camps). A similar pattern has been observed on the Andaman Islands at recently abandoned sites that people did not plan to reoccupy (Copper 1990). This situation may be a result of dogs displacing bones, particularly from features, at occupied camps. They often chew on bones near, but not necessarily at, a feature in use by humans who deliberately toss bones to the dogs waiting eagerly nearby (Kent n.d.b). Dogs do not often relocate bones at abandoned camps because they do not usually go to camps that are no longer inhabited. As noted by Tomka (1992:per. comm.), there might be a concomitant increase in the number of bones as sheet trash at sites where abandonment is anticipated (i.e. refuse spread across the site that is not confined to a feature) if the dispersal of bones is linked to a relaxation of site maintenance activities. This would mean there is an overall increase in the number of bones at abandoned camps, both within and between features. The data to evaluate this proposition have not yet been analyzed, although

they have been collected (and are the topic of future research). Other factors influencing the number of bones at features based on the category of Type also need to be assessed.

I expected abandoned camps to have fewer objects at features than occupied camps, which turned out to be the case (mean was 90.3 artifacts for abandoned camps and 120.3 for occupied camps). There are a number of factors one could posit for such a reduction; most obvious is the absence of still-functional objects at abandoned camps that were removed by occupants when they left. Although objects are less abundant at abandoned camps than at occupied camps, I had originally expected a larger difference. The smaller than expected difference between means, although still significant, may result from the free refuse available at the game scout camp, which constitutes the majority of possessions owned by people at Kutse. Objects are always available gratis from the trash dump and therefore there is little reason to curate them (i.e. replacement costs are low, so objects might be abandoned more readily than they would otherwise be, e.g. Binford 1979). If individuals leave tin cans and glass bottles at their abandoned camp, they can easily obtain new ones at the dump on the way to their only source of water. As noted earlier, although a few people store possessions not in use at abandoned camps, it is not a very common practice and, even when it occurs, relatively few objects are ever cached there. Fisher (1986) also noted the occasional storage of objects at abandoned Pygmy camps.

Actual length of occupation (Actual Mobility)

The means in Table 5.1 show a rise in the number of objects at features the longer the actual occupation. However, because of the within-group variation and the relatively small sample size, it is not a significant increase at the traditional threshold value of $p < 0.05$.[9] Nonetheless, I thought there probably are enough differences between means to examine the variable in a multivariate model. Hence, I included actual length of occupation in the multivariate model of statistically significant variables obtained from the original bivariate study (Table 5.3).[10]

By including Actual Mobility in the multivariate model, I was able to determine that actual length of occupation explains only a small amount of variation and that the rise in R^2 produced by adding it to the multivariate model is only 0.03, an insignificant amount. Also note the small drop in the Mallow's C_p statistic, which also indicates that Actual Mobility does not contribute much to explaining the variance in the number of objects. While other research has indicated a positive relationship between actual length of occupation and the accumulation of objects (e.g. Schiffer 1975, 1987; Shott 1989), this study shows that the number of objects at features is less influenced by Actual Mobility than it is by other variables.

The analysis also does not support the intuitively obvious relationship between the length of occupation and the number of bones that occur at features. While it is true that sites with longer occupations accumulate more faunal remains, as can be seen by comparing the means from short, medium, and long lengths of residence, the differences are not statistically significant and R^2 is relatively small (see Tables 5.1–5.3). These results highlight the need for future research to determine whether the lack of significance may be explicable in terms of facility maintenance, intercamp sharing of meat still on the bone, not including bones located between features (an area archaeologists have not systematically investigated), or other factors.

Anticipated length of occupation (Anticipated Mobility)

The analysis supports the hypothesis that people who plan to occupy a site briefly will have a different material culture assemblage, at least in size if not in kind, from those who anticipate a long occupation. In fact, anticipated mobility is one of the most significant variables tested and explains the second most unique variation (whether or not a site is occupied explains the most; see the standardized estimates in Table 5.3 which indicate rank importance of variables). This study reveals that people who plan a short occupation will maintain an inventory of fewer objects than those who plan a long occupation. Inhabited camps (Type 1) where residents plan a long occupation have a mean of 131 objects in contrast to a mean of thirty-four objects at an occupied camp where inhabitants plan a short occupation. Residents who plan to stay at Kutse for a short period of time (and tend in general to be more mobile than those who stay for long periods) have the same access to objects at the game reserve camp dump as others; they just possess fewer objects than residents who anticipate a long camp habitation. Abandoned sites (Type 2) at which occupants planned a short stay have a mean of nine objects in contrast to a mean of 108 objects from abandoned camps where occupants anticipated a long stay.

Another way to view the data is to examine cases where anticipated and actual length of occupation differ. Camps wherein residents planned a short occupation and also actually stayed a short period of time have a mean of thirty-four objects (Anticipated 1, Actual 1), whereas camps where residents planned a long occupation but were only at the camp for a short period (Anticipated 3,

Actual 1) have a mean of 95.3 objects. A t-test shows that the mean for Anticipated 3 but Actual 1 camps is not significantly different from Anticipated and Actual 3 camps, with a mean of 132.9 objects. The t-test indicates that camps where anticipated length of occupation are the same (e.g. anticipated long) but actual length of occupation differ (e.g. short versus long) have a more similar mean number of objects than have those camps with the same actual length of occupation but different anticipated lengths of occupation. This finding indicates that actual mobility is not the most influential variable in determining material culture abundance at features. Thus, people who plan to inhabit a camp for a shorter period of time will have and/or bring fewer objects to a site than those who plan to stay a long time. They concomitantly have less trash because they began with fewer possessions. It is possible that rates and amounts of artifact accumulation might change if people actually stay much longer than anticipated. Unfortunately, this cannot be tested empirically because I do not have any camps in my sample where inhabitants planned a short occupation but actually stayed much longer. However, the data presented in Kent and Vierich (1989:115–16) included a camp at which the inhabitants had anticipated a short occupation but ended up staying for a long period of time (Camp 2). The site exhibited more characteristics of camps where residents anticipated short occupations than they did with camps where inhabitants had anticipated long occupations.[11]

Because I suggest that the principle behind the model of mobility operates in societies with completely different patterns of movement, highly nomadic groups, which spend only a few weeks at a camp, should not be expected to have the same abandonment behaviors as sedentary or transhumant groups. I propose not only that highly nomadic peoples without animal or motorized transportation have fewer objects, but that the objects tend to be of a different kind, less durable and less bulky, and therefore less visible archaeologically (Kent 1990; Shott 1989). Thus, in addition to the distance and permanence of the move, abandonment behaviors are partly dependent on the amount and kind of material culture of a society. If this is true, different general models of abandonment need to be developed for groups with vastly different modes of mobility. The fact that the only significant variable in the model, besides whether or not a site is occupied, is mobility shows that mobility impacts the archaeological record in ways archaeologists must include in their models. Models of abandonment that incorporate these variables can then be used to examine intra-group or inter-group (i.e. cross-cultural) abandonment variability by comparing peoples with similar mobility patterns within and between regions.

It is not surprising that the number of faunal remains at features is not significantly associated with residents' anticipated mobility. There is no reason to expect sites where people planned a short versus long habitation to have more or less faunal remains.

Distance

Distance may not have been influential in the frequency of bones because dogs rarely go to camps other than their own, even if they live in the village core (i.e. observations suggest that canine scavenging in the village core is no greater than at the more isolated camps because dogs do not usually venture into different camps). If a dog wanders into a camp not belonging to its owner, it is usually chased away by people, by other dogs, or by both. I consistently observed dogs move bones around within a camp but not between camps. Faunal remains appear to be equally influenced by dogs at short, medium and long-term camps. In fact, at every camp I visited and/or lived in, dogs were an extremely influential agent responsible for the distribution and patterning of bones (Kent 1981; n.d.b). This seems to be the case for foragers and for pastoralists. If people do not actually give bones to the dogs, they take them when no one is watching. The only bones not spatially displaced by dogs are those eaten by people (for example, pulverized with meat in a wooden mortar). Dogs do not necessarily displace bones from the general area at which they are received, unless under pressure by other dogs. As a consequence, bones tend to cluster near features, such as hearths, or where people tossed them, but not necessarily in features.

On a number of occasions I observed the scavenging of building materials from huts and other structures by former occupants at abandoned sites in the village core. As a consequence, I expected the variable Distance to be significant. More research is necessary before attempting to explain the lack of significance between Distance and the number of objects present at features.

Ethnicity

The absence of a significant association between the number of faunal remains at features and ethnicity was predicted. At Kutse most Basarwa and Bakgalagadi hunt year-round, unlike Bakgalagadi residents of other villages in the Kalahari. In general, and based on data recorded on six hunters observed during thirteen episodes over a period of 378 observation days (between 1987 and 1991), Kutse Bakgalagadi males under 40–50 years old do not hunt more or less than Basarwa of the same age (a t-test of the number of hours spent hunting

was insignificant between ethnic groups; Kent n.d.c). Furthermore, for the purposes of this analysis, no distinction was made between domesticated goat and wild animal bones. That ethnicity does not influence the number of bones simply indicates that both ethnic groups are consuming a similar amount of meat.

The reason the ethnicity of the inhabitants does not significantly affect the total number of objects at features is because, unlike those elsewhere in the Kalahari, the Bakgalagadi[12] at Kutse are not generally wealthier in objects or prestige than the Basarwa. There are a number of reasons for this, including the lack of jobs at Kutse, the absence of a store, the particular history of the Bakgalagadi who occupy Kutse and who have tended to adopt Basarwa customs, and the free objects available to all at the game reserve refuse dump.

The influence of ethnicity on material culture varies greatly between regions. Differences depend on what symbols various ethnic groups employ to establish and signify their ethnicity (e.g. language, spatial patterning, refuse disposal as among the gypsies, economic pursuits, status, material culture, etc.; Hodder 1982). In some areas, wealth is an ethnic marker and in other areas it is not. For example, non-systematic observations of village Bakgalagadi living elsewhere in the Kalahari indicate that they may have a larger number of material goods, including more imported, store-bought objects, than the Kutse residents. In this case, ethnicity might significantly influence the abundance of objects at the camps they occupy in contrast to those occupied by Kutse Bakgalagadi or Basarwa (Kent n.d.a). The general lack of differentiation between Basarwa and Bakgalagadi at Kutse is unique to the Central Kalahari and Khutse Game Reserve areas and is at least partly a consequence of specific historical circumstances.[13] Therefore, although Bakgalagadi at Kutse do not have material culture inventories that differ significantly in abundance from the Basarwa, this finding is not generalizable for the rest of the Kalahari or for outside the Kalahari.

Gender and population

As stated above, gender was not one of the original variables tested, but was investigated after population was found to be non-significant. The lack of a significant relationship between gender and the number of objects (see Table 5.2) is probably due to the fact that most objects at Kutse are neither gender linked nor function specific. Spears are occasionally used by females to cut or stir something, and digging sticks are equally important to males and females. Some women make hunting snares out of mealie meal bag threads; the meat acquired in the snare trap technically belongs to them. In addition, the lack of employment at Kutse affects males and females equally.

Although perhaps seemingly counter-intuitive, it appears that the amount of material culture in features is influenced less by the number of people and more by how long people plan to stay at a camp. Camp population, whether measured in terms of all people residing at a camp, only adults, only males, or only females, is not significantly correlated and does not explain much variance in the number of objects at features.

In terms of population, faunal remains frequencies are similar to material culture frequencies. Camps with more adults (i.e. population excluding children) have a higher mean number of faunal remains than those with fewer (Adult category $1 = 6.8$, Adult category $2 = 23.7$, and Adult category $3 = 32.7$). However, these differences are not statistically significant even in a bivariate model partly because of within-group variation and partly because of sample size (Table 5.2). It is a little surprising that the number of men, the sex primarily responsible for hunting and butchering, at a camp does not influence the number of faunal remains in the multivariate model, but older non-hunting men were included in this category and may have caused the lack of significance and the small R^2.

The lack of a significant relationship between the number of bones and camp population, be it viewed as a whole, as the number of adults, or broken down into the number of males and females, might be explained by one of several factors. Bones, which are more common in areas between features than in features, may not, when examined from features alone, provide much information on population figures. It might be necessary to view bones from the entire camp – features and non-features together – and if so, this is important for archaeologists to know before formulating site sampling strategies. Another possibility which I personally favor stems from the common practice of sharing meat (with bones) between camps. Sharing appears to equalize the distribution of bones between camps with different numbers of inhabitants, as well as between camps with hunters who have different levels of skill (Kent n.d.b and c). Sharing is an important factor influencing the presence and frequency of faunal remains at Kutse. I suggest, then, that the prevalence of meat sharing within sharing networks plays an important role in the amount of meat and faunal remains at sites. Sharing, I propose, accounts for the lack of significance of camp population at the traditional threshold value of $p < 0.05$, the small amount of variance explained, and, when in a multivariate model, the high (i.e. non-significant) p-value.

Summary

The most important conclusion that can be drawn is that the number of objects located at features is influenced more by the length of time people plan to stay than by the length they actually do stay or the other variables tested, with the exception of Type. The reason is that people with anticipated short occupations tend to have fewer possessions, which are often less bulky and less durable, than people who plan to occupy a camp for a long time. This can produce variation in the archaeological record in two ways. First, inter-group or cross-cultural variation should be expected between societies with different mobility patterns. Consequently, there is a need for separate models of abandonment behavior for nomadic, semi-sedentary, and sedentary groups. When an archaeologist investigates a site, a general mobility pattern is usually at least implicitly assumed for the group (e.g. the occupants were nomadic foragers or sedentary year-round residents). Models of specific site abandonment need to be able to incorporate gross differences in mobility patterning. The details in abandonment models appropriate for highly nomadic groups might not be equally appropriate for very sedentary groups. Moreover, intra-group variation should be expected in societies that seasonally use different mobility patterns (i.e. sedentary with reoccupied base camps and briefly occupied special-purpose sites). Another source of potential variation in the archaeological record is from camps where people plan to spend a specific amount of time but either stay longer or shorter due to unforeseeable events. Since one of our tasks as archaeologists is to recognize and interpret variability in the archaeological record, it is important to establish models that take variability into account. Any model of mobility must be cross-culturally valid in that it describes consistent relationships that occur between groups, and therefore through time (i.e. are not culture- or time-specific). Abandonment models need to be formulated in such a way as to be relevant for the particular mobility pattern practiced by the society who produced the sites to which the model is applied.

Archaeological implications and future directions

A number of archaeological implications have already been alluded to above. It is suggested that the relationship between mobility and material culture is not linked to a specific culture or region. As a result, models developed from Kutse data provide a useful departure from which to understand different archaeological societies. Most Kutse residents are sedentary and their camps and material culture reflect this mobility pattern by the presence of formal storage features, more permanent architecture, and other aspects of site structure not found at highly nomadic !Kung Basarwa rainy season camps, for example. My research indicates that highly nomadic groups will have a different material inventory from sedentary groups. Therefore, if we use material culture in our models of abandonment, we must first take gross levels of mobility, such as nomadism versus sedentism, into account. While our understanding of Kutse sedentary camps provides an appropriate starting point from which to examine abandonment in sedentary societies, such as the Anasazi, abandonment practices at Kutse are not necessarily appropriate to understanding abandonment among Bolivian transhumant agro-pastoralists, who regularly practice reoccupation and cache a relatively large number of objects at abandoned sites (see Tomka, this volume).

We can apply our understanding of the influence of mobility patterns on object abundance and abandonment to Schlanger and Wilshusen's chapter (this volume) on abandonment in the Mesa Verde Anasazi region. They present an excellent analysis of abandonment modes tied to rates of abandonment. Schlanger and Wilshusen support their conclusions by correlating the amount of debris left on pit structure floors with abandonment modes (they used object weight inside a particular feature – pit structures – instead of frequency of objects in features, as was done here). Because their paper is so well thought out, it is possible to analyze their data from different perspectives. For instance, the above analysis indicates that the amount of material culture at a site, be it measured in terms of weight or frequency, is significantly related to the length of time occupants planned to stay at a camp within the larger category of sedentism. In other words, sedentary people can have base camps at which they anticipate a long stay and special-activity camps at which they plan a shorter stay. Not all camps occupied by sedentary peoples represent the same anticipated length of occupation, although this variable is not factored into Schlanger and Wilshusen's analysis. Moreover, the above suggests that variability resulting from a number of planned and unplanned situations should be expected, which will be reflected in the archaeological record.

It cannot be expected that sedentary horticulturalists on a different continent will have exactly the same patterns with precisely the same details of abandonment as recently sedentary Basarwa, but the impact of anticipated mobility is still an influential factor in both cases. Anticipated mobility needs to be taken into account in

models explaining diversity in the archaeological record everywhere. I am suggesting that mobility structures material culture in a predictable way and that this predictable relationship, based on a general principle of mobility, underlies abandonment processes that are not necessarily restricted to one ethnic group or to one time period (also see Schlanger 1991; Yellen 1977). In other words, the use of straight ethnographic analogy is problematic in most cases. However, the elucidation of relationships, and the principles behind them, are cross-cultural and atemporal, and therefore applicable to all societies, including prehistoric ones only known through the archaeological record. That is why cross-cultural relationships between mobility and material culture were emphasized in this analysis, rather than the details of specific abandonment behavior as practiced at Kutse. It is also why the relationships are applicable to different societies outside the Kalahari, including the prehistoric American Southwest. For example, how much of the variability Schlanger and Wilshusen (this volume) documented among Anasazi sites can be accounted for by diversity in anticipated and/or actual length of occupation? Were mobility patterns different enough between the periods examined to account for the differences in total number/weight of objects on pit structure floors? The study presented here suggests that mobility should be one of several factors tested in hypotheses to explain abandonment variability between the Anasazi periods.

In addition, nomadic settlement patterns influence the visibility of foragers in the archaeological record. Brooks and Yellen (1987) have already addressed this issue among the !Kung, noting that the only recognizable archaeological sites are those that people had planned to reoccupy. Sites that were permanently abandoned were simply invisible in the archaeological record. Research among diverse groups indicates profound differences in abandonment behavior between sites at which inhabitants had planned reoccupation and sites at which they had not (Tomka 1989, and this volume; Stevenson 1982).

Another important issue that needs to be included in models of abandonment is scavenging, a behavior that is particularly common at camps located within or near villages or communities. Ethnographic observations indicate that scavenging at least of building materials from abandoned camps is extremely common at Kutse. The reason the variable Distance is not significantly correlated with the amount of material culture in the analysis presented here might be that the camps examined are too close to one another so that there is not enough diversity within the sample to detect variability (e.g. many of the Distance 2 camps are located along paths people travel when foraging).

The amount of material at a camp is often used to infer mode of abandonment and there is some evidence to support such an inference in some cases (e.g. Stevenson 1982 and others). However, scavenging needs to be considered before conclusions are drawn about even seemingly isolated sites (Schiffer 1987). For example, we often do not take paths into consideration because we take shoes for granted. But people who are habitually barefoot tend to travel outside of camp on trails to avoid thorns and other potential dangers in the Kalahari. This is apparently also true in forested environments, such as those inhabited by African Pygmies (Laden 1990). Isolated abandoned camps that are located along a trail are vulnerable to scavenging, just as are the abandoned camps located within the dispersed community of Kutse (Kent 1990). Instances of unplanned abandonment might be masked in the archaeological record by scavenging. Despite the lack of association of the variable Distance and artifact abundance in the Kutse data, the role of scavenging in abandonment behavior and visibility needs to be systematically assessed in a variety of situations, environments, and cultures. It is obvious that postoccupation scavenging would occur in and near villages, but such scavenging may also occur at seemingly isolated camps. The location and relationship of sites and paths in the immediate environs need to be taken into account when model building.[14]

This study shows that faunal remains frequencies are not necessarily conditioned by the same factors that condition artifact frequencies, as can be seen by comparing the bivariate and multivariate models for each. As a consequence, bones need to be studied as a separate dependent variable. Although the distribution of faunal remains and artifacts is influenced by some of the same factors, such as Type, which is an indirect measure of site maintenance activities and perhaps hindrance values, other factors appear to impact the two quite differently. In other words, there are a number of variables that affect bone distributions that do not influence artifact distributions in the same way or to the same extent and vice versa. Anticipated Mobility does not influence faunal assemblages but does influence artifact assemblages. Variables that impact faunal remains but not necessarily artifacts include scavenging by dogs or wild carnivores and different cooking techniques (e.g. roasting versus boiling as described in Kent n.d.b).

The above ethnoarchaeological research is directly applicable to prehistoric archaeological investigations.

For instance, Pueblo II Anasazi sites excavated in southwestern Colorado were analyzed using the concepts of anticipated and actual mobility (Kent 1992b). On the basis of architecture, features, artifacts, faunal remains, and botanical remains, three of the sites analyzed were interpreted as anticipated and actual long occupations, the fourth was identified as an anticipated and actual short occupation, and the fifth was identified as an anticipated long but actual short occupation (Kent 1992b). Anticipated short occupations among sedentary societies tend to have fewer objects than longer ones because people take fewer possessions with them if they plan to stay at a special activity site for a brief period (i.e. they cache their things at the base camp).[15] The Basarwa data indicate that nomadic societies not only have fewer possessions in general than sedentary societies, but that people who plan short occupations will have the least number of objects within the range that is characteristic of nomadic groups.

Conclusions

Six variables were originally selected to test their significance in influencing the number of objects and faunal remains located in features at occupied and abandoned camps at a recently sedentary Kalahari community. The only significant variables that account for the variation in the number of objects at features in a multivariate model are Type and Anticipated Mobility, although the actual length of occupation is almost significant in a bivariate model. Of the independent variables thought to influence the number of faunal remains at camps, Type is the only significant variable, although the variable Males is just slightly non-significant in a bivariate model. However, because of shared variation the variable Males is completely non-significant in a multivariate model.

Anticipated Mobility significantly influences the total number of objects located at features, while Actual Mobility has a more borderline p-value and explains less variance. The reasons for the difference in significance and amount of variance explained lie in the nature of the material culture system. Simply stated, the more mobile a group, the less material culture they carry and/or abandon. This relationship should be visible cross-culturally between groups, such as nomadic hunter-gatherers and sedentary horticulturalists. The relationship should also be visible within groups, such as societies with year-round base camps and special-activity camps occupied for shorter periods.

That Anticipated Mobility influences material culture inventories and abandonment behaviors in predictable ways may seem at first to be a fairly simple and straight-forward proposition. However, its ramifications for model building and understanding diversity and variability in the archaeological record are far reaching. One consequence of this finding is the necessity first to establish the general mobility pattern of a prehistoric group, and therefore understand the context of the quantity of their material culture, before analyzing abandonment behavior. Otherwise we may confuse sites with an accumulation of material resulting from different mobility strategies with sites having an accumulation of material resulting from different modes of abandonment. The logical next question is: What conditions anticipated mobility? But that is beyond the scope of the chapter and the book. Nonetheless, it is hoped that this chapter contributes to the growing literature on abandonment behavior by pointing out some of the significant relationships necessary to include in models of abandonment and directions to explore with future research.

Appendix. Example of objects located at windbreaks at three Kutse camps.

CAMP 1 – Basarwa
Anticipated medium/actual short occupation
Site population = 10 people

Date of inventory: 7 June 1987

Windbreak 1:	*2 Water jugs
	2 Enamel bowls
	1 Long metal-tipped spear
	1 Blanket fragment
	*1 Vegetable oil square tin can "pot"
	*1 Broken brown plastic medicine bottle
	*1 Tablespoon
	1 Stirring stick
	*1 Tin can
	*1 Bone smoking pipe (goat proximal tibia shaft)
	1 Heavy cloth fragment
	1 Cloth bag
	1 Blanket
	1 Vegetable oil square tin can "pot"
	*1 Axe
	*1 Home-made grass sieve
	*1 Enamel tea cup
	1 Red fabric fragment
	1 Blue fabric fragment

1 Square vegetable oil square tin can "pot"
*1 Lid from soda pop can
4 Unidentifiable bird breast bones
1 Enamel bowl
1 Piece of steenbok trap fragment
1 Digging stick
*1 Stone anvil

CAMP 2 – Bakgalagadi/Basarwa
Anticipated long/actual long occupation
Site population = 7 people

Date of inventory: 28 June 1987

Windbreak 1:	*2 Goat hides
	1 Jackal (*Canis mesomelas*) hide
	1 Fox (*Octocyon megalotis*) hide
	1 Square cooking tin can "pot"
	*1 Hartebeest (*Alcelaphus buselaphus*) hide fragment
	*25 Small sticks for staking out hides
	*2 Large three-legged cast iron cooking pots with lids
	1 Piece of processed leather
	1 Steenbok (*Raphicerus campestris*) hide
	2 Steenbok horns
	1 Blackened tin can "pot"
	1 Steenbok articulated ulna and radius
	4 Blankets
	*1 Fox hide
	1 Pants fragment
	*1 Wooden pestle for pounding meat
	1 Thumb piano
	*5 Blankets
	*1 Sandal
	*1 Goat hide (to be made into mat)
	1 Tin can
	1 Fox hide
	*2 Pot lids
	*2 Water jugs
	*1 Mealie meal bag used as a mat
	*1 Enamel cup
	2 Hartebeest hide fragments
	1 Cloth bag with stakes (20) for hide preparation
	1 Stirring stick
	1 Enamel coffee cup
	1 Plastic bottle with clinic medicine;

```
 1  Coin envelope of pills from clinic
*2  Water jugs
 1  Cow horn with brains in it
 1  Plastic bag (empty)
 1  Small tin can with oil in it
 1  Goat cranium (used as hide scraper)
 4  Jackal feet with claws
 2  Water jugs
*1  White cloth
 2  Steenbok traps
 1  Goat hide strip
 1  Pair of children's sandals
*1  Empty mealie meal bag
*1  Small plastic water jug
 3  Fox hides
 1  Metal spear
 1  Mealie meal bag (full)
*1  Axe
*1  Wooden tray for grinding tobacco
 1  Piece of paper bag
*1  Blackened square tin can "pot"
*1  Little enamel pot with goat milk
```

* Lying on ground; not starred is in the branches of the feature.

Acknowledgments

I am most grateful to the people of Kutse and particularly Willy, my field assistant, for helping me in too many ways to recount. I thank the government of Botswana, including the Office of the President, Ministry of Local Government and Land, and the National Museum and Art Gallery of Botswana, for permission to conduct research in their country and for assistance in various bureaucratic matters. I also appreciate the financial support provided by Wenner-Gren Foundation for Anthropological Research, Fulbright Foundation, and Old Dominion University Arts and Letters.

Martha Graham, Sarah Schlanger, Bob Benfer, and Mike Schiffer provided excellent constructive comments that were most valuable in revising earlier rough drafts. I thank Steve Tomka and Cathy Cameron for inviting me to participate in their symposium and later book, and for their comments on a draft of this manuscript. I appreciate the quantitative advice provided by Steven Rhiel, Garland White, and Ed Markowski on the quantitative portion of the paper. However, and unfortunately, any inadequacies are solely my responsibility. I also thank Jim Railey for drafting Fig. 5.2, Old Dominion University Graphics for drafting Fig. 5.1 and 5.3, and Marion Blue and Liliane McCarthy for editorial comments.

Notes

1 I appreciate Steve Tomka (pers. comm. 1992) pointing out the possibility that while each household had equal access to the game reserve dump, they may not have collected the items in equal proportions if there were wealth differences between households before they moved to Kutse or before they moved to their current camp at Kutse. Although this may be the case for other groups, interviews, inventories, and direct observations indicate that it is *not* the case for most Kutse residents.

2 Most activities during the dry season take place around the hearth at the windbreak, including sleeping, eating, and entertaining. Windbreaks are also the major structures used for storing possessions during the dry season. Huts are used primarily for brief periods in the rainy season to escape the rain or the oppressive summer heat at midday. They are used year-round for storage and many huts at Kutse have an interior storage platform, unlike the huts built by more mobile groups.

3 For the most part, Kutse camps are abandoned permanently, unlike camps used by Mexican Rarámuri (Tarahamara) or Bolivian agro-pastoralists (see Graham, this volume and Tomka, this volume).

4 According to Neter, Wasserman, and Kutner 1990:149: "At times, it may be desirable to introduce a constant into a transformation of Y, such as when Y may be negative. For instance, the logarithmic transformation to shift the origin in Y and make all Y observations positive would be $Y' = \log_{10} (Y + k)$, where k is an appropriately chosen constant."

5 Interaction effects were also examined, but none was significant or explained much variability. As a consequence, interaction effects were not included in any of the models. Residuals were examined for normality by running SAS diagnostics and by examining plots of the residuals.

6 According to Tabachnick and Fidell (1989:128–9; original emphasis), if "either standard multiple or hierarchical regression is used, one would like to have 20 times more cases than IVs [independent variables] . . . . However, *a bare minimum requirement is to have at least 5 times more cases than IVs* – at least 25 cases if 5 IVs are used."

7 See Freedman *et al.* 1991:501: "The *P*-value of a test depends on the sample size . . . . [An] important difference may not be statistically significant if the sample is too small."

8 This type of analysis is sometimes called Ward's hierarchical regression.

9 It is well known that "An important regressor can have a large (nonsignificant) *p*-value if the sample is small ... " (SAS 1990:15; also see Freedman *et al.* 1991:501).

10 My justification for including Actual Mobility in the multivariate model is based on the well-known observation that many "coefficients are of real importance even though they are not significant. If one deletes them from the regression (or almost equally faultily, includes them but omits them from the ensuing report because they are 'not significant'), the result will be a regression chosen for irrelevant reasons ... " (Achen 1982:52). By using a $p < 0.06$ cutoff, I increase my chances of making a type I error to only 6 percent (i.e. rejecting a true null hypothesis; actual length of time a site was occupied had a $p = 0.0557$; see Table 5.2).

11 Although anecdotal and not based on systematically collected data, several Euroamericans have told me that they never purchased furniture for apartments they had rented for an anticipated short period, even though they ended up staying a long time. They kept thinking that they would leave soon and, as a consequence, did not want to acquire a bed, tables, and other furniture that they would have obtained if they had anticipated a long stay. This is consistent with the predictions of the model and the one site that was an anticipated short but actual long occupation in Vierich's data (Kent and Vierich 1989). We might expect people not to carry and/or acquire as many possessions if they plan a short stay, even if they end up staying a long time. Hopefully future research will permit the assessment of material culture assemblages and site structure of sites where inhabitants anticipated a short occupation but ended up staying for a long period of time.

12 There are a few Bakgalagadi at Kutse who do not regularly hunt or gather but instead rely more on their goat herds and gardens. They tend to be a very small minority, however, most of whom moved to Kutse in 1988 or later. After 1987 several Bakgalagadi households moved to Kutse who, as a group, tend to have more goats and donkeys than the other Kutse Bakgalagadi or Basarwa.

13 Most Kutse Bakgalagadi represent the first wave of migration of Bakgalagadi into the region. Unlike later immigrants, they did not incorporate as many Botswana customs, traits, or items of material culture. Instead, they adopted some of the Basarwa culture.

14 Equally important, but less often appreciated, is the fact that in many parts of the world today full-time foragers *and* full-time horticulturalists coexist in the same region. This occurs in South Africa, East Africa, Central Africa, India, the Philippines, and parts of South America (Bailey *et al.* 1989; Ellison and Brandt Chapter, this volume; Headland and Reid 1989; Hitchcock 1982; Kent 1992a; Sponsel 1989; Vierich 1981). For past societies, we tend to regard areas as either occupied by foragers or occupied by horticulturalists. Certainly this is not the pattern in many parts of the world today, and there is no reason to assume that the mixture of groups following different mobility and subsistence strategies was any less extensive in the past, after the advent of farming and/or pastoralism (e.g. one possible region traditionally thought to have been exclusively inhabited by horticulturalists, such as the Anasazi southwest, may, in fact, have been inhabited, at least on the margins, by foragers as well; also see Powell 1990). In these cases, it is important to distinguish situations such as anticipated short-term habitations from long-term ones (e.g. Kent 1992b), nomadic societies' base camps from sedentary societies' special-activity camps, and anticipated abandonments from unanticipated ones. In order to accomplish this, we need to understand abandonment behavior along with the implications of sedentism and anticipated short versus long occupations for material culture, site structure, and other aspects of behavior and culture.

15 One needs to study material culture in context of the entire site. For example, it is conceivable that an anticipated short occupation where a large number of lithic reduction activities occurred might have more flakes than an anticipated long occupation where tools were not commonly made. In the Pueblo II Anasazi example, I was able to distinguish anticipated long from short occupations based on abundance and other attributes of the lithic assemblage, in conjunction with the ceramics, faunal and botanical remains, and various facets of the site structure. Rather than focus on abundance as a sole factor divorced from all other kinds of data, it is necessary to examine the abundance of tools, in addition to the number of flakes, the tool to flake ratio, and the diversity of tool types and raw materials (e.g. Kent 1992b). No single criterion can be used to determine mobility patterns; instead, a number of different variables need to be investigated with competing hypotheses, as I did in this chapter. The testing of

competing hypotheses indicates that it is essential to take mobility into account as a potentially influential variable when formulating models of abandonment based on material culture frequencies. One should not make inferences from within a vacuum – it is necessary to include site structure data along with material culture abundance and other information to formulate appropriate models of abandonment and to construct appropriate inferences.

References

Achen, Christopher
1982 *Interpreting and Using Regression.* Quantitative Applications in the Social Sciences. Sage University Paper 29.

Ames, Kenneth
1991 Sedentism: A Temporal Shift or a Transitional Change in Hunter-Gatherer Mobility Patterns? In *Between Bands and States*, edited by Susan Gregg, pp. 108–34. Southern Illinois University Center for Archaeological Investigations, Occasional Paper 9.

Bailey, Robert, Genevieve Head, Mark Jenike, Bruce Owen, Robert Rechtman and E. Zechenter
1989 Hunting and Gathering in Tropical Rain Forest: Is It Possible? *American Anthropologist* 91(1): 59–82.

Binford, Lewis
1979 Organization and Formation Processes: Looking at Curated Technologies. *Journal of Anthropological Research* 35(3): 255–73.
1980 Willow Smoke and Dogs' Tails. *American Antiquity* 45(1): 4–20.

Blalock, Hubert
1979 *Social Statistics.* McGraw-Hill, New York.

Brooks, Alison and John Yellen
1987 The preservation of activity areas in the archaeological record: Ethnoarchaeological and archaeological work in Northwest Ngamiland, Botswana. In *Method and Theory for Activity Area Research: An Ethnoarchaeological Approach*, edited by Susan Kent, pp. 63–106. Columbia University Press, New York.

Brooks, Robert
1989 Planned versus Unplanned Abandonment of Dwellings: Impacts on the Context of House Floors. Paper presented at the 54th Annual Meeting of the Society for American Archaeology, Atlanta.

Cooper, Zarine
1990 Abandoned Onge Encampments and their Relevance in Understanding the Archaeological Record in the Andaman Islands. Paper presented at the 6th International Conference on Hunting and Gathering Societies, University of Alaska, Fairbanks.

Dowdy, Shirley and Stanley Wearden
1991 *Statistics for Research.* John Wiley and Sons, New York.

Fisher, John
1986 Shadows in the Forest: Ethnoarchaeology among the Efe Pygmies. Unpublished PhD Dissertation, University of California, Berkeley.

Freedman, David, Robert Pisani, Roger Purves, and Ani Adhikari
1991 *Statistics, 2nd Edition.* W. W. Norton & Company, New York.

Headland, Thomas and Lawrence Reid
1989 Hunter-Gatherers and their Neighbors from Prehistory to the Present. *Current Anthropology* 30(1): 43–66.

Hitchcock, Robert
1982 The Ethnoarchaeology of Sedentism: Mobility Strategies and Site Structure Among Foraging and Food Producing Populations in the Eastern Kalahari Desert, Botswana, PhD dissertation, University of New Mexico. University Microfilms, Ann Arbor.

Hodder, Ian
1982 *Symbols in Action.* Cambridge University Press, Cambridge.

Kent, Susan
1981 The Dog: An Archaeologist's Best Friend or Worst Enemy – The Spatial Distribution of Faunal Remains. *Journal of Field Archaeology* 8(3): 367–72.
1990 Invisible Foragers: The Archaeological Visibility of Foraging Hunter-Gatherers. Paper presented at the Conference for African Archaeology, Gainesville, Florida.
1991 The Relationship Between Mobility Strategies and Site Structure. In *The Interpretation of Spatial Patterning Within Stone Age Archaeological Sites*, edited by T. Douglas Price and Ellen Kroll, pp. 33–59. Plenum Publishing Corporation, New York.
1992a The Current Forager Controversy: Real versus Ideal Views of Hunter-Gatherers. *Man* 27(1): 40–65.
1992b Studying Variability in the Archaeological Record: An Ethnoarchaeological Model for Distinguishing Mobility Patterns. *American Antiquity* 57(4): 635–60.
n.d.a Bakgalagadi: The Other Inhabitants of the Kalahari. Manuscript submitted for publication.

n.d.b The Influence of Hunting Skill, Sharing, Mode of Cooking, and Dogs on Faunal Remains at a Sedentary Kalahari Community. Manuscript submitted for publication.

n.d.c Hunting Variability in the Kalahari. Manuscript submitted for publication.

Kent, Susan and Richard Lee

1992 A Hematological Study of !Kung Kalahari Foragers: An Eighteen Year Comparison. In *Diet, Demography, and Disease: Changing Views of Anemia*, edited by Patricia Stuart-Macadam and Susan Kent, pp. 173–200. Aldine de Gruyter, New York.

Kent, Susan and Helga Vierich

1989 The Myth of Ecological Determinism – Anticipated Mobility and Site Organization of Space. In *Farmers as Hunters – The Implications of Sedentism*, edited by Susan Kent, pp. 96–133. Cambridge University Press, Cambridge.

Laden, Gregory

1990 Ethnoarchaeology among African Pygmies. Paper presented to the Society for Africanist Archaeology, Gainsville, Florida.

Lee Richard

1979 *The !Kung San: Men, Women, and Work in a Foraging Society.* Cambridge University Press, Cambridge.

Lewis-Beck, M.

1990 *Applied Regression.* Quantitative Applications in the Social Sciences. Sage University Paper 22.

Littell, Ramon, Rudolf Freund, and Philip Spector

1991 *SAS System for Linear Models.* SAS Institute, Cary, NC.

Neter, John, William Wasserman and Michael Kutner

1990 *Applied Linear Statistical Models*, third edition. Irwin Publishers, Homewood, IL.

Powell, Shirley

1990 Sedentism or Mobility: What Do the Data Say? What Did the Anasazi Do? In *Perspectives on Southwestern Prehistory*, edited by P. Minnis and C. Redman, pp. 92–102. Westview Press, Boulder, CO.

SAS

1990 *SAS/STAT User's Guide*, Release 6.06 Edition. Cary, NC: SAS Institute.

Schiffer, Michael

1975 The Effect of Occupation Span on Site Content. In *The Cache River Archaeological Project: An Experiment in Contract Archaeology*, edited by Michael Schiffer and J. H. House, pp. 265–9. Arkansas Archaeological Survey Research Series 8.

1987 *Formation Processes of the Archaeological Record.* University of New Mexico Press, Albuquerque.

Schlanger, Sarah

1991 On Manos, Metates, and the History of Site Occupations. *American Antiquity* 56(3): 460–74.

Shott, Michael

1989 Diversity, Organization, and Behavior in the Material Record: Ethnographic and Archaeological Examples. *Current Anthropology* 30(3): 283–315.

Silberbauer, George

1981 *Hunter and Habitat in the Central Kalahari Desert.* Cambridge University Press, Cambridge.

Sponsil, Leslie

1989 Farming and Foraging: A Necessary Complementarity in Amazonia? In *Farmers as Hunters: The Implications of Sedentism*, edited by S. Kent, pp. 37–45. Cambridge University Press, Cambridge.

Stevenson, Marc

1982 Toward an Understanding of Site Abandonment Behavior: Evidence from Historic Mining Camps in the Southwest Yukon. *Journal of Anthropological Archaeology* 1:237–65.

1985 The Formation of Artifact Assemblages at Workshop/Habitation Sites: Models from Peace Point in Northern Alberta. *American Antiquity* 50: 63–81.

Tabachnick, Barbara and Linda Fidell

1989 *Using Multivariate Statistics.* Harper Collins, New York.

Taylor, Walter

1964 Tethered Nomadism and Water Territoriality: An Hypothesis. *Proceedings of the Acts 35th International Congress of the Americas. Mexico*, pp. 197–203.

Tomka, Steve A.

1989 The Ethnoarchaeology of Site Abandonment in an Agro-Pastoral Context. Paper presented at the 54th Annual Meeting of the Society for American Archaeology, Atlanta.

Vierich, Helga

1981 The Kūa of the Southeastern Kalahari: A Study in the Socio-ecology of Dependency. PhD dissertation, University of Toronto. Ann Arbor, University Microfilms.

Woodman, Craig

1987 Proxemic Analysis of Pithouse Sites. *American Archaeology* 6(3): 170–3.

Yellen, John

1977 *Archaeological Approaches to the Present.* Academic Press, New York.

6
Agricultural abandonment: a comparative study in historical ecology

GLENN DAVIS STONE

On the Nigerian savanna between Lafia and Shendam are thousands of farmsteads of sorghum, millet, and yam farmers. The area south of the small town of Namu is populated largely by Kofyar, who have been moving there from the hills of the Jos Plateau since the middle of this century. The Kofyar first came on a seasonal basis, living in ephemeral compounds, but by the time I came in 1984 they had established enduring settlements in many areas.

I had come to study the Kofyar settlement system, and I began by learning the local geography, especially the names of the various *ungwas*, or neighborhoods. While most of the place names were in Kofyar or Hausa, I would occasionally encounter names that referred to the Tiv, a tribe that had moved into the Namu area from the south. Place-names such as Koprume contained a small slice of settlement history – *kop* being the Kofyar term for the former residence of someone, *Rume* being the name of the Tiv who had abandoned the area. In fact, it turned out that our own compound had originally been built by Tiv and later abandoned.

Since a focus of my research was the evolution of settlement patterns, including the factors affecting farm abandonment, I was intrigued by the permanency of Kofyar settlement in precisely the same locales where Tiv settlement had been ephemeral. Kofyar and Tiv had apparently occupied the same ecological niche, clearing fields with fire and growing yams and interplanting millet and sorghum. But when land within easy reach of the compound was played out, the Kofyar and Tiv responses to the option of abandonment were completely different. Shifting cultivation, a well-known adaptation to land abundance, often involves shifting

settlement – periodic abandonments that ensure constant access to fresh farmland and game. But the Kofyar, at least those on the best agricultural soils, had spurned the idea of abandonment even when vast tracts of virgin land were available, and some of them now lived on spots named for Tiv who had been quick to shift.

This chapter deals with the particular type of abandonment that we can call "agricultural abandonment" – the abandonment of agrarian sites (normally farmsteads or farming hamlets) as a response to declining agricultural yields. Without intensification, cultivation almost always degrades agricultural resources,[1] and abandonment is a basic – but not ubiquitous – reaction. Of all the factors causing farmers to abandon the small sites that dominate so much of the archaeological record, this is probably the most important. Still, our understanding of agricultural abandonment is poor, and we have been slow in recognizing it as a problem in its own right.[2] My approach is to treat it as part of an *agrarian settlement system*, drawing on the fruitful research on hunter-gatherer settlement ecology (Struever 1968; Binford 1980). The agrarian settlement system can then be seen as embedded in social organization and in cultural institutions for mobilizing human resources.

The study of modern agrarian ecology is invaluable for understanding agrarian settlement systems in the past. Agricultural phenomena that can be studied today have parallels in past farming systems, including choices of crops, crop combinations, and crop scheduling; problems with weeds, insects, and diseases; issues of fertility, drainage, and texture; and the practical problems of storage, labor mobilization, and land tenure.

It is because there are constants in agricultural phenomena worldwide that we find use in such general concepts as *intensification*. And it is because of these constants that we find meaningful patterning in agrarian settlement systems. The adaptation called shifting cultivation, with its low labor investments in agriculture, high marginal returns to labor, and abandonment when yields decline, is a recurrent pattern worldwide. At the same time, intensive farmers endeavor to establish land tenure, and develop increasing reluctance to abandon their farms. Abandonment is an integral part of agricultural adaptation, but it figures in more than one pattern; the problem is in predicting when agricultural abandonment should and should not occur.

If we might take a lesson from the geographers who have outpaced us in building settlement theory, we might try to control as many variables as needed to isolate the most salient forces shaping the agrarian settlement system. The von Thünen/Chisholm theory of land use and the Christaller/Lösch theory of central places are built on perfectly isotropic, ahistorical plains populated by perfectly rational, knowledgeable people. Perhaps we could imagine an evolutionary trajectory for agrarian settlement on such an imaginary plain: put a population of farmers there, give them each a pig and a pouch of wheat, or a Sudanic hoe and some yam cuttings, or 40 acres and a mule, and build a theory of agrarian settlement.

A crucial parameter in any such model will have to be *occupation span*, which is a function of abandonment strategies: when population grows and resources degrade, are settlements completely abandoned, partially abandoned by fissioning, or is production intensified? In real life, all of these responses occur, but our models generally embody *a priori* assumptions about how farmers prioritize them.[3]

We don't yet know enough about the factors militating for and against agricultural abandonment to be able to predict its occurrence, and this obviates modeling agrarian settlement in the abstract. If there is no single, unambiguous trajectory that an agrarian settlement system should follow, even on a controlled artificial landscape, we will run into the question of determinism in cultural systems. Is the evolution of agrarian settlement deterministic, or "probabilistic" (Haggett 1965; Flannery 1976)? If the probable doesn't happen, what is the alternative? If there is no single trajectory, can we identify two or more modal trajectories, and predict the factors that determine which one occurs?

I am convinced that no single trajectory of settlement evolution can be defined without holding constant so many key variables that the model would become useless. However, there is something to be learned by exploring actual cases of agrarian settlement evolution (Stone 1991). I want to describe briefly two cases which on the surface seem quite different, but which both suggest the same two modalities in agrarian settlement evolution.

The first case is set on the frontier in the savanna of central Nigeria that I noted at the outset. The second case is set on a frontier in the Delaware Valley in the seventeenth century. We think of this area being wrested from the Indians by permanent settlers, yet there was a population of shifting agriculturalists, largely from Scandinavia, that preceded the small farming villages of English, German, and Dutch settlers. The Nigerian and American cases differ in their economic and historical matrix and the actual settlement forms and crops, but the parallels between them reveal something about the latitude of agricultural adaptations, and this provides a context for understanding the causes of farmstead abandonment.

The Nigerian frontier

What today we call the Benue Valley is a wide trough filled with limestones, sandstones and shales. Between the towns of Lafia and Shendam, near the geographical center of Nigeria, soils of high agricultural potential have developed. Raiding and slaving threatened agricultural settlements in the past, and during the early past of this century the Namu Plains contained only a handful of small, walled towns, separated by miles of vacant land. With the British pacification, the area became an agricultural frontier, and by the 1940s colonial officials began to report farmers in the area.

The Kofyar were one of several groups that, prior to pacification, had lived in the defensive hills of the Jos Plateau, just north of the Benue Valley. During the 1940s Kofyar began to establish migratory bush farms on the piedmont between the Plateau and the Benue Valley; by the early 1950s their farms had reached Namu and the frontier in the Benue Valley.

The frontier farms were visited by Robert Netting in the early 1960s (Netting 1968, 1969). The Kofyar were coming from a tradition of small contiguous farmsteads; the pattern that developed on the frontier was one of large contiguous farmsteads. By the early 1960s there were hundreds of single-household compounds scattered in the Benue Valley south of Namu and Kwande, predominantly along water courses.

Cultivation on the early frontier was extensive, which requires a relatively low ratio of population to productive resources. Over the years, population has increased and continual cropping has reduced soil productivity. The Boserup (1965) model predicts that farmers would perforce intensify cultivation, accepting the higher labor costs per unit of output. But, as an archaeologist interested in abandonment as a component in agrarian settlement systems, I was interested in whether Kofyar followed the Boserup route or simply shifted their settlement to where they could keep farming extensively. I have analyzed the settlement histories of several hundred Kofyar households (Stone 1988a, 1988b) and will summarize some of the findings here.

Kofyar farmers show a strong tendency to keep their farms, even if it means adopting the labor-expensive methods of intensification, *unless* they are on lands that offer especially poor returns to intensive labor. On the fertile and well-drained soils south of Namu, farms are virtually never abandoned. When households fission, the farm may be subdivided or the son's family may have to seek land elsewhere, but the original compound remains. These farms do indeed have to intensify their agriculture. Intensive techniques here include manuring, mulching, and additional field preparation, resulting in a lengthened agricultural season with high daily labor inputs (Stone, Netting, and Stone 1990).

This response to rising land pressure occurs consistently only where soils are both fertile and well drained. To the east of Namu, where there are granite-derived soils with lower fertility, residence times are highly variable, and on the poorly drained clay soils to the south, farms are commonly abandoned within ten years. But in the absence of such soil problems (and sometimes even when they exist), the Kofyar show a dependable preference for intensification over abandonment.

While the Kofyar have been colonizing the Namu Plains from the north, the Tiv have been moving in from the south. In contrast to the Kofyar, the Tiv traditionally maintained a system of extensive cultivation by continually expanding onto new lands throughout the Benue Trough. The British tried to check Tiv expansion in 1912 with the infamous "Munshi Wall" (Munshi being the Hausa name for the Tiv, used by colonial authorities), but, as the colonial archives admit, the Munshis simply "climbed over the wall" (Udo 1966:133).

Tiv expansion most often took the form of gradual encroachment on the land of other Tivs, with the outermost groups moving against non-Tiv farmlands (Bohannan 1954a, 1954b). Tiv movement also took the form of *disjunction*, or emigrating from the area controlled by one's agnatic kin. Emigration was usually to other areas controlled by Tiv, but by the 1940s the Pax Britannica allowed increasing movement into frontier areas (Bohannan 1954a). In location after location, exhaustion of the fields near the compound was remedied not by the heightened work of intensification but by emigration. Farm abandonment, in other words, was an integral part of the farming system.

Tiv movement in general is not only embedded in the agricultural system, it "is intimately associated with the social and political structure of the Tiv – is, in fact, a facet of it" (Bohannan 1954a:2). As described by Bohannan, and developed in an evolutionary context by Sahlins (1963), the hierarchical social organization called the segmentary lineage is singularly effective at mobilizing kin to contest the boundary disputes that inevitably result from constant encroachment of other farmers' lands. When a farm expands, it is against one's most distantly related neighbor, so that in the ensuing dispute, the antagonist will always have more closely related neighbors to call on.

The utility of this lineage and territorial system in pioneering new lands is clear, although it has not been studied. Bohannan did remark on the rapidity of movement, noting (1954a:2) that in "precisely those areas in which land shortage is least severe that the rate of migration appears to be the most rapid."

There were Tiv settlements south of Namu by the early 1950s; they probably preceded the Kofyar in the area, although the few recorded observations are ambiguous (Stone 1988b:130). The Tiv did establish one enduring settlement of several dozen huts north of Langkaku, named Takumburu. Other Tiv compounds were ephemeral, like the one headed by the aforementioned Rume, and their abandoned lands are now farmed by Kofyar. Kofyar who talked with Netting in 1962 were critical of the Tivs, deriding their planting of yams after the rains had started, their broadcasting of grains, and their propensity to abandon a locale as soon as the bush rats had been hunted out. The Tiv were, of course, simply using more extensive cultivation methods, and their preference for leaving rather than intensifying was perfectly consistent with this (Stone 1988b).

The Delaware Valley

The second case, set in the seventeenth century eastern US, is the subject of a recent historical ecological study by Jordan and Kaups (1989). These geographers describe two very different agrarian settlement systems in the Delaware Valley. The differences in these adaptations trace to their roots in Europe, where there existed what might be called an ecological core and periphery. The fertile Germanic core of Europe, with its stable (and partly intensive) three-field system of production, had a prosperous, conservative, agrarian population. Fringing the core were British hilly areas, the subarctic north, and the infertile Eastern European plain. Population here was sparse, and land productivity low. This area gave us Scotch-Irish, Welsh, Alpine Swiss, and Finnish settlers. Of particular import was an adaptive system originating in Eastern Finland, with its short growing season, thin morainic soils, and pine-spruce forests. In the *huuhta* farming system, cultivation was very extensive, with rye being grown in the ashes on swidden plots that were abandoned after a single year. The Finns kept open-range stock and also hunted and gathered. This system relied on an estimated 2500 acres per family. They lived in one-room cabins or small multi-structure farmsteads, which were usually abandoned every few years.

This highly extensive agrarian settlement system was banished to America when it started to encroach on the ecologic core. The swiddeners had colonized most of interior Finland and moved into Sweden and Norway in the 1600s. The valleys here supported stable, intensive-farming villages, and the Finns colonized the interfluves very successfully, sticking to the high ground, until "the Germanic Valley folk awoke to find Finns perched in the heights above them, and the new ethnic map of south-central Scandinavia had topographic lines as borders" (Jordan and Kaups 1989:51). Laws were enacted to constrain the wanton destruction of forest and game, and many swiddeners, perceived as landless vagabonds, were rounded up for transport to the rich deciduous Eastern Woodlands of America ("a bit like tossing Br'er Rabbit in the briar patch": Jordan and Kaups 1989:58n). A Finnish population was in place on the Delaware River in the 1650s, where they thrived – hunting, farming Indians' land, being imprisoned for wizardry, brewing beer and vodka, and farming very extensively.

The agrarian settlement system was preadapted to the woodlands, and it flourished in the backwoods frontiers where European settlement had yet to reach. Farmsteads with a log cabin and sometimes an outbuilding or two were established near old Indian fields which provided forage and attracted deer. The main agricultural job was tree-chopping, a task to which the Finns brought not only technologically superior axes but skill in their use, and an ethic that chopping was preferable to sodbusting. They also chopped trees for wages, and it was Finnish axemen the Dutch hired to clear Harlem in 1661.

Influenced by Indian agricultural tactics, they inter-cropped corn with squash, pumpkins or watermelons in fields where the treestumps were left standing. Vegetables and tobacco were grown in kitchen gardens. The only tree crop was peach, which bore fruit within three years, required less care than apples or pears, and produced brandy. They relied significantly on hunting and gathering.

An essential component of this adaptation was mobility. The backwoodsmen dispersed rapidly along water-courses, driven by what Jordan and Kaups call a "cultural resistance to intensification of land use." Their explanation is to the point:

> The backwoods folk had to choose between intensifying land use and preserving their traditional lifestyle through migration. Some contemporary observers, core Germanic types all, could not understand the motives of those who moved, believing instead that migration "prevented their enjoying the fruit of their labours." (1989:78)

But abandonment offered the pioneers a sweet fruit indeed; high marginal returns on their labor. The plots in forest clearings served for only three to five years. After that the high yields that followed the burning dropped off quickly, regardless of the native fertility of the soil, and weeds quickly became a problem demanding a large investment of labor. At that point the backwoods pioneers "had no ability or interest in restoring the productivity of the soil through manuring, and they refused to submit to a season of hard hoeing. Let their Germanic successors accomplish such intensifications of land use; the Midland pioneers preferred to make another clearing in a different place" (1989:100).

The Finnish system had in effect "skimmed the cream" from the woodlands; the price had been a high degree of mobility, which bothered them not a whit. In fact, for short moves, cabins could simply be dismantled and reassembled in the middle of a new field. The second wave of settlers were obliged to farm more intensively, to which they too were preadapted, as they came from the ecological core of Europe. These more permanent settlements varied from dispersed farmstead to small villages, but they shared a key set of characteristics that contrasted with those of the Finns who had come before. Most importantly, when faced with the choice of intensifying production or moving on, they intensified. This meant planting on bush-fallowed land, which meant plowing, which meant the arduous work of stump-clearing that the Finns had disdained.

Discussion

Jordan and Kaups present the Finno-Indian swidden system as an example of the "pioneer farmer" stage in Frederick Jackson Turner's history of the American frontier, and as an example of a singularly successful strategy of forest colonization (1989:7). They are critical of "normative" models, such as Green's (1979) model of temperate forest colonization, which levels differences among cultures and winds up with the rather awkward prediction of parallel adaptations in all temperate woodlands. Jordan and Kaups call their work "particularistic cultural ecology," a framework they believe anthropologists have discarded too hastily. In this framework, adaptive strategies result from the interplay between the unique history of a culture and its physical environment (see also Galt 1991 and Bennett 1976). They are explicitly interested in the particulars of this case, and they cite as a goal of cultural geography the gaining of "a better grasp of general process so to understand an immensely complicated history."

Since many archaeologists envision the opposite goal – a better grasp of complicated histories so as to understand general process – it is worthwhile to try to fit these cases into ecological principles. It is true that the first European settlers in the American midlands and the Tiv in the Namu savanna thrived precisely because they were preadapted to the system of extensive farming and rapid abandonment that frontiers select for. Margolis (1977) shows that this favored frontier adaptation conforms to the strategy of fugitive species (MacArthur and Wilson 1967) in newly opened habitats. The extensify/abandon strategy thrived on both early frontiers, while the intensifiers dominated the second stage, with their enduring settlements. The concept of cultures adapting to separate ecological niches (Barth 1956) is especially apt when the niches open serially, as in ecological succession (cf. Gall and Saxe 1977); in both of these cases, the intensifiers' niche was improved by the field clearing done by the extensifiers before them. It is equally consistent with economic models of land-use competition (Hudson 1977).

But there is more to it than this. The Tiv and Finnish agrarian settlement systems may have been especially adapted to frontier conditions, but some of the Germanic and Kofyar were there in the same conditions, at approximately the same time. I would say that both the intensifying and the extensifying systems make ecological sense, but only if we see the agrarian settlement system as embedded in social organization and labor mobilization.

In cultural ecology, causality tends to run from the effective environment to food acquisition systems to cultural domains such as social organization and settlement (Steward 1955; Flannery 1972a). Food acquisition tactics are selected according to their efficiency or marginal utility, intrinsic properties which are independent of culture. Thus, intensive agriculture is seen as less efficient than extensive, regardless of the farmers' culture.

But all strategies of food procurement and production require technology, including what we might call social technology – conventions for mobilizing human resources. Social technology that facilitates a food production strategy lowers the cost of that strategy. Earle (1980:4) writes that

> because social relationships play an important role in procurement strategies, the possible forms for the organization of labor in exploitative tasks are set by a group's structure ... as well as by the technical requirements of the work. To the degree that social

structure affects the possible organizational forms, it affects the costs of exploiting a resource and, thus, its importance in the subsistence economy.

Thus, efficiency of production strategies can vary culturally, and even a purely ecological analysis of basic strategies such as agricultural intensification vs. abandonment needs to consider social (or informational or even ideational) technology that affects costs and benefits.

The intensive agriculture that the Kofyar make look easy is remarkably difficult, not just because of the gross labor requirements but because of the confounding scheduling problems that arise in a system where the pivotal fuel of intensification is human labor. The Kofyars' "culture," or at least their experience over the past century, effectively lowers the cost of intensification via an intricate array of conventions for mobilizing labor (Stone, Netting, and Stone 1990), their reliance on the household as the basic productive unit, and even some of their fundamental values.

At the same time, abandonment and residential mobility were not a part of the pre-frontier Kofyar system. In the Jos Plateau homeland, a man usually changed residences only when leaving his natal household; if he inherited the family farm, he might never move. Not surprisingly, social technology provided little support for residential mobility. The Kofyar household was too small to act as a pioneering unit on the Benue frontier, and would-be pioneers had to persuade other households to join them in forming extemporaneous migrating groups (Stone 1992). Land disputes had traditionally been handled by village elders or clan members, procedures of no use when disputants were non-Kofyar. Intensification, which we usually see as the expensive way out, was cheaper for the Kofyar because of their social technology.

For the Tiv, social technology lowered the cost of abandonment by facilitating migration and expansion into new land. The segmentary lineage provided a ready principle for organizing pioneering units, such as the group claiming descent from Takumburu who settled in the Namu area early on. The lineage system was adept at mobilizing support for land disputes with non-Tiv and Tiv alike.

The contrast finds parallels on the American backwoods frontier and other multi-ethnic frontiers as well. It shows how land pressure may demand the end of extensive farming, but not dictate whether or not farms are abandoned. In many cases it is impossible to model farmstead abandonment without knowledge of (or assumptions about) other aspects of culture, which may include social organization and ideology. In order to understand abandonment, then, we must put it not only in the context of the agrarian settlement system, but in the context of fundamental questions of causality that have traditionally divided anthropologists.

The interpretive/idealist tradition in anthropology sees culture as the process of making collective sense of the world, especially by manipulation of symbols; the materialist/ecological tradition focuses on physical interaction with the world, especially the acquisition of basic provisions. At least a few archaeologists have sought a common ground; Flannery, for instance, has advocated the inclusion of information in ecological models for years (Flannery 1972b). But in exploring the mediation of idealist and materialist causality, Flannery has tended to focus on isolated fragments of ideology, such as the Zapotec concept of good farmland (1986:516) or the Andean ideas about propitiation of ancestors (Flannery, Marcus, and Reynolds 1989). To me, the events in the Namu savanna and the Delaware Valley suggest organic, structural linkages between agricultural tactics, residential mobility, social organization, and ideology, if I might borrow a little from both Radcliffe-Brown and Steward. In fact, it is useful to conceive of *suites* of such traits, and this may help in the study of the context of abandonment where we have no direct evidence of past ideology.

These case studies suggest two modes of agricultural adaptation which we might call intensifiers and extensifiers. My examples of frontier intensifiers (the Germanic types and the Kofyar) come from intensive farming traditions and the extensifiers (the Finns and the Tiv) come from extensive farming backgrounds, but my point should not be mistaken for cultural reductionism. It is rather a recognition that on these frontiers there was no single factor that dominated the unfolding of settlement patterns; there was no good analog for von Thünen's transport cost, Chisholm's time cost, or Christaller's efficiency of distribution. The common denominator on these frontiers is that as population grows and resources degrade, one must either intensify or leave. The balance may be tipped by local ecology, because the nature of intensification varies widely, depending on which factors most hinder production (Stone 1988a). But in many environments it's a close call, and the balance may be tipped by cultural factors that affect the relative costs of intensification and abandonment. There are technological factors: the Finns incessant chopping was underwritten by their superior axes and their skill at using them. There are social organizational factors: the Tiv's segmentary

lineage was ideally suited to squabbling over the land they encroached, while the Kofyar labor organization was adapted to the manpower demands of intensification. These are basic material conditions that affect the costs and benefits of abandonment as opposed to intensification.

And yes, there are also cultural values, which are strangely similar in these two very different frontiers. The Finns' disdain for the Germanic system, with its stumpless fields and tidy villages, finds an echo in the pioneering Tiv, climbing over the wall with their hoes slung over their backs, never stopping to question the cultural dictum that each farmer had the right to the land he needed (Bohannan 1954a:4).

The idea of two distinct modes of adaptation, the intensifiers and the abandoners, may or may not prove to be overly simple. Yet I find it an appealing heuristic device, which should help make sense of the variability in abandonment patterns elsewhere.

Acknowledgments

My Kofyar research was conducted with R. McC. Netting and M. P. Stone, with funding from the National Science Foundation (BNS-8308323 and BNS-8318569) and the Wenner-Gren Foundation. This paper also draws on analysis done under a Weatherhead Fellowship at the School of American Research. I am grateful to C. Cameron and S. Tomka for having organized this project, and to R. McC. Netting, M. P. Stone, and T. G. Jordan for commenting on this paper. I am clearly indebted to Netting and Jordan for their insights into the relationship between history and ecology, but I am solely to blame for flaws in this paper.

Notes

1 The principal exception is the cultivation of land surfaces that are regularly renewed by natural processes, such as mud-flat horticulture in the American midwest (Struever 1968) or *ak chin* farming in the desert Southwest (Castetter and Bell 1942).

2 Anthony (1990:901), for instance, lumps "most farmers" with industry-specialized laborers, herd-following hunters, and pastoralists in their practice of relatively frequent, long-distance migration.

3 The Boserup model of agricultural intensification implicitly holds constant the possibility of abandonment (Grigg 1979:69–70). Some archaeological models have retained the assumption of non-abandonment while others have assumed that farmers respond to pressure by abandonment whenever they

can (Schiffer and McGuire 1982:272; Gregg 1988:33) or by fission (Hamond 1981; Keegan and Machlachlan 1989).

References

Anthony, David W.
  1990 Migration in Archaeology: The Baby and the Bathwater. *American Anthropologist* 92:895–914.
Barth, Fredrik
  1956 Ecological Relationships of Ethnic Groups in Swat, North Pakistan. *American Anthropologist* 58:1079–89.
Bennett, John W.
  1976 *The Ecological Transition: Cultural Anthropology and Human Adaptation.* Pergamon Press, New York.
Binford, Lewis R.
  1980 Willow Smoke and Dogs' Tails: Hunter-Gatherer Settlement Systems and Archaeological Site Formation. *American Antiquity* 45:4–20.
Bohannan, Paul
  1954a The Migration and Expansion of the Tiv. *Africa* 24:2–16.
  1954b *Tiv Farm and Settlement.* HMSO, London.
Boserup, Ester
  1965 *The Conditions of Agricultural Growth.* Aldine, New York.
Castetter, Edward F. and Willis M. Bell
  1942 *Pima and Papago Indian Agriculture.* University of New Mexico Press, Albuquerque.
Earle, Timothy K.
  1980 A Model of Subsistence Change. In *Modeling Change in Prehistoric Subsistence Economies*, edited by T. K. Earle and A. L. Christenson, pp. 1–29. Academic Press, New York.
Flannery, Kent V.
  1972a The Origins of the Village as a Settlement Type in Mesoamerica and the Near East: A Comparative Study. In *Man, Settlement and Urbanism*, edited by P. J. Ucko, R. Tringham and G. W. Dimbleby, pp. 23–53. Schenkman, Cambridge, MA.
  1972b The Cultural Evolution of Civilizations. *Annual Review of Ecology and Systematics* 3:399–426.
  1976 Evolution of Complex Settlement Systems. In *The Early Mesoamerican Village*, edited by Kent V. Flannery, pp. 162–73. Academic Press, New York.
  1986 A Visit to the Master. In *Guilá Naquitz: Archaic Foraging and Early Agriculture in Oaxaca, Mexico*, edited by K. V. Flannery, pp. 511–19. Academic Press, Orlando.

Flannery, Kent V., J. Marcus, and R. Reynolds
  1989 *The Flocks of the Wamani: A Study of Llama Herders on the Punas of Ayachucho, Peru.* Academic Press, San Diego.
Gall, P. L. and A. Saxe
  1977 The Ecological Evolution of Culture: The State as Predator in Succession Theory. In *Exchange Systems in Prehistory*, edited by T. Earle and J. Ericson, pp. 255–67. Academic Press, New York.
Galt, Anthony H.
  1991 *Far from the Church Bells: Settlement and Society in an Apulian Town.* Cambridge University Press, Cambridge.
Green, Stanton W.
  1979 The Agricultural Colonization of Temperate Forest Habitats: An Ecological Model. In *The Frontier: Comparative Studies*, Vol. II, edited by W. W. Savage and S. I. Thompson, pp. 69–103. University of Oklahoma Press, Norman.
Gregg, Susan A.
  1988 *Foragers and Farmers: Population Interaction and Agricultural Expansion in Prehistoric Europe.* University of Chicago Press, Chicago.
Grigg, David
  1979 Ester Boserup's Theory of Agrarian Change: A Critical Review. *Progress in Human Geography* 3:64–84.
Haggett, Peter
  1965 *Locational Analysis in Human Geography.* Edward Arnold, London.
Hamond, Fred
  1981 The Colonisation of Europe: The Analysis of Settlement Process. In *Pattern of the Past: Studies in Honor of David Clarke*, edited by Ian Hodder, G. Isaac, and N. Hammond, pp. 211–48. Cambridge University Press, Cambridge.
Hudson, John C.
  1977 Theory and Methodology in Comparative Frontier Studies. In *Frontier: Comparative Studies*, Vol. I, edited by D. H. Miller and J. O. Steffen, pp. 11–31. University of Oklahoma Press, Norman.
Jordan, Terry G. and Matti Kaups
  1989 *The American Backwoods Frontier: An Ethnic and Ecological Interpretation.* The Johns Hopkins University Press, Baltimore.
Keegan, William F. and Morgan D. Machlachlan
  1989 The Evolution of Avunculocal Chiefdoms: A Reconstruction of Taino Kinship and Politics. *American Anthropologist* 91:613–30.
MacArthur, Robert H. and E. O. Wilson
  1967 *The Theory of Island Biogeography.* Princeton University Press, Princeton.

Margolis, Maxine
   1977 Historical Perspective on Frontier Agriculture as an Adaptive Strategy. *American Ethnologist* 4:42–64.
Netting, Robert McC.
   1968 *Hill Farmers of Nigeria: Cultural Ecology of the Kofyar of the Jos Plateau.* University of Washington Press, Seattle.
   1969 Ecosystems in Process: A Comparative Study of Change in Two West African Societies. *National Museum of Canada Bulletin* 230:102–12.
Sahlins, Marshall D.
   1963 The Segmentary Lineage: An Organization of Predatory Expansion. *American Anthropologist* 63:322–45.
Schiffer, Michael B. and Randall H. McGuire
   1982 The Study of Cultural Adaptations. In *Hohokam and Patayan: Prehistory of Southwestern Arizona,* edited by R. H. McGuire and M. B. Schiffer, pp. 223–74. Academic Press, New York.
Steward, Julian H.
   1955 The Concept and Method of Cultural Ecology. In *Theory of Culture Change,* by Julian H. Steward, pp. 30–42. University of Illinois Press, Urbana.
Stone, Glenn Davis
   1988a Agricultural Intensification and Residential Mobility: An Archaeological Perspective on Boserup. Paper presented at the meeting of the Society for American Archaeology, Phoenix.
   1988b Agrarian Ecology and Settlement Patterns: An Ethnoarchaeological Case Study. PhD Dissertation, University of Arizona. University Microfilms, Ann Arbor.
   1991 Settlement Ethnoarchaeology: Changing Patterns among the Kofyar of Nigeria. *Expedition* 33(1):16–23.
   1992 Social Distance, Spatial Relations, and Agricultural Production among the Kofyar of Namu District, Plateau State, Nigeria. *Journal of Anthropological Archaeology* 11:152–72.
Stone, Glenn Davis, R. McC. Netting, and M. P. Stone
   1990 Seasonality, Labor Scheduling, and Agricultural Intensification in the Nigerian Savanna. *American Anthropologist* 92:7–23.
Struever, Stuart
   1968 Woodland Subsistence-Settlement Systems in the Lower Illinois Valley. In *New Perspectives in Archaeology,* edited by S. R. Binford and L. R. Binford, pp. 285–312. Aldine, New York.
Udo, Reuben K.
   1966 Transformation of Rural Settlement in British Tropical Africa. *Nigerian Geographical Journal* 9:129–44.

PART III

Regional abandonment processes: archaeological cases

7
Local abandonments and regional conditions in the North American Southwest

SARAH H. SCHLANGER and
RICHARD H. WILSHUSEN

Introduction

The Four Corners country of North America was the heartland of Anasazi farmers for almost a thousand years before AD 1300. Today, the country is a sparsely populated rural setting. For every farmstead or small town established since the nineteenth century, there are many ancient ruined hamlets and villages in the surrounding fields. With so many ruins so close at hand, the hows and whys of abandonments, the subject of this volume, have been at the center of Southwestern archaeology from its earliest days.

When the field was young and there were few archaeologists and many ruins, the general opinion was that a widespread drought had forced the Anasazi to abandon their homes. By the first decade of this century, as the number of archaeologists rose but the general state of knowledge remained unchanged, A. V. Kidder pronounced Southwestern archaeology to be a "sucked orange" (Kidder 1958:322) and suggested that archaeology abandon the Anasazi. Kidder, one of the founders of the field, left for the lusher environs of lowland Mexico and Central America.

Archaeology did not abandon the Anasazi, however, and the field revived as A. E. Douglass' tree-ring studies began to yield a double harvest of absolute dates and data on paleoclimatic patterns. By 1929, Douglass thought he had identified the cause of "the abandonment" as the Great Drought of the later thirteenth century, AD 1276–99 (Douglass 1929). Today, eighty years after Kidder's sucked orange prognosis, dendrochronology has given us evidence for myriad droughts, and for drought relief, for myriad abandonments and for

frequent reoccupations. There seems to have been no single abandonment; rather, the area was occupied and abandoned repeatedly over the course of the Anasazi millennium.

Although we have lost the consensus that marked the early days of the field, environmental causes continue to play a large part in discussions of abandonments in the Southwest. Population patterns in areas as small as a single valley and as broad as the entire Southwest have been found to be correlated with low and high-frequency variation in rainfall, streamflow, and temperature (Berry 1982; Burns 1983; Cordell 1975; Dean et al. 1985; Euler et al. 1979; Gumerman 1988; Larson and Michaelsen 1990; Schlanger 1988). While crop failure from drought or short growing seasons and degradation of arable fields through arroyo cutting and falling water tables are most frequently implicated in the analysis of area-wide abandonments, deforestation and depletion of critical wood resources have been blamed as well (Kohler and Matthews 1988; Stiger 1979; Wyckoff 1977).

Our work brings a new perspective to the study of abandonments and environment in the North American Southwest. Here we move the scale of analysis from geographical units and long time periods – a valley, a drainage, or a larger region over the course of several hundred years – to individual houses and short-term but potentially critical fluctuations in environmental conditions. This is the scale at which we can most readily identify the relations that hold between our postulated cause – drought – and our predicted response – abandonment.

Whatever their cause, all abandonments are part of a general process of adjustment between local populations, local conditions, and regional conditions. When abandonments occur, however, they occur as local events: houses are abandoned as regions are depopulated. In Southwestern archaeology, thanks again to Douglass and dendrochronology, we are afforded a rare opportunity to test models of environmental causation with the data that we gather directly from abandoned houses. With the wood we collect from abandoned structures we can reconstruct a record of temporal variability in local construction and repair. This same wood gives us the data necessary to reconstruct a matching, but independent, record of variability in regional environmental conditions. Within the houses, too, the floors and fill yield details of the events following closely on the decision to leave.

In the following analyses, we use archaeological samples from the Dolores area of southwestern Colorado to examine the correspondence between local abandon-

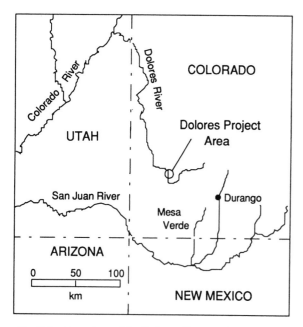

Fig. 7.1   Location of the Dolores Project Area.

ments and regional conditions in the American Southwest. These samples were collected during the course of a large cultural resources mitigation program (Robinson *et al.* 1986). Program archaeologists recorded over 1000 sites in the area; 102 of these were tested or excavated during fieldwork at Dolores.

A brief overview of the Dolores area

The Dolores area (Fig. 7.1) falls in the extreme southwestern corner of Colorado and is part of the larger Four Corners country occupied by the prehistoric Anasazi horticulturalists and their forebears between the AD/BC boundary and about AD 1300. Historically, growing seasons are short and rainfall is low; although the area today produces dry-farmed wheat and beans, crop failures and shortfalls are not uncommon.

In the Dolores area, the earliest horticultural settlers appear about AD 600. They established small, single-household and two-household settlements with semisubterranean, earthen-walled and earth-covered residential structures. These pit structures had roofs supported by wooden post-and-beam construction. They were usually a single chamber, but sometimes exhibited a small antechamber that served as a ventilation device and afforded some interior storage space.

The Anasazi occupation in the Dolores area peaked

around or slightly before AD 875. By that time, the small hamlets had been replaced by large multifamily villages; long, arcing, single-story pueblos, containing both storage facilities and living rooms, were built to accompany the pit structures that were now shared between families.

The research program

Our analysis begins with a critical appraisal of occupation periods. If we are to study the relations that hold between environmental conditions and local abandonments, we must know when people were living in the area and when they were not. To fix occupations and abandonments in time, we need very precise and accurate determinations of site occupation periods. When do abandonments begin? When does residential use cease?

Thereafter we turn our attention to the temporal variations in local climatic conditions registered by paleoclimatic proxy records. Which of these paleoclimatic changes would be apparent and meaningful to local decision makers in the Dolores area? What is the level of correspondence between perceptible and significant climatic changes and residential abandonments within the study area? Can we find any support for the idea that droughts were causing abandonments?

Finally, we focus on three different aspects of individual abandoned structures. First, we want to know how individual structure abandonments relate to the detailed occupation picture presented earlier. When were structures abandoned? Early in an occupation period? All through the period? Primarily at the end of a period? Second, we are concerned with the way in which the structures were treated at abandonment. Were the structures stripped of timber? Were they left to fill naturally? Were the roofs collapsed intentionally? How does abandonment treatment fit with the larger occupation pattern? Third, we look into what was left behind on the structure floors and begin the work of setting floor inventories into the larger context of structure, site, and regional abandonment.

Periods of human occupation between AD 600 and 910

The Anasazi occupation of the Dolores area is concentrated primarily between AD 600 and 910. Fig. 7.2 depicts the general population pattern as reconstructed from estimates of site population in the Dolores area (Schlanger 1985:fig. 4.1; Schlanger 1988:fig. 3). This reconstruction shows a gradual rise in average, momentary population from AD 600 to 800, then a period of very rapid growth, from AD 800 to 880, followed by a

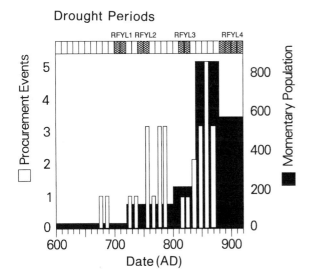

Fig. 7.2   *Estimated momentary population in the Dolores area compared with procurement events at Dolores (ten-year groupings).*

sharp decline around AD 900, and a virtual abandonment of the area for the next 100 years. Orcutt, Blinman, and Kohler (1990) note the possibility of an abandonment of the area between AD 800 and 829; otherwise, the site-count curve shows the area to have been steadily occupied as a residential locale between AD 600 and 910.

There are also data on beam procurement illustrated in Fig. 7.2, and these data suggest a different interpretation of occupation patterns at Dolores. The tree-ring dated record of pit structure construction and abandonment that can be developed from an analysis of the beams recovered from excavated houses may offer a more accurate picture of the Dolores occupations.

"Timber procurement events," construction, and abandonment at Dolores

Pit structure roofs are built from many beams, each of which may or may not be amenable to dating through dendrochronological analysis. In order to use the tree-ring samples from Dolores to analyze construction activity and abandonments, we must first make adjustments for the way in which the samples are clustered in individual structures. Giving each dated sample an equal weight runs the risk of including numerous dates from a few well-preserved structures, and few dates from poorly preserved structures. Assigning a single construction

date to each pit structure that has yielded datable construction wood ignores the tree-cutting activities associated with structure repair, rebuilding, and remodeling, and the not uncommon practice of incorporating old wood (harvested at an earlier date, or taken from dismantled roofs) to new structures.

To counter these difficulties, we used the idea of a timber "procurement event." While it is possible to use downed timber as construction material for roofs, the need for precisely sized pieces makes it likely that most roof beams were cut from living trees. It is also very difficult to cut or shape dead wood with stone axes. Cutting, or "death" dates from construction timbers, then, are ordinarily closely related to the date of tree harvesting and timber procurement. Timber procurement episodes can be independent of pit structure construction, however, and if much time elapses between beam procurement and construction, or if a structure contains reused beams, or if a deteriorating structure is repaired with new wood, a given structure may contain beams from more than one procurement event.

We deal with these possibilities by adopting the following conventions. First, we assume that pit structures last for no more than ten years on average without refurbishing (Ahlstrom 1984; Schlanger 1988; Cameron 1990a). This means that pit structures with suites of dates spanning more than ten years were either repaired or remodeled during use, or were constructed with old beams. In either case, they include beams from more than one general period of procurement. Our second convention follows on the first. Each date cluster from a given pit structure is counted as an individual timber procurement episode. For a pit structure to contribute more than one procurement date, the clusters must be separated by ten years. The focus is on modal "events" that primarily characterize periods of beam procurement in the locale, and that only secondarily characterize the dates of specific pit structure construction. In short, our primary interest is in demonstrating whether people are in the region and chopping down trees.

Fig. 7.2 shows the distribution of procurement events as reconstructed from the twenty-eight pit structures with datable roof timbers in the Dolores excavation record (Table 7.1) in relation to the reconstruction of average momentary population. For the tree-ring data, cutting dates[1] were given precedence over "v" or "vv" clusters, and the date with the highest frequency of occurrence within any ten-year span was taken to represent the primary procurement event for that decade. For example, if five timbers with cutting dates were recovered from a single structure (874r, 875r, 876r, 876rG, and

Table 7.1. *Tree-ring dates plotted in Fig. 7.2*

Site	Structure	Dates	Plot
5MT23	PS 3	852r	852
	PS 7	735vv, 738vv	738
	PS 10	856 + r	856
		867 + r	867
	PS 13	786rG, 794rB, 795 + vv, 797 + vv	794
	PS 16	737vv, 740vv	740
	PS 32	836 + vv, 836 + vv	836
	PS 43	856r	856
	PS 51	864 + vv, 865 + r, 870vv	865
	PS 82	767v, 768v	768
5MT2162	PS 1	691vv, 692vv	692
5MT2181	PS 1	779vv, 780v	780
5MT2182	PS 1	780r, 780r, 781v	780
	PS 1	789vv, 790r (5), 793r, 793vv (2)	790
	PS 201	866rG	866
5MT2193	PS 2	763vv, 764vv, 765vv (3), 766vv (2), 767vv, 768vv (2), 769vv (6), 770vv	769
5MT2236	PS 1	758vv, 760vv, 761vv, 762vv (2), 765vv, 765r	765
5MT2848	PS 1	783vv, 784r	784
	PS 1	684v, 685v	685
5MT4475	PS 3	874vv, 874v, 874r, 875v, 874 + r	874
	PS 7	865r, 870v, 871r (4)	871
5MT4477	PS 2	870 + v (2), 871v (2), 871r (2), 871B	871
5MT4480	PS 1	864B, 868 + vv, 874vv	864
5MT4644	PS 1	787v, 793vv	793
	PS 2	775vv (3), 776v (4), 776vv (3)	776
5MT4725	PS 4	845v, 845r (3)	845
5MT5107	PS 2	823r, 827vv, 829v (7), 830r	829
	PS 2	842 + r, 843r	843
	PS 2	863vv, 865vv	865

877B), the date with the highest frequency, i.e. 876, is taken as the primary procurement event. For the structures where there are only "v" or "vv" clusters, the date with the higher frequency is treated as the primary procurement event. In the case of a tie, the latest date takes precedence. As Table 7.1 shows, in twenty-one cases, the procurement event is identical to the latest date from the

structure. In eight cases, the primary procurement event is earlier than the latest date. In no case is the difference more than ten years, of course, and in all but one case, the difference is less than five years.

Our analysis of procurement events shows four distinct clusters of activity associated with the construction of pit structures in the Dolores area: an early cluster in the decades of the AD 680s and 690s; another brief period of timber procurement in the 730s and 740s; a distinct, and substantial renewal in beam procurement between 760 and the 790s; and a last cluster spanning the decades between 830 and the 870s. Note that these patterns would not change if we dated the procurement event strictly on the basis of the latest cutting, "v" or "vv" dates from structures.

Clearly, this analysis identifies periods of construction rather than abandonment, but at the same time, the clusters and their chronological order point to abandonments as well as peaks in occupation and beam cutting. The procurement clusters are separated by twenty to forty years, while the average life-span (without significant rebuilding) of a Dolores area pit structure is closer to ten or fifteen years (Schlanger 1985, 1988). This makes it possible to use procurement patterns as clues to abandonments: if the area were continuously occupied, we would expect a more continuous procurement record based on new construction, repair, remodeling, and beam reuse (Eighmy 1979; Schlanger 1980). Gaps of twenty to forty years mark long intervals when little, if any, new construction or repair was taking place. We believe the Dolores area was not occupied as a residential locale during these periods.

Paleoclimatic reconstruction and periods of expected abandonment

If the Anasazi did abandon the Dolores area, or any other area of the Southwest, because of drought they were probably responding to the effects of drought on their corn crops. The most important economic resource for the Dolores Anasazi between AD 600 and 910 was corn, or maize (Matthews 1988; Minnis 1989), and precipitation is the factor most directly responsible for the success of maize agriculture in the northern Southwest. Most traditional agriculturalists in the region attempted to maintain a one to two-year storage reserve (Bradfield 1971; Ford 1968). Faced with a drought long enough to exhaust their reserves, Puebloan peoples sometimes resorted to "short- and long-term migration" (Zubrow 1974:64). We imagine that the prehistoric peoples in the

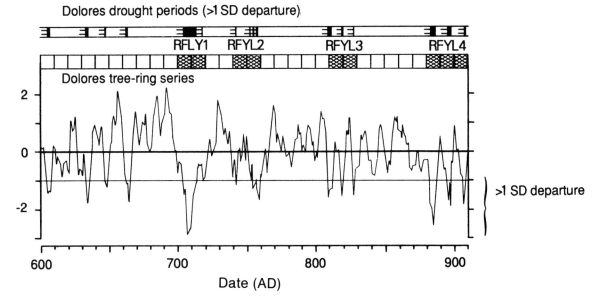

Fig. 7.3   Five-year unweighted running means of Dolores tree-ring departures. Tree-ring data are from Petersen 1987 and figure is adapted from Blinman 1988:Figure 2.2.

Dolores area faced the same problems and exercised similar solutions.

When did the Dolores people face droughts? Wood samples provide critical data for this question as well. Precipitation figures prominently in tree growth, which makes it possible to use tree-ring samples to construct estimates of past environmental conditions. Trees add relatively wide annual rings when moisture available during that growing season is high and the tree is able to draw on food reserves held over from the previous growing season (Fritts 1976:231–8). Trees produce narrow rings when growing-season moisture and held-over food reserves are low. Proxy records of past rainfall and moisture conditions can be created by calibrating tree-ring width with precipitation records. Petersen (1987) has developed such a proxy record for the Dolores area.

Fig. 7.3 illustrates five-year unweighted running means of the Dolores area tree-ring width indices for the period AD 600 to 910. We have followed Petersen (1987) and Orcutt (1987) in defining critical periods as those in which negative departures from the mean exceed one or more standard deviations. (Petersen calibrated this drought measure with tree-ring indices from the historic droughts of the 1890s and the 1950s in the Dolores area.)

This treatment of the proxy precipitation record shows four major drought episodes, which we have labelled "Run For Your Life" (RFYL) periods, and

Table 7.2. *Drought episodes and benign intervals at Dolores*

Climatic period	Timespan
DWBH 1	AD 650–700
RFYL 1	AD 700–20
DWBH 2	AD 720–40
RFYL 2	AD 740–60
DWBH 3	AD 760–810
RFYL 3	AD 810–30
DWBH 4	AD 830–80
RFYL 4	AD 880–920

four intervening intervals of relatively benign climatic conditions, herein referred to as "Don't Worry, Be Happy" (DWBH) periods (Table 7.2 and Figs. 7.2 and 7.3).

Construction behavior, paleoclimate, and abandonments

A comparison of the beam procurement record and the reconstructed drought periods (Fig. 7.2) shows a remarkable correspondence between clusters of procurement events and our "Don't Worry, Be Happy" periods. Building appears to have occurred primarily during those periods that have no extended droughts. Beam procurement is concentrated in four periods: (1) the AD 680s and 690s; (2) the 730s and 740s; (3) the 760s through 790s; and (4) the 830s through the 870s. The "Don't Worry, Be Happy" periods run from (1) AD 650 to 700; (2) 720 to 740; (3) 760 to 810; and (4) 830 to 880.

Conversely, there appears to be little construction activity during the "Run For Your Life" periods. We are inclined to interpret these gaps as periods when the Dolores area was abandoned. It may be, of course, that these gaps are simply an artifact of our small sample size, or that they represent periods when new construction and repairs were delayed. We cannot overcome the small sample size problem, but we can suggest that it is unlikely that Pueblo I pit structures could be maintained without significant construction or repair over the ten to thirty-year gaps seen in the Dolores record as we know it today. All in all, the drought record and the timing of abandonments at Dolores seem to be closely tied. A. E. Douglass would be pleased with the correspondence between occupation and favorable environmental conditions, abandonment, and drought. A. V. Kidder, on the other hand, would probably still bring up sucked oranges.

The archaeology of abandonment at Dolores

The abandoned houses of the Dolores area do contain more than old wood, of course, and their other contents are equally critical to understanding abandonment patterns at Dolores. We turn now to a discussion of house treatment and house content for those structures abandoned between AD 600 and 910. We begin with a general discussion of the abandonment strategies that may have been practiced (and indeed, carried out) by the Dolores Anasazi, then move on to identify archaeological correlates of these strategies, and then bring these together in a discussion of the materials we find in the abandoned houses.

Abandonment strategies

We see four strategies for structure abandonment, differentiated along the vectors of distance moved and expectations for return. Much of the warranting research for our discussion is summarized in this volume, and is especially well outlined in Lightfoot's contribution; see also Schiffer's excellent summaries (1985:24–31; 1987:89–98).

Strategy 1: short-distance move/return anticipated. When the distance to be moved is short and a return is expected, we anticipate that structures will be left intact

so that they may be refurbished and reoccupied at a later date. Household furnishings may be either left in place or removed for use elsewhere. If the move is part of a seasonal shift in residence, some household equipment may be transported to the next residential site. Houses left intact, with roofs still in place, may attract scavengers, however. If an owner fails to return, the house may be stripped of useful materials.

Strategy 2: Long-distance move/return anticipated. When the distance moved is long and the period of anticipated absence is short, we expect that people will take steps to protect their houses, perhaps caching valuable house furnishings and equipment (either in the structure or elsewhere), and sealing entrances and features. Such a strategy may result in large material inventories on structure floors, and in the event that a structure is not reopened the floor assemblage may be unusually rich. Under conditions of regular, seasonal abandonment, however, as discussed above, household furnishings may be alternately depleted and restocked (Schiffer 1987:93). Again, these houses may be scavenged while they are abandoned; if the owners fail to return, these too may be stripped of materials.

Strategy 3: Short-distance move/long term of absence or no anticipated return. For short-distances moves, with no anticipated return, we expect that structural elements such as roofs will be salvaged, and house contents will be removed to the new residence. These structures will be emptied at the time of abandonment. There are two different situations where this strategy may be employed. First, structures may be abandoned with no intention of return when an entire settlement is being abandoned. In this case, it is the place that is being abandoned, rather than simply the structure. Alternatively, an individual structure may be abandoned without a corresponding abandonment of the surrounding settlement. Insect infestation may lead to such abandonments (Cameron 1990a; McGuire and Schiffer 1983; Seymour and Schiffer 1987), as may changes in the circumstances of an occupation or the needs of site occupants. Burning as a form of abandonment behavior is also associated with some ritual and burial practices (Cameron 1990b; Wilshusen 1986). When a structure is simply abandoned, without burning, it may be converted to another use, with appropriate changes in tool and equipment inventories. Once the roof timbers are removed or the roof burned and collapsed, what material remains on the floor is effectively sealed within the structure and is not subject to scavenging.

Strategy 4: Long-distance move/long term of absence or no anticipated return. We find it hard to imagine how people will treat structures under these circumstances. We do expect that people will salvage some portable equipment, but may abandon much of the heavier, bulkier, less valuable material. If roofs are left intact, floor inventories may be depleted through scavenging. If roofs are destroyed, relatively rich floor inventories may be preserved.

Archaeological correlates

We have identified a number of archaeological correlates for these abandonment strategies. The least ambiguous is roof treatment, which we discuss first. Less easily interpreted is the general category of floor assemblage materials, to which we turn after a consideration of roofs. We consider here a subsample of the entire excavation data set (Appendix A) consisting of twenty-six structures in which at least two-thirds, and usually the entire floor surface, was exposed during excavation. Most of these structures can be dated to ten to twenty-year periods based on dendrochronological samples or stratigraphic relations with other, better-dated structures. Because only a limited sample of known burned structures at Dolores was fully excavated and because not all burned structures produced datable timbers, the overlap between Table 7.1 (burned structures with datable timbers) and Appendix A (fully or nearly fully excavated structures that can be confidently assigned to a DWBH or RFYL episode) is necessarily limited.

Roof treatment

The four abandonment strategies outlined above lead us to expect three different roof treatments: roofs that are simply left intact, roofs that are salvaged, and roofs that are intentionally burned. The first treatment stems from situations in which Strategies 1, 2, and possibly 4, are employed, whereas roofs are salvaged or burned under Strategy 3.

There are three obvious roof treatments in the Dolores data set. Five of the structures in our sample had roofs that were simply left to collapse in place; nine roofs had been salvaged; and twelve of the structures in our sample had roofs that were partially or completely burned.

At Dolores, abandoned pit structures are often burned. We have detailed elsewhere why we believe these structures were intentionally burned (Wilshusen 1986; 1988). In our sample, a typical stratigraphic profile from this type of structure shows a 20 to 40 cm layer of burned or partially burned roof-fall in direct contact with the pit structure floor. Portions of walls and floor show signs of oxidation and suggest that a large internal fire was set to ignite the structure roof. At Dolores, these burned

structures rarely have significant trash deposits in their structure fill. Evidently, in most cases, occupation ceased in the local area at the time, or soon after, the structure burned. This kind of abandonment may signal a long-distance move with no expectation of return; certainly no one can live in one of these structures after it has been burned down.

Another common form of intentional destruction of a pit structure, but one that has rarely been recognized, consists of salvaging roof timbers and allowing the remaining roof superstructure to collapse on the pit structure floor. We feel this behavior is a signature of our short-distance move/no anticipated return model. Here, the timbers are most probably either reused as construction material for a nearby new pit structure or other building, or eventually consumed elsewhere as fuel. In stratigraphic profile, the roofing material shows as a uniform, massive deposit. Thin lenses of organic material within this deposit are the remains of twigs, branches, and brush used to stabilize the roof and keep dirt from leaking into the structure. These roof deposits lie directly on the pit structure floor. In some cases, partially re-excavated postholes, missing posts, and postholes filled with fallen roof debris attest to salvage of the main roof supports. The upper fill of such structures typically contains trash deposits, suggesting that while the structure was abandoned the local area continued to be occupied.

The final roof or structure treatment consists of abandoning a structure intact, so that it eventually deteriorates and fills entirely through natural processes. The stratigraphic signature of this treatment is similar to that of the salvaged structure, but the lower fill is not deposited as a single massive unit, and what stratigraphic breaks exist are related to natural, geomorphic or soil-forming processes, and not to cultural processes. This sort of abandonment, where the structure was left intact to decay naturally, may represent cases where structures were recycled for other, non-habitation purposes prior to site or area abandonment. Such older structures were neither protected nor intentionally destroyed when the area was later permanently abandoned.

Floor assemblages

When structures are abandoned, people are forced to make decisions about what to take and what to leave, and how to adjust the household tool inventory to changes in structure function. Here we monitor these decisions with a very simple measure: the total weight of the floor assemblage. DeBoer (1983) suggests that artifact weight is a useful dimension for predicting discard behavior, remnant use-life (or the amount of use still remaining in an artifact), replacement cost, and portability. We use weight here because it provides a clear summary of the total amount of material remaining on a pit structure floor at abandonment. To the degree that weight is also associated with remnant use-life, portability, value, and replacement cost, weight provides a convenient summary of these aspects of abandoned floor assemblages as well. In very basic terms, the more material left on pit structure floors, the higher the eventual replacement costs, the higher the value of the assemblage, and the higher the remnant use-life of the abandoned assemblage. Although we concentrate here on assemblage weight, we can see that fuller treatments of this problem will lead to models that exploit other aspects of assemblages, including item condition, material sources, material value, and material function.

We consider four classes of artifacts in our weight totals: ceramics, here tabulated and summed as individual sherds, regardless of total amount of the vessel present; ground-stone artifacts; flaked-stone tools; and debitage. These four classes represent the most common materials in Dolores area assemblages. By far the heaviest materials are ground-stone tools and ceramic sherds. In our 26-floor data set, ground-stone items and sherds contribute approximately evenly to the total, and comprise over 90 percent of the floor assemblages by weight. Flaked-stone tools and debitage contribute very little to the total floor samples, in contrast. It was felt that other material types would contribute vanishingly small proportions of the total, and so were excluded.

The four elements may be contrasted in terms of weight: ceramic vessels and sherds are both relatively heavy and bulky; ground-stone tools are both heavy, and quite heavy in some cases, and also bulky; flaked stone tools are neither heavy nor bulky; and debitage is neither heavy, nor bulky, nor valuable in any sense.

Interestingly, the contributions of these four material types to the total floor assemblage is far from constant. Both ground-stone tools and sherds are highly correlated with total assemblage weight ($r = 0.90$ and 0.87, respectively), while flaked-stone tools and debitage show only slight associations with total floor artifact weight ($r = 0.38$ and 0.37, respectively). Both the general categories of ground-stone tools, which includes a wide variety of food processing equipment, and ceramic vessels may be considered as stable elements of household furniture. Flaked stone tools appear to occur in household assemblages on more of an "as needed basis" and may be removed far more frequently at structure abandonment, or be introduced into structures much more infrequently. This same argument holds for debit-

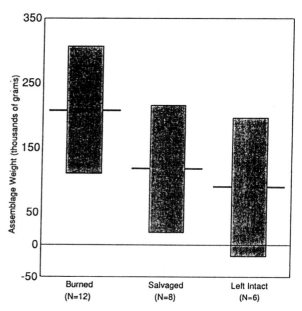

Fig. 7.4   *Mean weight of floor assemblages in structures with different roof treatments. The standard deviation for each group is illustrated with a bar.*

age, which is essentially a by-product of stone tool production, and may occur on floors only infrequently, and then may signal a breakdown in household cleaning activities.

Floor assemblages and roof treatments

Floor assemblages show some very clear patterning with regard to the roof treatments outlined earlier. Structures with burned roofs contain the heaviest floor assemblages, salvaged structures the next heaviest total, and structures that were simply left intact the lightest floor assemblages (Fig. 7.4). Regardless of the connection between roof treatment and abandonment strategy, as we suggested above, we might expect structures with burned roofs to contain heavier floor assemblages – more stuff on the floors – simply because the circumstances of structure abandonment make it impossible to retrieve any items left in the structure after the roof collapses. Similarly, the circumstances that promote roof salvage might well promote salvage of other house contents as well. When roof timbers are salvaged, however, the roof collapses onto the structure floor and traps any artifacts not retrieved before the beginning of the salvage operation. In contrast, the contents of structures that were simply left intact could be removed at any time. As seen in Fig. 7.4, structures in this class show the lowest

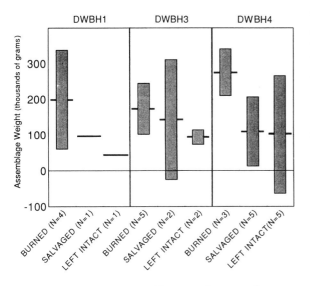

Fig. 7.5 Mean floor assemblage weight per roof treatment and period. The standard deviation for each group is represented with a bar.

average floor assemblage weight total. This low weight signals either a depletion in ordinary house inventories, or a change in house contents. Either way, house function appears to have changed, and both roof treatment and depleted or otherwise altered house inventories are pointing to a deliberate reshaping of the role of the house.

Floor assemblages, roof treatments, and environmental conditions

Fig. 7.5 shows the breakdown of average floor assemblage weight per roof treatment per period. The overall scheme follows the general pattern established in Fig. 7.4: in each period, structures with burned roofs contain the heaviest floor assemblages, followed by structures with salvaged roofs, and then structures with roofs left intact. What is interesting here are the small differences between the three occupations.

The final favorable period in the Dolores area, DWBH 4, marks the end of the use of the Dolores area as a residential locale. This appears to be marked in the floor assemblages by a slight, but clear rise in the average weight of material abandoned on the floors of structures with burned roofs. It is also marked by a lessening of the weight differences of floor assemblages in structures with intact roofs and structures where roofs were salvaged. The assemblage values for DWBH 1 show a similar distance between the weight of material in structures

with burned roofs and those not burned at abandonment. The second period, DWBH 3, lacks the relatively large difference between the assemblage weight in burned structures and the other two types, but shares the DWBH 1 pattern of relatively large differences between structures with salvaged roofs and structures with roofs left intact.

Although the small samples involved make any conclusions we might draw highly speculative, we feel we can suggest several possibilities. First, it may be that the similarities in DWBH 1 and DWBH 3 arise from a shared abandonment strategy. Perhaps the people leaving their homes during these times were thinking about moves of similar distance or duration, moves that were somewhat shorter than those undertaken during DWBH 4. The slight rise in the amount of material found on the floors of structures with intact roofs is also intriguing. This change suggests that either there were fewer people around to make use of this material or there was no one around for most of the time the structures were decaying naturally, or material needs shifted so that the materials available for scavenging and recycling were no longer valuable to later occupants. In any case, the abandonments in DWBH 4 seem different from previous abandonments of the Dolores area.

Although the sample sizes are too small to support definite conclusions about the timing of abandonments and the kind of roof treatment adopted for any given structure, there are some slight trends in the roof data that deserve mention here. Most burned structures appear to have been constructed in the second half of one of the DWBH periods, or within twenty years of one of the major, Run For Your Life episodes. However, given the short, ten-year use-life of a pit structure and our limited ability to place use and abandonment of pit structures more finely than twenty-year periods, it is not possible to show that these structures were abandoned, and their roofs burned, in response to the onset of severe drought conditions. Why the structures should be deliberately burned down and decommissioned is not clear. What is clear, however, is that burned structures give no opportunity for later reuse, and that the abandonment is both deliberate and permanent. In contrast to this pattern, roof timber salvaging and structure abandonments which did not involve roof collapse occurs all through the periods.

Burning roofs is a very costly proposition. It uses up valuable resources, closes off structures permanently, and may even pose a hazard to other structures in the vicinity. Burning as a form of abandonment behavior may be related to a host of causes, including insect infestation, ritual, warfare and burial practices (McGuire and Schiffer 1983; Seymour and Schiffer 1987; Cameron 1990b; Wilshusen 1986). Certainly this sort of behavior will be curtailed by the use of structures that are integrally tied together with wooden elements, such as the shared walls and wood roofs of pueblo architectural forms.

The observations we have made on structure roof treatments and on floor assemblages constitute our second test of the environmental conditions/abandonment model. How well does the model hold up? Despite the correspondence between construction and periods of relatively benign environmental conditions and apparent abandonment during periods of adverse conditions, many of the structures in the Dolores data set appear to have been abandoned without regard to the timing of droughts. That is, we do not find structure abandonments clustered at the end of the DWBH periods, but instead find them scattered through the periods. Most structures seem to have been abandoned under circumstances that must have been the norm for this area: the houses simply wore out. The houses were dismantled and their roof timbers used for other projects, household furnishings and equipment were scavenged and salvaged, houses were recycled for other purposes, but left standing, and, in general, houses and their contents were used and reused long after they were originally constructed and furnished.

Structures with burned roofs may have been abandoned with the onset of drought conditions, although the data are weak on this point. When structures are abandoned in this way, a good deal of apparently valuable material is abandoned as well. Not only are the roofs destroyed and the facilities made completely unusable, but a significant quantity of household goods are abandoned on the structure floors. We have not analyzed the exact make-up of these floor assemblages, but we expect that the assemblages contain usable materials. Why? Floor assemblages from scavenged or standing houses are much lighter – either materials are removed as part of the abandonment process and are not used elsewhere, or the materials taken from these structures still have some value as tools. The heavy assemblages associated with burned structures are either functionally distinct, or less depleted. Although this suggestion needs further testing, we feel that burned roof abandonments result in the deliberate destruction or discard of valuable materials. This abandonment strategy appears to relate to the conditions of our long-distance/no anticipated return model.

Summary and conclusions

We have moved here from a very large picture, with the single Great Abandonment and Great Drought theory of Southwestern abandonments, to a closer focus that shows episodic abandonments governed by episodic droughts, to a very fine-scale analysis that lets us look at individual structures as they are abandoned and recycled throughout the course of an occupation. Our analysis of the relationship between environmental conditions and structure abandonment has yielded a number of interesting observations.

First, our understanding of Dolores area abandonments changes considerably as we change analytic scale. By moving the level of analysis from synthesized reconstructions of population growth and decline to a chronology of construction and abandonment of individual structures, we have identified several abandonments of the Dolores area between AD 600 and 910. By analyzing precipitation patterns at a temporal scale that directly affects farming success, we have identified several periods when drought might have brought on abandonments. Matching the scales of analysis in this way gives us a heightened confidence in our ability to identify abandonments and to identify the underlying causes of these abandonments.

This brings us to our second point, which is that some of the results of our finest-scale analyses – the analyses of individual structures – appear to contradict the drought/abandonment picture that we gained through our comparison of tree-ring dated construction activity and tree-ring calibrated drought periods. In our sample of Dolores houses, structures are abandoned throughout occupation periods, not in clusters at the ends of the occupation periods. If structures were being abandoned in response to drought, we might expect them to be abandoned after drought conditions develop, but not before drought conditions develop. Actually, however, given the short use-life of pit structures, and the need for occupants to build, repair, or replace these structures fairly frequently, we should not expect to find all structures abandoned at the end of our "Don't Worry, Be Happy" climatic periods. What look like non-patterned abandonments, at least in the temporal sense, may have been a consequence of the vernacular architecture or of expectations for residential mobility, or of some as yet unrecognized set of circumstances. The abandoned structures do share some characteristics of roof treatment and floor assemblage, however, that add important details to our understanding of Dolores abandonments.

How a structure is treated at abandonment and what happens to the structure after it is abandoned tell us different things about the long-term use of places. In the Dolores area, roof treatment appears to be tied to the scale of the area that is being abandoned and to the circumstances forcing the abandonment. When only the structure is abandoned, the roof may be scavenged, or left in place. When the local area is abandoned as well, the roofs may be burned.

Our floor assemblage weight measure is more closely connected to what happens to a structure after it is abandoned. We have not been able to explore all the implications and possibilities offered by analyses of assemblage weight, but it appears to have some potential for answering questions of how far people moved when they abandoned structures and whether or not they returned or reused structures. Again, the data are slight, but the patterns are intriguing. During some abandonments, people move out of the area, but they do not stop using it or treating the features on the cultural landscape as valuable resources. The first abandonments of the Dolores area seem to have been of this type, with area abandonment as a residential locale followed by continued visitation of local sites by people with some use for household inventory items. Other abandonments may mark the end of the use of the area altogether for a considerable length of time. The last of the abandonments examined in this study fits this type. In this case, residential sites were not revisited, or at least houses were not scavenged for usable goods quite as heavily as they were before. Why would the region fall out of use? This kind of abandonment may follow human degradation and depletion of local resources such as wood (Kohler and Matthews 1988), game, or arable soil. In these cases, occupational hiatuses may last until the resource is replenished. Whatever the cause of this abandonment pattern, it is interesting to note that abandonments that are followed fairly shortly by renewed residential use and abandonments that have no closely succeeding residential reoccupation generate slightly different floor assemblages.

We expect that our analysis of abandonment patterns at Dolores, and especially our suggestion that the abandonments were closely tied to high-frequency variation in precipitation and maize harvests, will be overturned in the future as others rise to the challenge of the "sucked orange" that is Southwestern archaeology. For the present, however, we are satisfied that a change of scale – from Great Droughts to drought episodes, and from site-based population curves to abandoned structures – is as good as a change of scene. We see no reason to abandon the Southwest or to abandon abandonments just yet.

Appendix A. *Structures in data set*

Site	Pit structure	Period	Date	Roof treatment
5MT4545	1	DWBH 1	640–80	Salvaged?
5MT2378	1	DWBH 1	660–700	Left intact
5MT4684	1	DWBH 1	670–700	Burned
5MT4684	4	DWBH 1	670–700	Burned
5MT2858	1	DWBH 1	680–700	Burned
5MT2848	2	DWBH 1	685–700	Burned
5MT2854	1	DWBH 3	750–70	Salvaged
5MT2193	1	DWBH 3	760–70	Burned
5MT2854	2	DWBH 3	770–90	Left intact
5MT2194	1	DWBH 3	760–800	Left intact
5MT4644	1	DWBH 3	760–76	Salvaged
5MT2182	1	DWBH 3	780–800	Burned
5MT2193	2	DWBH 3	770–85	Burned
5MT4644	2	DWBH 3	776–800	Burned
5MT4644	3	DWBH 3	790–800	Burned
5MT2182	2	DWBH 4	860–80	Salvaged
5MT4475	5	DWBH 4	870–80	Burned
5MT5106	3	DWBH 4	860–80	Salvaged
5MT5106	4	DWBH 4	860–80	Left intact
5MT5106	2	DWBH 4	860–80	Left intact
5MT5107	1	DWBH 4	860–80	Left intact
5MT5107	2	DWBH 4	870–80	Burned
5MT5107	9	DWBH 4	860–80	Salvaged
5MT5107	10	DWBH 4	860–80	Salvaged
5MT5108	1	DWBH 4	860–80	Salvaged
5MT5108	2	DWBH 4	860–80	Salvaged

Acknowledgments

The data used here were gathered by the Dolores Archaeological Program (Contract No. 8–07–40–S0562), funded by the Bureau of Reclamation, US Department of the Interior. Additional support was provided by the Museum of New Mexico Foundation and the Museum's Office of Archaeological Studies. David Underwood and James N. Morris drafted our figures. Our presentation was greatly improved by the thoughtful comments of Eric Blinman, Cathy Cameron, Jeffrey Dean, Signa Larralde, Barbara Montgomery, Kenneth Petersen, Michael Schiffer, and Steve Tomka; we also wish to extend our thanks to Cathy Cameron and Steve Tomka for organizing an excellent symposium on abandonment behavior and analysis.

Notes

1 The tree-ring data from Dolores pit structures (Breter-nitz, Robinson, and Gross 1986: Appendix A) that can be used to analyze construction activity and aban-donments are reported in the form of "cutting dates" and "non-cutting dates." Cutting dates, which identify the year in which a tree died, are coded as "r," "G," or "B," which are assigned to samples with consistent outer rings; samples with beetle galleries, which occur directly under the tree bark; and samples with bark, respectively (Robinson, Harrill, and Warren 1975:6). Non-cutting dates are coded as "v," or "vv," where "v" signifies that the samples are missing no rings, but do lack the attributes of "r," "G," or "B" samples, and "vv" signifies that any number of rings may be missing. Clusters of non-cutting dates can approximate a cutting date under certain circumstances (Dean 1978:148; Bannister 1962:512).

References

Ahlstrom, Richard V. N.
 1984 A Comparative Approach to the Interpretation of Tree-Ring Data. Paper presented at the 49th Annual Meeting of the Society for American Archaeology, Portland, Oregon.
 1985 The Interpretation of Tree-Ring Dates. PhD dissertation, University of Arizona, Tucson. University Microfilms, Ann Arbor.
Bannister, Bryant
 1962 The Interpretation of Tree-Ring Dates. *American Antiquity* 27:508–14.
Berry, Michael S.
 1982 *Time, Space, and Tradition in Anasazi Prehistory.* University of Utah Press, Salt Lake City.
Blinman, Eric
 1988 The Interpretation of Ceramic Variability: A Case Study from the Dolores Anasazi. PhD dissertation, Washington State University, Pullman. University Microfilms, Ann Arbor.
Bradfield, Maitland
 1971 *The Changing Pattern of Hopi Agriculture.* Royal Anthropological Institute Occasional Papers 30. Royal Anthropological Institute of Great Britain and Ireland, London.
Breternitz, David A., Christine K. Robinson and G. Timothy Gross
 1986 Appendix A. Dating, In *Dolores Archaeological Program: Final Synthetic Report*, compiled by D. A.

Breternitz, C. K. Robinson and G. T. Gross, pp. 709–91. Bureau of Reclamation, Engineering and Research Center, Denver, Co.
Burns, Barney T.
 1983 Simulated Anasazi Storage Behavior Using Crop Yields Reconstructed From Tree Rings: A.D. 652–1968. PhD dissertation, University of Arizona, Tucson. University Microfilms, Ann Arbor.
Cameron, Catherine
 1990a The Effect of Varying Estimates of Pit Structure Use-Life on Prehistoric Population Estimates in the American Southwest. *The Kiva* 55:155–66.
 1990b Pit Structure Abandonment in the Four Corners Region of the American Southwest: Late Basketmaker III and Pueblo I Periods. *Journal of Field Archaeology* 17:27–37.
Cordell, Linda S.
 1975 Predicting Site Abandonment at Wetherill Mesa. *The Kiva* 40:189–202.
Dean, Jeffrey S.
 1978 Tree-Ring Dating in Archaeology. Miscellaneous Paper Number 24. University of Utah Anthropological Papers 99. University of Utah Press, Salt Lake City.
Dean, Jeffrey S., Robert C. Euler, George J. Gumerman, Fred Plog, Richard H. Hevly, and Thor N. V. Karlstrom
 1985 Human Behavior, Demography, and Paleoenvironment on the Colorado Plateaus. *American Antiquity* 50(3):537–54.
DeBoer, Warren R.
 1983 The Archaeological Record as Preserved Death Assemblage. In *Archaeological Hammers and Theories*, edited by J. A. Moore and A. S. Keene, pp. 19–36. Academic Press, New York.
Douglass, Andrew Ellicott
 1929 The Secret of the Southwest Solved by Talkative Tree Rings. *The National Geographic Magazine* 56:736–70.
Eighmy, Jeffrey L.
 1979 Logistic Trends in Southwest Population Growth. In *Transformations: Mathematical Approaches to Culture*, edited by C. Renfrew and K. L. Cooke, pp. 205–20. Academic Press, New York.
Euler, Robert C., George J. Gumerman, Thor N. V. Karlstrom, Jeffrey S. Dean, and Richard H. Hevly
 1979 The Colorado Plateaus: Culturela Dynamics and Paleoenvironment. *Science* 205:1089–1101.
Ford, Richard I.
 1968 An Ecological Analysis Involving the Population

of San Juan Pueblo, New Mexico. PhD dissertation, University of Michigan. University Microfilms, Ann Arbor.

Fritts, Harold C.
1976 *Tree Rings and Climate.* Academic Press, New York.

Gumerman, George J., ed.
1988 *The Anasazi in a Changing Environment.* Cambridge University Press, Cambridge.

Kidder, Alfred V.
1958 *Pecos, New Mexico: Archaeological Notes.* Papers of the Robert S. Peabody Foundation for Archaeology No. 5.

Kohler, Timothy A. and Meredith H. Matthews
1988 Long-Term Anasazi Land Use and Forest Reduction: A Case Study from Southwest Colorado. *American Antiquity* 53:537–64.

Larson, Daniel O. and Joel Michaelsen
1990 Impacts of Climatic Variability and Population Growth on Virgin Branch Anasazi Cultural Developments. *American Antiquity* 55:227–49.

McGuire, Randall H. and Michael B. Schiffer
1983 Theory of Architectural Design. *Journal of Anthropological Archaeology* 2:277–303.

Matthews, Meredith H.
1988 McPhee Community Cluster Macrobotanical Data Base: Testing the Concept of Agricultural Intensification. In *Dolores Archaeological Program Anasazi Communities at Dolores: McPhee Village*, compiled by A. E. Kane and C. K. Robinson, pp. 1097–127. Bureau of Reclamation, Engineering and Research Center, Denver, Co.

Minnis, Paul E.
1989 Prehistoric Diet in the Northern Southwest: Macroplant Remains from Four Corners Feces. *American Antiquity* 54:543–63.

Orcutt, Janet
1987 Modeling Prehistoric Agricultural Ecology in the Dolores Area. In *Dolores Archaeological Program Supporting Studies: Settlement and Environment* compiled by K. L. Petersen and J. D. Orcutt, pp. 649–77. Bureau of Reclamation, Engineering and Research Center, Denver, Co.

Orcutt, Janet, Eric Blinman, and T. A. Kohler
1990 Explanations of Population Aggregation in the Mesa Verde Region Prior to A.D. 900. In *Perspectives on Southwestern Prehistory*, edited by P. E. Minnis and C. E. Redman, pp. 196–212. Westview Press, Boulder, Co.

Petersen, Kenneth L.
1987 Reconstruction of Droughts for the Dolores Project Area Using Tree-Ring Studies. In *Dolores Archaeological Program Supporting Studies: Settlement and Environment*, compiled by K. L. Petersen and J. D. Orcutt, pp. 89–102. Bureau of Reclamation, Engineering and Research Center, Denver, Co.

Robinson, Christine K., G. Timothy Gross, and David A. Breternitz
1986 Overview of the Dolores Archaeological Program. In *Dolores Archaeological Program Final Synthetic Report*, compiled by D. A. Breternitz, C. K. Robinson and G. T. Gross, pp. 3–50. Bureau of Reclamation, Engineering and Research Center, Denver, Co.

Robinson, William J., Bruce G. Harrill, and Richard L. Warren
1975 *Tree-Ring Dates from Arizona H-I: Flagstaff Area.* Laboratory of Tree-Ring Research, University of Arizona, Tucson.

Schiffer, Michael B.
1985 Is There a "Pompeii Premise" in Archaeology? *Journal of Anthropological Research* 41(1):18–41.
1987 *Formation Processes of the Archaeological Record.* University of New Mexico Press, Albuquerque.

Schlanger, Sarah H.
1980 Demography and Dendrochronology: A Critical Examination of a Proposed Population Index. MA thesis, Washington State University, Pullman.
1985 Prehistoric Population Dynamics in the Dolores Area, Southwestern Colorado. PhD dissertation, Washington State University, Pullman. University Microfilms, Ann Arbor.
1988 Patterns of Population Movement and Long-Term Population Growth in Southwestern Colorado. *American Antiquity* 53:773–93.

Seymour, Deni and Michael Schiffer
1987 A Preliminary Analysis of Pithouse Assemblages from Snaketown, Arizona. In *Method and Theory for Activity Area Research: An Ethnoarchaeological Approach*, edited by S. Kent, pp. 549–603. Columbia University Press, New York.

Stiger, Mark A.
1979 Mesa Verde Subsistence Patterns from Basketmaker III to Pueblo III. *The Kiva* 44:133–44.

Wilshusen, Richard H.
1986 The Relationship between Abandonment Mode and Ritual Use in Pueblo I Anasazi Protokivas. *Journal of Field Archaeology* 13:245–54.
1988 The Abandonment of Structures. In *Dolores*

Archaeological Program Supporting Studies: Additive and Reductive Technologies, compiled by E. Blinman, C. J. Phagan and R. Wilshusen, pp. 673–702. Bureau of Reclamation, Engineering and Research Center, Denver, Co.

Wyckoff, Don G.
1977 Secondary Forest Succession Following Abandonment of Mesa Verde. *The Kiva* 42:215–31.

Zubrow, Ezra B. W.
1974 *Population, Climate and Contact in the New Mexican Pueblos.* Anthropological Papers of the University of Arizona, No. 24.

8

An assessment of abandonment processes in the Hohokam Classic Period of the Tucson Basin

SUZANNE K. FISH and PAUL R. FISH

Treatments of abandonment in the archaeological literature of the southwestern United States have commonly focused on adverse conditions precipitating departure from a previously inhabited locale. However, decisions as to the timing and mode of prehistoric abandonments were made in the light of conditions at destinations as well as points of departure, and cannot be fully understood from either partial perspective. The more inclusive process, which includes departure and relocation, is less amenable to study in the archaeological record because of the difficulty in establishing synchroneity between locationally disparate sets of events and their remains. Furthermore, material culture is seldom sufficiently distinctive to permit the tracking of particular persons or groups from one place to another.

In spite of these difficulties, additive trends in abandonment behavior can be approached through chronological change in comprehensive settlement patterns. Large-scale abandonments characterize the late prehistoric era throughout the Southwest. Within these broader developments, an instance of regional abandonment is examined among the Hohokam of southern Arizona (Fig. 8.1). Population dynamics that could account for patterns of Hohokam abandonment in the Tucson Basin are discussed in terms of cultural and environmental correlates. Evidence is reviewed for the nature of subsequent low-level use of abandoned territory and the relationship of this use to the economies of persisting communities.

A general model

Defining the archaeological parameters of abandonment

Abandonment is defined archaeologically as the absence or near absence of evidence for habitation of appreciable magnitude or duration in a locus of previous occurrence (Fish *et al.* in press). Significant reduction of earlier resident population is a corollary. Temporally, abandonment behavior may be so compressed as to constitute a brief event or so extended as to represent a trend or process; such distinctions may be difficult to discern in the archaeological record. Populations utilizing or remaining in the abandoned territory have low archaeological visibility.

Abandonment is subject to investigation at variable geographic scales. Cordell (1984) identifies site, local, and regional scales as typical foci of Southwestern study. Cultural and ecological factors most significant in abandonments of small scales may be different in kind and frequency from factors shaping abandonment phenomena of more encompassing extent. Factors influencing smallest-scale abandonments cumulatively account for larger-scale phenomena only if there are sufficient elements of causal interrelationship and locational and temporal synchroneity. Site abandonments are commonplace throughout Southwestern prehistory, abandonments of locales are less frequent, and regional abandonments are most restricted in time and space.

Even where contemporary site and local abandonments are so widespread as to create regional patterns, different scales of archaeological analysis result in emphasis on different aspects of the overall phenomenon. Studies focused at the levels of sites, locales, or regions experiencing abandonment are informative on environmental and cultural factors affecting the endurance and success of populations in those respective categories. However, variables limited to negative ones in abandoned areas represent incomplete data for reconstructions in which effects of external factors such as long-distance trade are considered.

Smaller scales of analysis are most relevant to detailed documentation of disadvantageous circumstances that may have precipitated abandonment decisions. They may provide evidence bearing on relocation such as pre-existing patterns of exchange relationships. A fine focus also may be needed to examine postabandonment land use. Nevertheless, the larger process of abandonment, including alternatives and outcomes, can be fully understood only at scales encompassing points of both departure and destination.

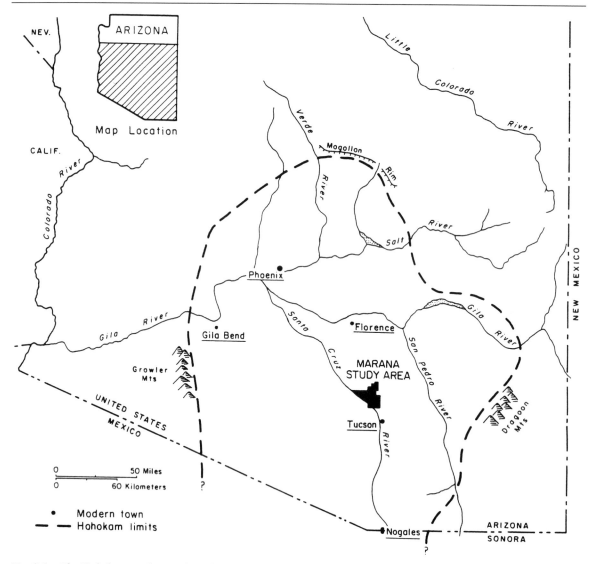

Fig. 8.1   The Hohokam tradition of southern Arizona.

Chronological trends in Southwestern abandonments

Abandonment decisions were solutions to problems. The perceived outcome of abandonment must have been considered more acceptable, under given circumstances, than remaining in the same location. Conditions in the area of destination, as well as in the area being abandoned, would have affected the timing and manner of departure.

We have argued elsewhere (Fish *et al.* in press) that large-scale abandonments across the Southwest in late prehistoric time can be related to the development of organizational modes accommodating relatively denser, integrated populations, and to the areally intensified production underlying these aggregates. The relationship between aggregated configurations and regional abandonments is not necessarily one of cause and effect. In some instances, concentrations of well-integrated settlement may have developed in place without marked effect on populations elsewhere. However, the development of such aggregates provided new alternatives to outlying groups experiencing social or environmental stress. At times, aggregated entities also may have contributed to pressures on smaller enclaves in surrounding regions or represented competing attractions.

Concentrations of denser population in the Southwest shifted toward areas capable of supporting intensified agriculture and particularly riverine irrigation after AD 1300. It is assumed that these aggregated entities based on intensive production incorporated some significant proportion of formerly more dispersed populations. Organizational structures had to be sufficiently flexible to incorporate incoming groups, to assign them social roles, to mediate interactions among the increasingly numerous members, and to provide newcomers access to the means of production such as land and water. Further, productive capacities had to be expandable in order to absorb the increased labor of abandoning groups and, with it, to support the higher population totals.

Initial frameworks for aggregated living and intensified production had to be in place before abandoners could consider such alternatives. Absorption may have involved increased labor input or lower production per unit area, but with possible trade-offs in greater subsistence security and survival through the stress initiating abandonment. From the viewpoint of existing aggregates, abandoning groups could have represented a potential for additional labor and productive expansion. Emigrating personnel may have been utilized readily in riverine irrigation and other labor intensive or differentiated subsistence activities (e.g. extractive specialties or farming in adjacent and more marginal uplands). Thus, the development of aggregated configurations presented new alternatives for regional inhabitants experiencing stress, as well as some probable attractions or benefits.

The role of destinations in abandonment behavior is hard to isolate, requires broader-based evidence, and has been relatively neglected. Typically, chronological precision and methods for distinguishing cultural identity are inadequate for conclusively linking specific populations and areas. Nevertheless, expectations concerning destinations must have strongly influenced abandonment decisions, which were based upon homeland conditions and the perception of alternatives. Where aggregated settlements served as destinations, their subsequent development was also affected by abandonment decisions.

The range of solutions for the integration of abandoning populations into existing aggregates is poorly understood. Ethnographically, puebloan arrangements include recognition of incoming group identity by accretion as separate clans (e.g. Hopi, Zuni) and the acceptance of ethnically distinct groups conditional to fulfilling particular functions or roles (e.g. the Tewa at Walpi on the Hopi Mesas). Unfortunately, analogies for the Hohokam and other non-puebloan peoples of the Greater Southwest are less plentiful and illuminating. Almost certainly, anticipated methods of incorporation at destinations would have influenced the staging of abandonments. Numbers of related persons abandoning and arriving *en masse* might be more apt to achieve acceptance as a group, while single or few households might be assimilated into existing organization. In all but the most catastrophic cases of abandonment, negotiation between abandoners and inhabitants at destinations probably preceded departures.

Subsequent use of abandoned areas

In many instances, low-level succeeding occupations or utilizations of abandoned areas also may be linked to processes of abandonment and relocation. At issue are the characteristics of ensuing or residual occupations, the degree to which they were disjunct or retained personnel and organization of the previous populations, and their relationship to the aggregated settlement systems joined by at least some of the former inhabitants. These questions have constituted a subject of recent interest and debate (e.g. Ambler and Sutton 1989; Upham 1984, 1988; Plog 1983; Stuart and Gauthier 1984; Sullivan 1987).

For the time-span following AD 1350 in many parts of the Southwest, the difficulties of recognizing and interpreting archaeological evidence dating to periods of abandonment are compounded. The manufacture of localized styles in decorated ceramics declines, while trade wares and pan-regional styles rise in prominence. By latest prehistoric time, a limited number of widespread ceramic types apparently circulate from relatively restricted locales of manufacture (e.g. Jeddito or Sitkyaki pottery from the area around modern Hopi and Ramos polychrome from the vicinity of Casas Grandes), yet may represent the major chronological markers in geographically distant areas. In the Tucson Basin and other Hohokam subareas, the numerically significant late prehistoric diagnostics are Salado polychromes, which are usually considered to have been acquired partly or wholly through trade.

There has been little exploration of potential modes of post-abandonment utilization directly linked with contemporary and adjacent population aggregates. Small-scale farming and gathering in the most favorable situations of abandoned regions may have provided short-term but critical supplements during episodes of agricultural calamity, such as flood damage to canals or severe drought. Depleted natural resources in the vicinities of aggregated populations also may have occasioned extractive specializations in outlying areas. If abandoning groups joined nearby aggregates, members would be optimal candidates for economic specialties of hunting, gathering, or quarrying in their former territories. Rights to land and resources in abandoned areas may have been retained, with such continuities structuring use of sparsely settled hinterlands by inhabitants of aggregated settlements. For example, at Hopi, periodic visits are made to boundary markers on distant lands that belonged to ancestral clans (Page 1940; James 1974).

The Tucson Basin Hohokam case study

The region furnishing a case study of Hohokam abandonment in the deserts of southern Arizona lies in the lower basin of the Santa Cruz River (See Fig. 8.1). The Tucson Basin proper, a 45 mile (75 km) segment between the San Xavier Indian Reservation to the south of Tucson and the town of Marana to the north, is the center of a red-on-brown variant within the Hohokam ceramic sequence. Topographic diversity from river floodplain to mountain ranges bounding the basin occurs within a valley width from 8 to 15 miles (13 to 25 km). Average rainfall is between 9 and 12 ins (225 to 300 mm), and perennial surface flow is confined to limited stretches of the river and major tributaries.

The lack of absolute dates, especially from tree rings, in Hohokam archaeology makes it difficult to achieve internal distinctions within relatively broad ceramic phases. However, at the chronological precision of phases, large-scale survey (Fish, Fish, and Madsen 1989, 1990, 1992) provides systematic coverage for 700 sq miles (1800 sq km) centered on the northern Tucson Basin, and serves to unify more scattered results throughout the region. An area dramatically abandoned during the Tanque Verde phase (*c.* AD 1150–1300) of the early Classic Period lies within this study area, as do some of the later Classic clusters of aggregated settlement that are likely destinations. Full-coverage data from the Marana Community, a territorial unit integrating multiple sites, permit a quantified assessment of population dynamics prior to abandonment and an exhaustive distribution of postabandonment activities.

Preclassic settlement and abandonment

Late Archaic sites in the northern Tucson Basin and those of succeeding periods are concentrated in two bands paralleling the valley axis. One linear array follows the Santa Cruz River, including both irrigable floodplain and adjacent alluvial fans on the lower valley slope that are suitable for floodwater farming. The second band follows the bordering mountain flanks in a broad swath along the upper valley slope. These settlement emphases remain stable until the Classic Period, with sites somewhat variably dispersed throughout the two topographic bands according to greater or lesser local opportunities (Fig. 8.2).

Settlement differentiation beyond distinctions in size and general function emerges in the study area during later Preclassic time in the form of sites with ballcourts in each band. Multisite territorial units, integrated about central sites with public architecture, typify Hohokam settlement organization after the earliest phases (Fish and Fish 1990). These clusters of inter-related sites are called communities. Earthen banked ballcourts are the common form of public architecture in central sites of Preclassic communities, superseded by mounds in the Classic Period. Separate Preclassic communities, each containing ballcourt centers, cover 27 sq miles (70 sq km) in the band of settlement along the river and 22 sq miles (57 sq km) on the upper valley slope, respectively.

Preclassic abandonments (prior to AD 1150) of a regional scale have not been identified in the Tucson Basin, although there are instances of areally restricted abandonments of multiple sites. One such example involves a group of four sites along the northern Santa Cruz River whose arrangement suggests a shared canal line. Abandonment of these sites by the Classic Period could be the result of localized change in river morphology as has been suggested for one portion of the southern basin (Doelle, Dart and Wallace 1985; Waters 1988), or could be correlated with population reorganization and aggregation at the beginning of the Classic Period.

Early Classic settlement and abandonment

Near the beginning of the Tanque Verde phase of the Classic Period, at about AD 1100, accelerating aggregation and reorganization becomes apparent (Fish, Fish, and Madsen 1989). Sites span the valley slope between the two previous communities, which coalesce into a single new territorial entity centered on a site with a platform mound. A canal 6 miles (10 km) long originates in the riverine band of settlement and extends to the newly settled mound site in an intermediate valley slope location (Fig. 8.3). The early Classic community encompasses both a larger territory (56 sq miles or 146 sq km) and more numerous sites than its combined Preclassic precursors. A new level of architectural differentiation can be distinguished among Classic habitation sites in the unequal distribution of substantial adobe structures and compounds, as well as the unique occurrence of a platform mound.

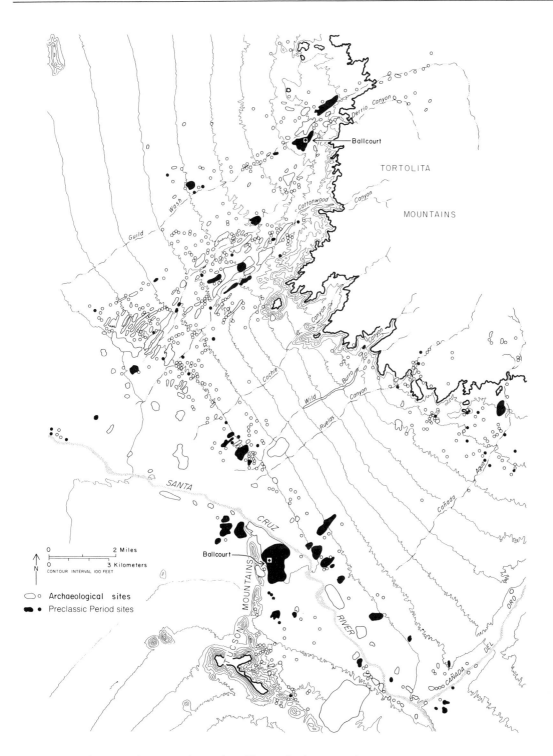

Fig. 8.2   *Preclassic settlement in the northern Tucson Basin.*

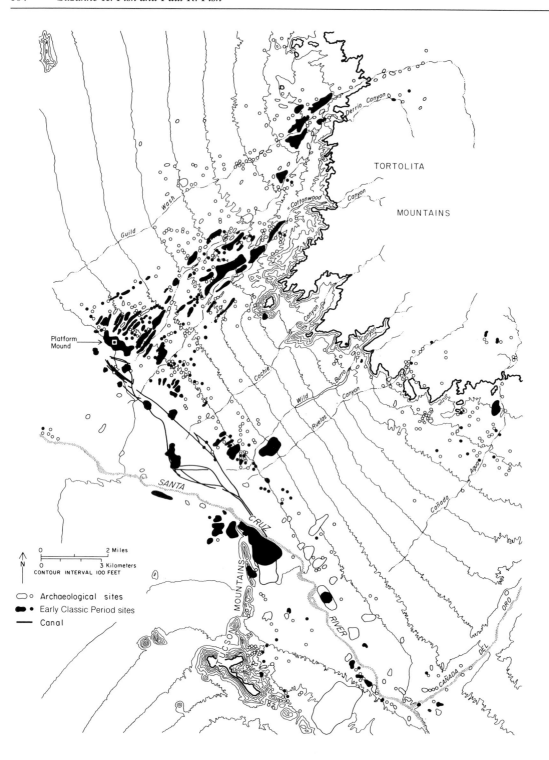

Fig. 8.3   Early Classic Period settlement in the northern Tucson Basin.

It is clear that the Classic Marana Community incorporates a greater population than the total for the two preceding ones. Because structure numbers cannot be tabulated from surface indications with Hohokam architecture, square meters of habitation area serve as a reasonable proxy for chronological comparison. Approximately 2,300,000 sq m are recorded in sites of the two Preclassic communities, while early Classic habitation area totals 6,100,000 sq m. This contrast becomes greater if relative duration is considered; although the Tanque Verde phase is poorly bounded by absolute dates (Eighmy and McGuire 1989; Dean 1991), it represents a clearly shorter interval than the Preclassic timespan. Some Preclassic sites are no longer occupied in the following period (Fig. 8.2 and 8.3), and may have contributed former population to areas more densely settled during Classic times. Nevertheless, the greater magnitude of habitation area in Classic Period sites by a factor of three implies substantial growth of the existing population and the probable inclusion of persons from outside the confines of the two prior communities. Places of origin for external increments are not known at this time.

Contemporary with the development of the larger, more aggregated and differentiated early Classic community is widespread evidence of intensified subsistence production (Fish, Fish, and Madsen 1990). Indeed, such intensification must have been essential for supporting the enlarged population. Agriculture is expanded into hydrologically marginal and previously unused land of the middle valley slope through the construction of cobble mulches or rock piles, and similar features are utilized along the mountain flanks. Drought resistant agave, planted in complexes of rock pile features, becomes an important crop in the expansion of cultivation beyond optimal settings (Fish *et al.* 1985). Settlements appear in poorer floodwater situations along the edge of the lower valley slope and are serviced by a canal constructed at this time. Intensification can also be recognized in non-agricultural production by the occurrence of huge extractive sites in portions of the middle slope containing dense saguaro cactus.

Identifiable inhabitation ceases by about AD 1350 throughout the 56 sq miles (146 sq km) of the early Classic Marana Community, a segment of the Tucson Basin continuously inhabited since the beginning of the Hohokam sequence (Fig. 8.4). The abandonment of this large area appears generally synchronous as measured with the low resolution of Hohokam ceramic phases. Salado polychromes, the markers for the transition from the early Classic Tanque Verde phase to the late Classic

Tucson phase, are exceedingly rare and virtually absent from contexts suggesting residence.

An environmental trigger for this abandonment is not apparent. Locally derived environmental sequences are unavailable for the Tucson Basin. In a climatic reconstruction from tree ring records in northern Arizona by Graybill (1989), summer precipitation, the critical factor in Tucson agricultural production, was found to be surprisingly consistent between AD 750 and 1350. Systemic disruptions of Salt River canals are posited at about AD 1350 (Nials, Gregory and Graybill 1989) owing to flood-induced changes in Phoenix intake locales. The morphology and seasonal flow regime of the Santa Cruz River is not similar to that of the Salt River, but even in the event of contemporary flood damage, occupation and production could have continued in the long-standing mountain flank settlements of the Marana Community.

The early Classic Marana Community could be viewed as an instance of aggregated living and intensified production in an environment with natural upper limits for subsistence potential. A riverine irrigated core may have contributed disproportionately to the supply of annual crops for the whole community. River flow is not perennial in this area, however, restricting the magnitude of productivity of canal systems compared to those on the Salt and Gila Rivers and even those on perennial, upstream stretches of the Santa Cruz to the south. The diversity of farming techniques and locations in the Classic Period implies that a residential population could have persisted in parts of the community under any conceivable conditions of environmental change. Nevertheless, a consensus for abandonment was reached by all inhabitants. In this sense, the decision to abandon can be viewed as a social as well as an economic choice among a large population whose strong interconnections are emphasized by such joint action.

Late Classic settlement and abandonment

The abandonment phenomenon of the later Tanque Verde phase is of a truly regional scale and involves more than a single multisite community unit. The absence of residential occupations between the midpoint of the Tucson Mountains and the southern edge of the Picacho Mountains (500 sq miles or 1300 sq km) has been established by systematic survey coverage. Areas to the north and south that continue to be occupied into the interval marked by Salado polychromes coincide with the distribution of large sites of the late Classic Period (Fig. 8.5).

Barring catastrophic population loss, it is reasonable

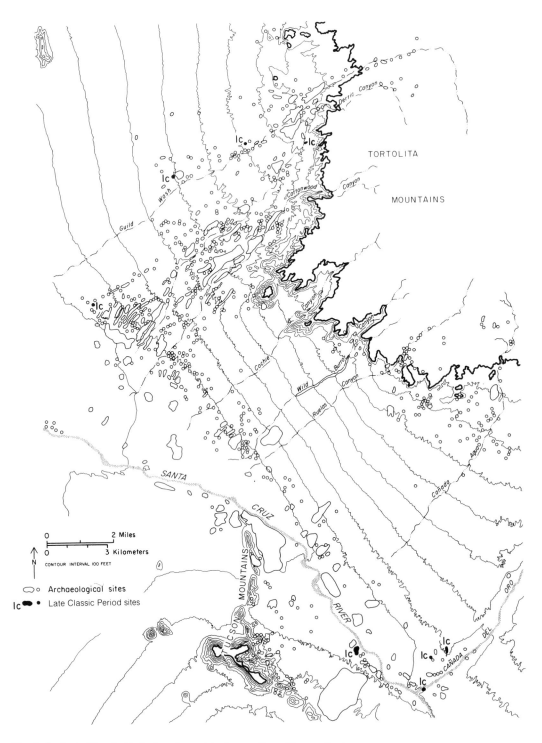

Fig. 8.4   Late Classic Period settlement in the northern Tucson Basin.

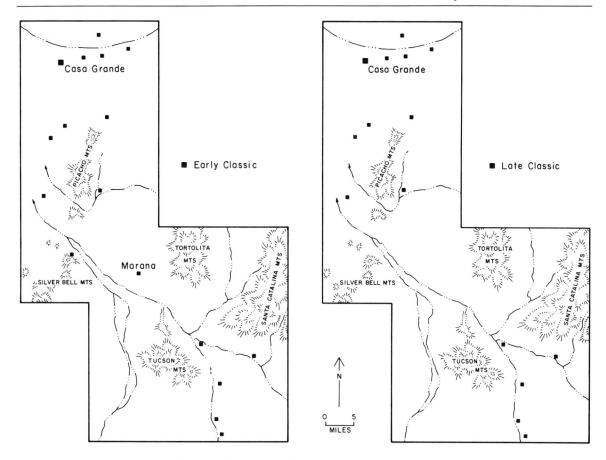

Fig. 8.5   Distribution of early Classic and late Classic Period platform mounds near Tucson.

to assume that inhabitants of the northern Tucson Basin were incorporated into late Classic settlement concentrations to the north and south. It further follows that productive capacities in these areas must have been sufficient to absorb the increased labor force as well as to satisfy the greater consumption demands. Heightened aggregation would have necessitated social structures capable of integrating significant increments of immigrants and maintaining stability in the face of higher numbers in closer proximity.

Later settlements of the Classic Period occur in situations with potential for agricultural intensification. Surface indications at large sites in these areas suggest that the late Classic Period witnessed the highest residential densities and the greatest investment in public architecture of presumed integrative function. Large late Classic Tucson phase sites in the southern Tucson Basin are situated along stretches of the Santa Cruz with perennial surface flow or along major tributaries with

extensive upland watersheds that would ensure reliable agricultural water. Historic gravity irrigation was practiced in the vicinity of all these sites. Each of the late Classic southern sites in Fig. 8.5 are known to have had multiple compounds. At the three sites where preservation allows any assessment, densities of surface remains are maximal compared to regional occupations of all other periods, and a platform mound is present. During this time in the southern Tucson Basin, there is a decrease in numbers of small sites (Doelle, Dart, and Wallace 1985). Correspondingly increased labor pools at large settlements may have intensified irrigated production.

Late Classic sites to the north of the Tucson Basin occur in proximity to the Picacho Mountains. Five sites with platform mounds are found in areas with long histories of habitation, but represent the largest and densest occupations for the area's Hohokam sequence. One of these is adjacent to the Santa Cruz. The others are located along watercourses which are ephemeral but have watersheds of significantly greater size than Santa Cruz tributaries in the abandoned northern segment of the Tucson Basin. A number of large reservoirs demonstrate the potential for water management to prolong availability. The three northernmost mound sites are from 9 to 15 miles (15 to 25 km) from the pre-eminent site of Casa Grande on the Gila River and may be integrated into its sphere in some manner.

Late Classic utilization of abandoned areas

The late Classic abandonment of the northern Tucson Basin is well documented. Areas occupied at this time, presumably incorporating some large proportion of the previous northern basin population, are equally well identified. Distributional data pertaining to a continued late Classic presence in the abandoned territory illustrate the difficulty of understanding relationships between such remains and inhabitants of contemporary aggregated settlements in surrounding areas.

Fig. 8.4 shows the northern Tucson Basin distribution of sites with Salado polychromes, the only chronological diagnostics in this region for Hohokam occupations of the later Classic. Each of the few sites yielding polychromes within the former early Classic Marana Community contains at most a handful of sherds; all are small sites which also lack assemblages that would suggest significant habitation during either late Classic or earlier times. Because diagnostics are typically rare at small sites and because polychromes may be trade items, late Classic utilization of the area could be under-represented. However, these wares occur consistently in late sites of all sizes to both north and south of the abandoned area. The distributional patterns indicate an ephemeral presence primarily reflecting extractive activities or travel between late settlement concentrations in the northern and southern basin. Near the Tortolita Mountains, co-occurrence of polychrome sherds and projectile points on one small site suggests hunting.

Several lines of evidence raise the intriguing possibility of continued agave production in rock pile fields of the former Marana Community. A radiocarbon date in the late Classic Period was obtained on charred agave from a roasting pit in a large field. Additionally, polychrome sherds associated with ground stone and a relatively diverse lithic assemblage occur at one small site on the northern edge of the series of fields producing this date. Without maintenance, canals to the mound site near these fields would no longer have functioned. Natural water sources lie at least 6 miles (10 km) distant. The location of this small site therefore would have been inconvenient for even extended camping in the absence of an over-riding, location-specific function.

Field complexes of rock piles and other simple stone features remained intact as agricultural facilities after the early Classic exodus. Agaves require less direct tending than annual crops. It is thus possible that at least a reduced level of production might have been maintained by former community residents or other persons living at a distance, perhaps in conjunction with seasonal fieldhouse residence. Distances from late Classic settlement clusters to either the north or south of the intervening abandoned area might have permitted such intermittent activity.

Widespread patterns and cumulative process

Hohokam residents departed *en masse* from an early Classic community of the Tucson Basin, in spite of the fact that sectors of their diverse territory should have remained productive under any scenario of environmental change. Natural or societal limits that were eventually exceeded may have precipitated the dissolution of this community as an aggregated entity. However, accommodation to early Classic levels of density and integration may represent a precondition that facilitated the ultimate incorporation of members into the more highly aggregated systems of late Classic society. From this perspective, escalating scales of aggregation and abandonment over time would be outcomes of cumulative and interrelated developmental processes.

The linkage of regional abandonments with aggregation and intensified production in the late prehistoric Southwest has validity only as a model of the broadest scope. Parallels to many of the forces and conditions initiating episodes of large-scale abandonment must have occurred throughout regional chronologies. Nevertheless, earlier solutions to such stresses failed to produce equally widespread archaeological patterns of regional extent, in which residential occupations were virtually lacking. Populations increasing even at low rates over time may have progressively eliminated a number of prior options. Regional abandonments became pervasive in an era of increasing alternatives in the form of aggregated settlements that possessed the potential for organizational and productive expansion.

References

Ambler, J. Richard and Mark Q. Sutton
    1989 The Anasazi Abandonment of the San Juan Drainage and the Numic Expansion. *North American Archaeologist* 10:39–53.

Cordell, Linda S.
1984 *Prehistory of the Southwest*. Academic Press, Orlando.

Dean, Jeffrey S.
1991 Thoughts on Hohokam Chronology. In *Exploring the Hohokam: Prehistoric Desert People of the American Southwest*, edited by George Gumerman, pp. 61–150. University of New Mexico Press, Albuquerque.

Doelle, William H., Allen Dart, and Henry Wallace
1985 *The Southern Tucson Basin: An Intensive Survey Along the Santa Cruz River*. Technical Report 85–3. Institute for American Research.

Eighmy, Jeffrey and Randall McGuire
1989 Dating the Hohokam Phase Sequence: An Analysis of Archaeomagnetic Dates. *Journal of Field Archaeology* 16:215–31.

Fish, Paul R., Suzanne K. Fish, George Gumerman, and J. Jefferson Reid.
In press. Toward an Explanation for Southwestern Abandonments. In *The Structure and Evolution of Prehistoric Southwestern Societies*, edited by George Gumerman and Murray Gell-Mann. School of American Research, Santa Fe.

Fish, Suzanne K. and Paul R. Fish
1990 An Archaeological Assessment of Ecosystems in the Tucson Basin of Southern Arizona. In *The Ecosystem Approach in Anthropology: From Concept to Practice*, edited by Emilio Moran, pp. 159–88. The University of Michigan Press, Ann Arbor.

Fish, Suzanne K., Paul R. Fish, and John Madsen
1989 Differentiation and Integration in a Tucson Basin Classic Period Hohokam Community. In *The Socio-Political Structure of Prehistoric Southwestern Societies*, edited by Steadman Upham, Kent Lightfoot, and Roberta Jewett, pp. 237–67. Westview Press, Boulder.

1990 Analyzing Prehistoric Agriculture: A Hohokam Example. In *The Archaeology of Regions: The Case for Full-Coverage Survey*, edited by Suzanne K. Fish and Stephen A. Kowalewski, pp. 189–218. The Smithsonian Institution Press, Washington DC.

1992 *The Marana Community in the Hohokam World*. Anthropological Papers of the University of Arizona Number 56. University of Arizona Press, Tucson.

Fish, Suzanne K., Paul R. Fish, Charles Miksicek, and John Madsen

1985 Prehistoric Agave Cultivation in Southern Arizona. *Desert Plants* 7:102–16.

Graybill, Donald
1989 The Reconstruction of Prehistoric Salt River Streamflow. In *The 1982–1984 Excavations at Las Colinas*, by Donald Graybill, David Gregory, Fred Nials, Suzanne Fish, Charles Miksicek, Robert Gasser, and Christine Szuter, pp. 25–38. Arizona State Museum Archaeological Series 162. University of Arizona Press, Tucson.

James, Harry C.
1974 *Pages from Hopi History*. University of Arizona Press, Tucson.

Nials, Fred, David Gregory, and Donald Graybill
1989 Salt River Streamflow and Hohokam Irrigation. In *The 1982–1984 Excavations at Las Colinas*, by Donald Graybill, David Gregory, Fred Nials, Suzanne Fish, Charles Miksicek, Robert Gasser, and Christine Szuter, pp. 59–78. Arizona State Museum Archaeological Series 162. University of Arizona Press, Tucson.

Page, Gordon B.
1940 Hopi Land Patterns. *Plateau* 13:29–36.

Plog, Fred
1983 Political and Economic Alliances on the Colorado Plateaus, A.D. 400–1450. *Advances in World Archaeology* 2: 289–330.

Stuart, David and Rory Gauthier
1984 *Prehistoric New Mexico: Background for Survey*. New Mexico Archaeological Council, Albuquerque.

Sullivan, Alan P.
1987 Artifact Scatters, Adaptive Diversity, and Southwestern Abandonments: The Upham Hypothesis Reconsidered. *Journal of Anthropological Research* 43:345–60.

Upham, Steadman
1984 Adaptive Diversity and Southwestern Abandonments. *Journal of Anthropological Research* 40:235–56.

1988 Archaeological Visibility and the Underclass of Southwestern Prehistory. *American Antiquity* 53:245–61.

Waters, Michael R.
1988 The Impact of Fluvial Processes and Landscape Evolution on Archaeological Sites and Settlement Patterns along the San Xavier Reach of the Santa Cruz River, Arizona. *Geoarcheology* 3:205–19.

9

Regional settlement abandonment at the end of the Copper Age in the lowlands of west-central Portugal

KATINA T. LILLIOS

[The Copper Age of Iberia] arose suddenly and ... attained a rich flourishment; but this brilliance lasted only a short time and it disappeared at last without leaving any trace of itself.

(Åberg 1921:1)

Introduction

A major challenge prehistorians face is explaining regional settlement abandonment among sedentary agricultural communities, particularly those who have invested a significant amount of energy and time in constructing and maintaining settlements. There are, indeed, many examples of regional abandonment among such communities in the prehistoric past; these include the depopulation of the Four Corners area of the southwest United States around AD 1300 and the abandonment of Mycenaean palaces in the Argolid plain of Greece at about 1200 BC. Attempts to explain these abandonments have often focused on the occurrence of a social or environmental catastrophe, such as a war, flood, drought, or volcanic eruption, which directly affected the entire region. In some causes, these events can be documented (see Cameron 1991a:178–81). In general, however, I would argue that unicausal explanations can not account for the archaeological or paleoenvironmental data associated with most regional abandonments. This is principally because the landscapes that prehistoric communities inhabited were rarely so environmentally uniform or sociopolitically integrated that one catastrophic event would have affected an entire region to the extent that all settlements in that region would have been abandoned. In the abandonment of a regional settlement

system for which there is evidence of unequal access to raw materials, land, or power, or some degree of economic, territorial, or ideological domination, a more appropriate explanatory framework would recognize the possibility of different but interdependent abandonment mechanisms having taken place throughout a region. The conceptual language of center–periphery relations provides such a framework (Champion 1989; Chase-Dunn and Hall 1991; Rowlands, Larsen, and Kristiansen 1987).

In this paper, I examine the widespread abandonment of settlements that occurred at the end of the Copper Age (2000 BC) in the lowlands of west-central Portugal (Fig. 9.1) within a center–periphery model. The archaeological and paleoenvironmental data suggest that in the center (Lisbon and Setúbal peninsulas) and the periphery (interior lowlands) different but related processes resulted in lowland abandonment at the end of the Copper Age. I propose that abandonment in the center occurred as a result of social tensions heightened by environmental degradation. The cases for abandonment in the periphery, where social differentiation was less marked and population not as dense, are not clear; they may have occurred to accommodate the shifts in exchange alliances resulting from center abandonments.

In the following discussion, I first briefly review the history of Copper (3000–2000 BC) and Bronze Age (2000–1000 BC) research in Portugal, describe the nature of the archaeological data, and evaluate previous explanations for lowland abandonment. The principal characteristics of center–periphery relations are outlined and compared to the archaeological evidence for the lowlands. Finally, I propose a mechanism for abandonment in the Portuguese lowlands, which takes into account the different trajectories of the center and periphery.

History of research

The Copper Age (or Eneolithic) of Portugal has been the focus of intensive research since the late 1800s, when prehistoric archaeology was first recognized as a scholarly pursuit in Portugal (Santos 1980). The period generated fervent interest throughout the European archaeological community (Åberg 1921; Cartailhac 1886; Déchelette 1906) after the discovery of wealthy tombs in the Lisbon and Setúbal areas, such as Monte Abraão (Ribeiro 1878), Palmela (Costa 1907), and São Martinho de Sintra (Apolinário 1896). These burials were replete with decorated ceramics, finely flaked flints, objects made of North African ivory, carved limestone idols, ground stone tools, gold, and copper. Copper Age hilltop settlements throughout west-central Portugal,

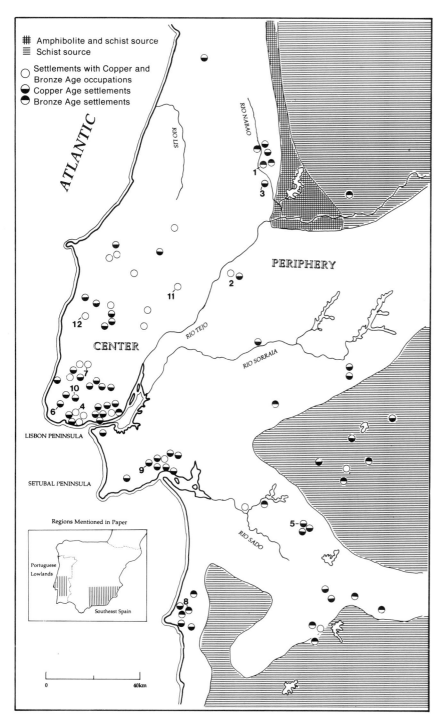

Fig. 9.1   Location of Copper and Bronze Age settlements in the Portuguese lowlands. Sites mentioned in text: 1 Agroal; 2 Alpiarça; 3 Fonte Quente; 4 Liceia; 5 Monte da Tumba; 6 Olelas; 7 Penedo de Lexim; 8 Quitéria; 9 Rotura; 10 Serra das Baútas; 11 Vila Nova de São Pedro; 12 Zambujal.

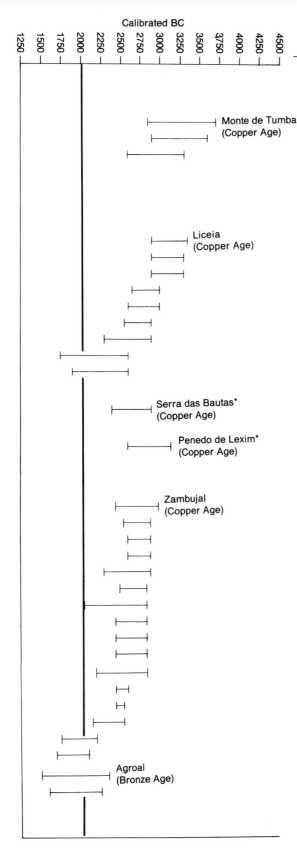

Calibrated BC

Monte de Tumba
(Copper Age)

Liceia
(Copper Age)

Serra das Bautas*
(Copper Age)

Penedo de Lexim*
(Copper Age)

Zambujal
(Copper Age)

Agroal
(Bronze Age)

such as Liceia, Olelas (Ribeiro 1878), and Rotura (Simões 1878), similarly received a good deal of attention for their impressive structural remains, including fortifications and semi-circular towers, and abundant artifacts. More recent excavations at some of these sites, such as Rotura (Silva 1966–7, 1968–9) and Liceia (Cardoso 1982, 1989), as well as other settlements, such as Vila Nova de São Pedro (Paço 1947; Paço 1939 [1970], 1942 [1970]), Zambujal (Sangmeister and Schubart 1981), Monte da Tumba (Silva and Soares 1985, 1987), Serra das Baútas (Arnaud and Gamito 1972), and Penedo de Lexim (Arnaud 1974–7; Arnaud, Salgado de Oliveira, and Jorge 1971), have provided the best data available on stratigraphy and occupational histories for the Portuguese Copper Age (Fig. 9.2). Portuguese nationalism has been well served by the discovery of Copper Age sites; in the words of Jalhay and Paço, the early excavators of Vila Nova de São Pedro, the Copper Age was glorified as "one of the most wonderful pages of Portuguese prehistory" (Jalhay and Paço 1945:91).

The settlements of Copper Age communities, whose subsistence economies were based on the intensive farming of wheat and barley and the herding of cattle and ovicaprids (Correia 1980), represent significant investments in energy and time. Typically they are hilltop sites overlooking river valleys and they range in size from 0.1 ha (Penedo de Lexim) to 1.0 ha (Rotura). Most were surrounded by enclosure walls which in some cases (e.g. at Vila Nova de São Pedro and Zambujal) underwent repeated consolidation up to a thickness of 4 m (Harrison 1977:30). Domestic structures (*cabanas*) are generally found within the confines of these walls; they tend to be circular in plan, 2–3 m in diameter, with stone foundations, and are often associated with grinding stones (e.g. at Vila Nova de São Pedro – Paço 1970[1939]:235). Evidence for local manufacturing activities, such as the production of ceramics and schist plaques (Vila Nova de São Pedro), textiles, flaked and ground-stone tools, and copper objects (Zambujal), can also be found within these enclosure walls.

Copper Age settlements often show a high degree of occupational continuity; at the site of Vila Nova de São Pedro, house foundations were built over older house foundations (Paço 1970[1942]:280); at Zambujal, one of the houses had numerous superimposed hearths (Harrison 1977:33). At a few sites, some contraction in the area occupied between the pre-Beaker (3000–2500 BC) and

Fig. 9.2   Absolute dates for lowland Copper and Bronze Age settlements in Portugal (thermoluminescence date; all others are radiocarbon dates).*

Beaker (2500–2000 BC) phases of the Copper Age seems to have occurred (Harrison 1977:30).

During the Copper Age, lowland communities were integrated by an exchange system involving engraved schist plaques, copper axes, and ground stone tools made of amphibolite. The sources of schist and amphibolite are found in the eastern half of Portugal, and the distribution of finished products made of these raw materials throughout the lowlands indicates an effective exchange network. There are copper sources in the areas north of Lisbon, with minor ores sources found throughout the lowlands (Harrison 1974). Nevertheless, it is highly probable that some of the copper objects on archaeological sites at which there is no evidence for local smelting were acquired through exchange.

The archaeological record for the Copper Age indicates that there was significant variability in the consumption of prestige goods, settlement density, and proximity to important raw materials, particularly schist and amphibolite, between the interior and coastal zones, suggesting some level of sociopolitical control, exploitation, or domination. I propose that this variability reflects a center–periphery relationship, with the center at the Lisbon/Setúbal peninsulas, in some way controlling the critical resources of the interior periphery.

Coastal settlements amassed prestige goods in greater quantities and variety than interior settlements, suggesting a difference in social complexity between these two areas. Beaker ceramics, for example, which have been argued to be prestige goods since they are often associated with gold and copper, craft specialist objects, or non-local items (Harrison 1977), are found predominantly at Portuguese coastal sites (Spindler 1981:fig. 49). Differences in consumption of luxury goods between the coast and interior may partially explain the difference in the degree to which settlements were fortified in these two areas. Settlements of the littoral tend to be more heavily fortified than those of the interior. Walls of interior settlements appear to be enclosure walls for game, wind breakers, or simply markers of territory, e.g. Fonte Quente (Oosterbeck and Cruz, in press).

The density of Copper Age settlements is also much higher along the Atlantic littoral than in the interior. While there has certainly been more research conducted along the coast, a recent systematic survey of late prehistoric sites conducted in the Nabão Valley did not yield the abundance of Copper Age settlements found along the coast (Lillios 1991). There are, on average, five Copper Age settlements per 100 sq km along the littoral, compared with only two to three settlements per 100 sq km in the interior. This difference may reflect the higher productivity of the coast and Tejo estuary; the varied resources that are found at the coast include fertile soils, fish and shellfish, and forest products.

The coast and interior contrast most dramatically, however, in their access to critical raw materials, particularly amphibolite. Amphibolite is a metamorphic mafic rock, which is dark green to black in color. The nearest sources to the lowlands are found in the Portuguese interior uplands. The stone was the raw material used to make the ground stone tools that were necessary to the survival of these agricultural communities, including axes, adzes, chisels, hammerstones, and wedges, and which are found in great abundance on Copper Age settlements. Additionally, amphibolite objects served as prestige or ritual goods, as suggested by the fact that unused ground stone axes and adzes are often found in Copper Age burials along the coast (e.g. at Cascais), as are limestone representations of adzes (e.g. at Praia das Maças, Palmela, Cascais, São Martinho de Sintra, Anta de Estria, Pai Mogo, Baútas, Samarra, and Tojal de Vila Cha). I argue that differential access to schist played a less important role for two reasons: (1) schist sources are much more abundant than amphibolite sources, and (2) schist was used principally in the production of ritual plaques, while amphibolite was used for both utilitarian and ritual purposes. Although there are basalt sources in the lowlands, they were rarely quarried for stone tools in Portuguese prehistory. The reason for this preference of amphibolite over basalt seems to lie in the physical properties of the two stones. As a metamorphic rock, amphibolite's foliated structure renders it less likely to fracture during use (W. Barnett: pers. comm.).

Although the source of amphibolite is nearer to communities of the interior, the settlements of the coast accumulated more finished products made of amphibolite. At the site of Vila Nova de São Pedro, located along the Rio Tejo, halfway between the amphibolite source and the coast, approximately 1000 ground stone tools were found (Leisner and Schubart 1966). At Liceia, located a few kilometers from the coast, over 300 were found. Groundstone tools in this abundance have not been found at interior settlements. Furthermore, some of the ground stone items found at Liceia and Vila Nova de São Pedro appear to be blanks, which are roughly the size and shape of an adze or axe, but with none of the sides completely polished. A type of redistributive network is suggested by this distributional pattern (Renfrew 1977). In such a system, high concentrations of objects made of amphibolite would be expected to be found in the areas which had preferential access to the material. That the highest concentrations of ground stone tools are not found nearest the source and that production areas are found at a distance from the source suggest that coastal groups had some level of control over the raw material. Such control over a distant raw material, which did not necessarily involve a highly integrated political system, can be documented ethnographically among the Maori. "Natives state that when a good quality of stone was found . . . the situation of the deposit was kept secret as far as possible, so that other tribes, and even other divisions of the same tribe, should not become acquainted with it" (Best 1912:24). Control of the raw material may have been facilitated if the inhabitants of the source area were particularly unfriendly: "In obtaining material for his stone implements, the Maori was often much hampered by the restriction of his social system – the division of people into tribes, independent of each other, and often at war, certainly always suspicious of each other. Hence he could not range at will over distant lands in search of desirable material for his implements" (Best 1912:24).

The case of the Yanomamo as described by Chagnon (1968, 1979) bears an important similarity to the archaeological evidence for the Portuguese lowlands. Where the villages of the Yanomamo are larger, more densely packed, and palisaded, large-scale competitive feasting takes place. In the area where settlements are more dispersed, "the entire complex of alliances based on formal, reciprocal trading, and feasting, is either greatly diminished in scale or, in some areas, nonexistent" (Chagnon 1979:114). The accumulation of ground stone tools, as well as other prestige goods at the densely distributed Portuguese coastal sites and the contrasting pattern in the interior parallels the Yanomamo case.

Such competition may have had something to do with the fact that by the end of the Copper Age, at about 2000 BC, most lowland settlements were abandoned permanently. Settlements with initial occupation in the Early Bronze Age (2000–1500 BC) have been notoriously difficult to locate; those that are known to have been occupied during this period include Quitéria, along the Atlantic coast (Silva and Soares 1981) and Agroal, in the interior (Lillios 1991). At present, Agroal is the only settlement radiocarbon dated to this period in Portugal. Agroal is a hilltop site, whose inhabitants practiced intensive herding of ovicaprids and cattle, farming, and fishing, and carried out local manufacturing activities such as copper smelting. In contrast to Copper Age sites, Agroal is not walled and lacks goods that can be considered prestige items (i.e. goods produced by craft specialists or obtained by long-distance exchange). Other settlements purported to have been occupied in the Early Bronze Age, such as Quitéria, have a similar artifact assemblage to that of Agroal. The excavations at Agroal conducted in conjunction with a re-evaluation of other purported Bronze Age lowland settlements (Lillios 1991) indicate a shift from a clustered hilltop settlement pattern in the Copper Age, particularly in the Lisbon and Setúbal areas, to a dispersed distribution of hilltop and valley bottom settlements in the Bronze Age.

Some burials dated to this period have been identified in caves and stone-lined cists, such as Almonda (Paço, Vaultier, and Zbyszewski 1947), Pessegueiro, and Provença (Silva and Soares 1981), and these generally contain a few undecorated ceramics and a copper dagger. The available settlement and burial data suggest that the Copper to Bronze Age transition was also characterized by significant social and economic changes in addition to shifts in settlement pattern. Specifically, the marked decline of prestige and non-local goods between the Copper and Bronze Ages suggests a decrease in the vertical and horizontal differentiation of lowland society. Ground stone tools ceased to be used as prestige goods, although they are still found as utilitarian goods on settlements. This contrast between the Copper and Early Bronze Ages did not go unnoticed by nineteenth-century prehistorians: "We do not find in Lusitania the wonderful civilization of villages that is known in Fuente Alamo, El Argar, etc., [Early Bronze Age settlements in southeast Spain] . . . " (Siret and Siret 1887:241).

The question of abandonment at the end of the Copper Age has most often been treated within the context of overall sociocultural change. According to Savory, the Copper to Bronze Age transition of Portugal, as well as Spain, was characterized by "progressive isolation" and "stagnation" resulting from aridity associated with the sub-boreal climatic phase (Savory 1968:198). It is unclear to what degree the climatic sequences derived for northern Europe can be applied to southern Europe, particularly to a transitional Mediterranean/Atlantic area such as Portugal. Even if a generalized phase of dessication could be documented for southern Europe, it would not explain why widespread abandonment did not occur in southeast Spain, the other region in Iberia for which there is a well-established Copper to Bronze Age sequence. Many Copper Age sites in southeast Spain, whose culture sequence most closely resembles that of the Portuguese lowlands, were, in fact, not permanently abandoned between the Copper and Early Bronze Ages; some of these settlements include

Cerro de la Virgen (Schüle and Pellicer 1966) and Gatas (Chapman *et al.* 1987).

There are, nevertheless, indications that abandonment in the lowlands was related to a phase of environmental degradation, rather than a climatic shift which was proposed by Savory (1968). Palynological data from the vicinity of Alpiarça, a Copper Age settlement on the southern bank of the Rio Tejo, documents a phase of environmental degradation in the form of deforestation in the early second millennium BC (Leewaarden and Janssen 1985). The ratio of non-arboreal to arboreal pollen (principally pine) peaks at this point in the sequence; the causes for this event, the authors argue, are anthropic (Leewaarden and Janssen 1985:229). Activities of the Copper Age that might have contributed to this process include agriculture, forest clearance for wood products, and metallurgy.

Chapman (1982, 1990) has emphasized the relationship between increasing social complexity, continuity of settlement occupation, and the management of scarce resources in prehistoric Iberia. According to Chapman, in Portugal, unlike in southeast Spain, neither water nor arable land can be considered critical resources and thus there was no significant need for human groups to invest in water control systems or the development of elite managers. The absence of these ties created weak links between human groups and their land, and thus, in the presence of any social stress, fission and settlement abandonment would present itself as a viable option. While it is true that water availability is not as much of a problem in the Portuguese lowlands as it is in the sub-arid conditions of southeast Spain, precipitation levels are, nonetheless, low enough (annual mean = 400–800mm) to produce a Mediterranean landscape (Lines Escardó 1970:215). Despite this, Chapman has raised the issue of cost benefits in relation to abandonment but, I would argue, he has focused on the maintenance of food production to the neglect of social reproduction.

Gilman, on the other hand, has approached the changes between the Copper and Bronze Ages of Portugal from the perspective of social reproduction (Gilman 1987). He has argued that Copper Age elites financed their power through wealth distribution; that is, they converted their surplus into prestige or non-local goods, with which reliable exchange partners to secure more of these goods could be maintained. They did not, according to Gilman, engage in the other form by which elites support their position, namely through the extraction of surplus from peasant cultivators. They either employ coercive measures, which, he argues, are risky in non-industrial societies, or aid in the capital intensification of

production through the construction of, for example, irrigation systems. Gilman suggests that the changes accompanying the Copper Age to Bronze Age transition in lowland Portugal were the result of an inherently unstable system – "a victim to the changes of fashion and the vulnerability to import substitution which characteristically beset wealth distribution" (Gilman 1987:29). It is unclear what import was substituted in the Early Bronze Age to set off a phase of "devolution" between the Copper and Bronze Age. Nonetheless, I would agree that exchange of prestige goods was a significant factor in the changes between the Copper and Bronze Ages, but only in those areas of the coast in which consumption of prestige goods was significantly greater than their interior partners.

As the above discussion demonstrates, the issue of lowland abandonment has not been addressed explicitly. While important factors that diminished the ties prehistoric communities in Portugal had toward the land and each other have been identified by Chapman and Gilman, little attempt has been made to discover the source of the cleavages that resulted in the abandonments, nor has there been much recognition of the variability between the evolutionary trajectories of Copper Age lowland communities.

Center–periphery relations in the Portuguese lowlands

In a center–periphery relationship, a center is defined as the area which controls the distribution of manufactured goods through the domination or exploitation of a periphery, which produces or has direct access to the necessary raw materials (Eckholm 1980; Eckholm and Friedman 1982). Different levels of social complexity or population density characterize a center–periphery relationship (Chase-Dunn and Hall 1991:19). The implication of this model is that the history of a periphery is to a large extent determined or strongly influenced by the events of a center.

When Wallerstein (1974) discussed center–periphery relations in the context of world systems theory, he intended it to be a framework for understanding the history of capitalist societies, and, in particular, the role that developed nations had in the "under-development" of other nations. The exchange of prestige goods was not thought to be important in social transformations. Since Wallerstein's thesis was proposed, archaeologists and social anthropologists have been stimulated by world systems theory and have applied it to the histories of pre-capitalist societies, even those not existing in a state of mutual interdependence (see Kristiansen 1987;

Peregrine 1991). The term "world network" has recently been proposed for such cases and has been defined as "intersocietal networks in which the interaction (trade, warfare, intermarriage, etc.) is an important condition of the reproduction of the internal structures of the composite units and importantly affects changes which occur in these local structures" (Chase-Dunn and Hall 1991:7). A further modification to Wallerstein's original thesis was proposed by Schneider (1977), who argued that in precapitalist societies the exchange of prestige goods, rather than bulk goods, is a more potent force in social cohesion and change.

I suggest that the Portuguese lowlands in the third millennium BC functioned, *on a smaller scale*, as a world network. There is some evidence for the control by coastal communities of critical raw materials, such as amphibolite, which would have been necessary to both coastal and interior groups. I also suggest that the exchange of goods, such as amphibolite, copper, and schist, was an integral component in the reproduction of the social order.

In the remainder of this paper, I will examine the abandonments of the lowlands at the end of the third millennium BC within the framework of a world network. Possible mechanisms for abandonment in the center and periphery will be considered.

Center–periphery abandonments

In what I designate as the center, that is, in the Lisbon and Setúbal peninsulas, the Copper to Bronze Age transition was associated with the following changes in the archaeological record:

1. a shift from clustered to dispersed settlement pattern,
2. a shift from principally hilltop fortified settlements to both hilltop and lowland unfortified sites, and
3. a decline in non-local goods consumption.

In the periphery, or the Portuguese interior, the Copper to Bronze Age can be characterized by:

1. little change in the overall pattern of settlement, that is, dispersed settlement pattern in both Copper and Bronze Ages,
2. a shift from hilltop walled settlements, without the defensive qualities of the center, to hilltop unwalled settlements, and
3. a decline in non-local goods consumption.

At the transition between the third and second millennium BC, the center and periphery both suggest a phase of social fragmentation or fission. I use the term "fission"

in a loose way to refer to the splitting up, and migration of, social groups. Although the material or archaeological indicators of fission are rarely discussed by ethnographers, the literature that does exist (e.g. Cameron 1991b; Friedman 1975; Gulliver 1977; Leach 1954; Petersen 1982; Stephenson 1990; Whiteley 1988) indicates the following as correlates of fission events among sedentary or shifting agricultural communities:

1. long-term abandonment of settlements,
2. decline in average size of settlements or range of settlement sizes, and
3. a shift from clustered to dispersed settlement distribution.

Because the archaeological data for the center and periphery are significantly different, I suggest that the mechanisms for abandonment must have also been different. In general, abandonment of the center is comparable to the transformations documented for the Kachin of Burma (Friedman 1975; Leach 1954), the Awak of Micronesia (Petersen 1982), and the Hopi of Arizona (Cameron 1991b; Whiteley 1988).

Among the Kachin, groups oscillate between *gumlao* (stratified) and *gumsa* (egalitarian) forms of social organization. These shifts occur in association with fission events and result in changes in settlement distribution. In *gumlao* phases settlements are clustered and in *gumsa* phases they are dispersed. The transformation occurs when swidden gardens are cultivated to the point of degradation and populations can no longer be supported by them (Friedman 1975). This shift from clustered to dispersed settlement is documented for the coastal communities of Portugal.

The fission events documented for the Awak of Ponape, Micronesia, also bear a resemblance to the Portuguese case (Petersen 1982). Population levels for the Awak, who cultivate yam, taro, fruits, and other vegetables, reached a central point in 1975. At that time, they numbered 700 individuals inhabiting an area of 2.5 sq km. Fission occurred, and the group split into two factions, the Upper and Lower Awak; in 1979, the Upper Awak group splintered into two groups. Both splits resulted in population movement and the establishment of new settlements. Population factors were cited by the Awak as one cause for the splits. As populations grew, males perceived less chance for themselves to be promoted (Petersen 1982:22). In addition, the larger population made effective leadership more difficult; as one section chief stated: "one man cannot rule a thousand" (Petersen 1982:22). Other reasons that were recognized as factors were the unequal production of crops displayed at competitive feasts and envy resulting from that. In 1975, the people of Lower Awak had become more wealthy than those of Upper Awak; their land was more productive and they outdid the Upper Awak at competitive feasts.

The Awak example has important implications for the Portuguese case. It suggests that those coastal Portuguese groups who could not compete effectively in feasting or gift-giving, which would be comparable to the situation of the less well-off Upper Awak, may have initiated the fission events. Such a proposition would be testable by comparing the abandonment dates for settlements with differing accumulations of prestige goods, such as schist plaques and ground stone tools. One would expect the earliest abandonment among those sites with lower quantities of such prestige goods.

The Oraibi Hopi of northeastern Arizona underwent a dramatic fission event in 1906 which led to the establishment of new settlements at Hotevilla and Bacavi. There are many interpretations of the Oraibi split (Whiteley 1988). Generally, it has been viewed as the consequence of disagreements over positions toward the US government, although the Oraibi themselves say that the split was prophesied as a way of dealing with overpopulation, water scarcity, and the depletion of arable land. The importance of this split in relation to the Portuguese case is that in the Oraibi split the role of religious specialists was eliminated and, thus, the social hierarchy conflated. In a statement of an older Hotevilla male, this process was described:

> Those claiming authority in Hotevilla, or anywhere else on Third Mesa, by their religious offices, don't really have it. Everyone nowadays is just a commoner; the religious leaders who led the people to Hotevilla lost all their authority the moment they turned to go back to Oraibi ... [T]he split itself involved making everyone equal as commoners, so there were no chiefs who would be superior to anyone else. (Whiteley 1988:258)

Although the archaeological evidence for the Early Bronze Age of Portugal is poor, what is known suggests a marked decline in consumption of prestige goods and ritual activity associated with burials, and an overall decrease in the variability of settlement size and structure.

The abandonments in the periphery of the lowlands, as mentioned above, do not reveal such marked changes as in the center. In fact, the archaeological record suggests more continuity in the interior between the Copper and Bronze Ages in terms of settlement and burial occupation

and artifact types (Lillios 1991). It is unlikely that events as dramatic as those described for the Awak and Hopi fissions led to the settlement changes that have been documented. Most probably, they represent the shifts in alliances and exchange networks resulting from the fissions in the center.

Discussion

Based on the archaeological, paleobotanical, and ethnographic data, the following model for regional abandonment in the Portuguese lowlands can be proposed.

- Lowland communities, beginning in the Neolithic and throughout the Copper Age, required ground stone tools to fill their fields, cut trees, and work wood. The raw material for these tools was amphibolite, the nearest source of which was in the interior of Portugal.
- Although communities on the coast enjoyed the benefits of a rich and diverse subsistence base, they were more dependent on reliable exchange partners to obtain ground stone than groups in the interior, who lived closer to the source of the amphibolite.
- As a way of engaging these resources, competitive feasts (with offerings of wild game, seafood, agricultural produce) were given. Women may also have been a medium of exchange. This feasting would have been most pronounced in those areas furthest from the amphibolite sources, that is, in the center.
- This feasting increased in intensity; possible evidence for the intensification of feasting behavior is the sharp rise in wild fauna (e.g. deer) at some Late Copper Age sites of the center (e.g. Vila Nova de São Pedro).
- The environment of the lowlands, particularly along the coast, became degraded as a consequence of this intensification.
- Coastal groups whose land quality was declining were not able to engage in exchange alliances, and may have felt envious of their more wealthy neighbors (as in the Awak case). As a result, they abandoned their settlements and moved.
- Shifts in regional exchange alliances, initiated by the center, led to some abandonment in the periphery.

Conclusion

Attempts to explain regional abandonment in the archaeological record tend to be too simplistic in not addressing intra-regional variability, both in the evidence prior to the abandonment process and the evolutionary trajectories after the abandonment. Center–periphery relations provide a means of analyzing the dynamics between prehistoric communities within a region which, although not necessarily existing in a state of interdependence, were certainly affected by non-local events. Testing center–periphery models in the archaeological record requires fine-grained chronological understanding of settlement abandonment in a region. While this is currently not possible for the later prehistory of Portugal, detailed and accurate settlement histories do appear attainable for the prehistoric Southwest (see Schlanger and Wilshusen, and Fish and Fish, this volume).

Regional settlement abandonment is often correlated with a phase of social fragmentation or fission, as it is in the Portuguese case. As such, a better understanding of the mechanisms involved in regional abandonment is necessary in order to refine archaeological modeling of social devolution in general. Explanations for these processes remain in an immature phase of prime-mover models; only when the multivariate factors involved in these processes are recognized can archaeologists do justice to the complexity of past human behavior.

Acknowledgments
I would like to thank the editors, Catherine Cameron and Steve Tomka, for their insightful comments and suggestions. I am especially grateful to Antonio Gilman and Philip Kohl for their critical reading of drafts of this paper.

References

Åberg, N.
  1921 *La Civilisation enéolithique dans la péninsule ibérique*. Vilhelm Ekmans Universitetsfond, Uppsala.
Apolinário, M.
  1896 Necrópole neolítico do Valle de São Martinho. *O Arqueólogo Português* 2:210–21.
Arnaud, J. M.
  1974–7 Escavações no Penedo de Lexim. *O Arqueólogo Português* 7–9:398–406.
Arnaud, J. M., L. V. Salgado de Oliveira, and V. O. Jorge
  1971 O povoado fortificado neo- e eneolítico do Penedo de Lexim (Mafra). *O Arqueólogo Português* 5:97–138.
Arnaud, J. M. and T. Gamito
  1972 O povoado fortificado neo- e eneolítico da Serra das Baútas. *O Arqueólogo Português* 6:119–62.
Best, E.
  1912 *The Stone Implements of the Maori*. New Zealand Dominion Museum. Bulletin No. 4, Wellington.

Cameron, C.
  1991a Structure Abandonment in Villages. In *Archaeological Method and Theory*, edited by M. B. Schiffer, Vol. III, pp. 155–94. University of Arizona Press, Tucson.
  1991b The Relationship of Residential Patterns to the Oraibi Split. Unpublished paper presented at Society for American Archaeology meeting, New Orleans, 1991.
Cardoso, J. L.
  1982 *O Castro de Leceia*. Câmara Municipal de Oeiras, Oeiras.
  1989 *Leceia: Resultados das Escavações Realizadas 1983–1988*. Câmara Municipal de Oeiras, Oeiras.
Cartailhac, E.
  1886 *Les Ages préhistoriques de L'Espagne et du Portugal*. C. Reinwald, Paris.
Chagnon, N.
  1968 Yanomamö Social Organization and Warfare. In *War: The Anthropology of Armed Conflict and Aggression*, edited by M. Fried, M. Harris, and R. Murphy, pp. 109–59. The Natural History Press, New York.
  1979 Mate Competition, Favoring Close Kin, and Village Fissioning among the Yanomamo Indians. In *Evolutionary Biology and Human Social Behavior*, edited by N. Chagnon and W. Irons, pp. 86–132. Duxbury Press, North Scituate, MA.
Champion, T. C. (ed.)
  1989 *Centre and Periphery*. Unwin Hyman, London.
Chapman, R.
  1982 Autonomy, Ranking, and Resources in Iberian Prehistory. In *Ranking, Resources, and Exchange: Aspects of the Archaeology of Early European Society*, edited by A. C. Renfrew and S. T. Shennan, pp. 46–51. Cambridge University Press, Cambridge.
  1990 *Emerging Complexity: The Later Prehistory of South-East Spain, Iberia and the West Mediterranean*. Cambridge University Press, Cambridge.
Chapman, R., V. Lull, M. Picazo, and M. E. Sanahuja
  1987 *Proyecto Gatas I. La Prospección Arqueoecológica*, BAR Int. Series 348, Oxford.
Chase-Dunn, C. and T. D. Hall (eds.)
  1991 *Core/Periphery Relations in Precapitalist Worlds*. Westview Press, Boulder, CO.
Correia, S. H.
  1980 Povoados calcolíticos da estremadura portuguesa: tentativa de abordagem economica. *Arqueologia* 2:24–9.

Costa, A. J. M. da
1907 Estações préhistóricas dos arredores de Setúbal. *O Arqueólogo Português* 12:206–17.

Déchelette, J.
1908 Essai sur la chronologie préhistorique de la péninsule ibérique. *Revue Archéologique* 12:219–65.

Eckholm, K.
1980 On the Limitations of Civilization: The Structure and Dynamics of Global Systems. *Dialectical Anthropology* 5:155–66.

Eckholm, K. and J. Friedman
1982 "Capital" Imperialism and Exploitation in the Ancient World-Systems. *Review* 6:87–110.

Friedman, J.
1975 Tribes, States, and Transformations. In *Marxist Analyses and Social Anthropology*, edited by M. Bloch, pp. 161–202. Malaby Press, London.

Gilman, A.
1987 Unequal Development in Copper Age Iberia. In *Specialization, Exchange, and Complex Societies*, edited by E. M. Brumfiel and T. K. Earle, pp. 22–9. Cambridge University Press, Cambridge.

Gulliver, P. H.
1977 *Networks and Factions: Two Ndenduli Communities. A House Divided.* Social and Economic Papers, No. 9, Memorial Institute of Newfoundland.

Harrison, R. J.
1974 A Reconsideration of the Iberian Background to Beaker Metallurgy. *Palaeohistoria* 16:63–105.
1977 *The Bell Beaker Cultures of Spain and Portugal.* American School of Prehistoric Research, Bulletin 35, Peabody Museum, Harvard.

Jalhay, E. and A. do Paço
1945 El castro de Vilanova de San Pedro. *Actas y Memórias de la Sociedad Española de Antropologia, Etnográfia, y Préhistória, Madrid, 1945* 20:5–91.

Kristiansen, K.
1987 Center and Periphery in Bronze Age Scandinavia. In *Centre and Periphery in the Ancient World*, edited by M. Rowlands, M. Larsen, and K. Kristiansen, pp. 74–85. Cambridge University Press, Cambridge.

Leach, E. R.
1954 *Political Systems of Highland Burma.* G. Bell and Sons Ltd, London.

Leewaarden, W. van and C. R. Janssen
1985 A Preliminary Palynological Study of Peat Deposits near an Oppidum in the Lower Tagus Valley, Portugal. *I Reunião do Quaternário Ibérico, Lisbon, 1985*, Vol. II, pp. 225–36.

Leisner, V. and H. Schubart
1966 Die Kupferzeitlich Befestigung Pedra do Ouro. *Madrider Mitteilungen* 7:9–60.

Lillios, K. T.
1991 Competition to Fission: The Copper to Bronze Age Transition in the Lowlands of West-Central Portugal (3000–1500 BC). PhD thesis, Yale University.

Lines Escardó, A.
1970 The Climate of the Iberian Peninsula. In *Climates of Northern and Western Europe*, edited by C. C. Wallén, pp. 192–239. Elsevier, Amsterdam.

Oosterbeck, L. and A. R. Cruz
In press O Rio Nabão ha 4000 anos: o povoado da Fonte Quente e o mais antigo povoamento no vale do Nabão. *Boletin Cultural da Câmara Municipal de Tomar.*

Paço, A. do
1947 Castro de Vila Nova de São Pedro. *Arqueologia e Historia* 3:31–80.
1939[1970] A póvoa eneolítica de Vila Nova de S. Pedro. *Trabalhos de Arqueologia de Afonso do Paço*, Vol. I, pp. 229–74.
1942[1970] A póvoa eneolítica de Vila Nova de S. Pedro. *Trabalhos de Arqueologia de Afonso do Paço*, Vol. I, pp. 275–306.

Paço, A. do, M. Vaultier, and G. Zbyszewski
1947 Gruta da nascente do Rio Almonda. *Trabalhos de Antropologia e Etnologia* 11:171–87.

Peregrine, P.
1991 Prehistoric Chiefdoms on the American Midcontinent: A World System Based on Prestige Goods. In *Core/Periphery Relations in Precapitalist Worlds*, edited by C. Chase-Dunn and T. Hall, pp. 193–211. Westview Press, Boulder, CO.

Petersen, G.
1982 *One Man Cannot Rule a Thousand: Fission in a Ponapean Chiefdom.* University of Michigan Press, Ann Arbor.

Renfrew, C.
1977 Alternative Models for Exchange and Spatial Distribution. In *Exchange Systems in Prehistory*, edited by T. K. Earle and J. E. Ericson, pp. 71–90. Academic Press, New York.

Ribeiro, C.
1878 *Noticias de algunos estações e monumentos préhistóricos.* Academia Real das Ciências, Lisbon.

Rowlands, M., M. Larsen, and K. Kristiansen (eds.)
1987 *Centre and Periphery in the Ancient World.* Cambridge University Press, Cambridge.

Sangmeister, E. and H. Schubart
  1981 *Zambujal. Die Grabungen 1964 bis 1973.* Phillip von Zabern, Mainz am Rhein.
Santos, M. F. dos
  1980 Estudos de pré-história em Portugal de 1850 a 1880. *Anais* 26:253–97.
Savory, H. H.
  1968 *Spain and Portugal.* Thames and Hudson, London.
Schneider, J.
  1977 Was There a Precapitalist World-System? *Peasant Studies* 6:20–9.
Schüle, W. and M. Pellicer
  1966 *El Cerro de la Virgen, Orce (Granada) I.* Excavaciones Arqueológicas en España 46, Madrid.
Silva, C. T. da
  1966–7 O povoado pré-histórico da Rotura. *Arquivo de Beja* 23–4:164–72.
  1968–9 O povoado pré-histórico da Rotura. Vestigios de estratigrafia. *Arquivo de Beja* 25–7:31–56.
Silva, C. T. da and J. Soares
  1981 *Pré-historia da Area de Sines.* Gabinete da Area de Sines, Sines.
  1985 Monte da Tumba (Torrão): eine befestigte Siedlung der Kupferzeit im Baixo Alentejo (Portugal). *Madrider Mitteilungen* 26:1–21.

  1987 O povoado fortificado calcolítico do Monte da Tumba. *Setúbal Arqueológica* 8:29–79.
Simões, A. F.
  1878 *Introducção á Archeologia da Peninsula Iberica.* Lisbon.
Siret, H. and L. Siret
  1887 *Les Premiers âges du metal dans le sud-est de l'Espagne.* Alvum et Texte, Anvers.
Spindler, K.
  1981 *Cova da Moura.* Madrider Beiträge 7.
Spindler, K. and L. Trindade
  1969 A pôvoa eneolítica do Penedo-Torres Vedras. *Actas das Ias Jornadas Arqueológicas, Lisboa,* Vol. II, pp. 57–192.
Stephenson, K.
  1990 The Emergence of Virtual Groups. *Ethnology* 29:279–96.
Wallerstein, I.
  1974 *The Modern World-System,* Vol. I. Academic Press, New York.
Whiteley, P. M.
  1988 *Deliberate Acts.* University of Arizona Press, Tucson.

PART IV

Abandonment processes within sites: ethnoarchaeological cases

10
Abandonment at Zuni farming villages

NAN A. ROTHSCHILD, BARBARA
J. MILLS, T. J. FERGUSON, and
SUSAN DUBLIN

Introduction

The pueblo of Zuni, in western New Mexico, is currently the major year-round residence of most of the Zuni people. Within 30 miles of Zuni is a series of small villages (Fig. 10.1), called Ojo Caliente, Tekapo, Pescado, and Nutria, the latter two being divided by some residents into Upper and Lower segments. Until about fifty years ago these villages were occupied on a seasonal basis by many of the Zuni while they farmed or herded sheep. Today almost no one lives in them.

Portions of at least two of the villages were built on top of prehistoric sites dating to the fourteenth century (Kintigh 1985:45, 53–4). The historic occupation for several of the villages dates to the mid-nineteenth century, and for most of them their population peaked around the end of the nineteenth century. The total population of Zuni at that time was 1600, of which about 1400 were associated with one of the farming villages. According to a census taken by Frank Hamilton Cushing, 473 used Nutria, 580 used Pescado, and 440 used Ojo Caliente (Ferguson 1985:58–9; Mills and Ferguson 1980:1). Although they are now mostly not occupied each village has one or two resident families, and there is some occasional transient use of the houses by sheepherders. This lack of use is the product of environmental and cultural changes that made agriculture difficult or impossible on the nearby farmlands and altered patterns of land tenure. The water table has been lowered because of dam construction and local water sources have dried up. There has been major soil erosion, resulting from clear-cutting of the adjacent National

Forest land by the federal government (Ferguson 1989:89–107; Hart 1991:2–6).

The Zuni economy changed from one based on agriculture (both for subsistence and for market) and herding at the beginning of the twentieth century, to one in which silversmithing, wage labor, and welfare are the mainstays, while the pursuit of subsistence agriculture has declined. The agriculture practiced today is often directed toward alfalfa production for fodder (Ferguson 1985:136; Holmes and Fowler 1980:211), and since trucks have become widely used those who do farm can commute to their farms on a daily basis. In spite of the fact that neither farming nor herding, at present, require constant use of the structures at these villages, the buildings and the villages themselves continue to be used in a number of less intense ways.

The farming village study

In 1979, Barbara Mills and T. J. Ferguson began a study[1] of the so-called abandoned farming villages (Mills, Holmes, and Ferguson 1982). This project recorded the traditional architecture of the villages in great detail, and documented the presence of features around houses as well as artifacts that lay on the ground surface. The recording system described walls, roofs, apertures, masonry style, and the size of the structural elements (adobe or stone); it has since been incorporated into the recording system used by the Zuni Archaeology Program. In 1989, Susan Dublin and Nan Rothschild began a second study of the unrecorded villages, using the same system of documentation. Also surveyed

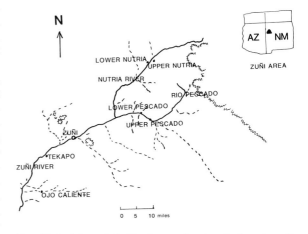

Fig. 10.1 Map of the Zuni area showing the location of the farming villages and Zuni pueblo.

during the second season was a 50 percent sample of those structures examined during the earlier study to see what kinds of changes had taken place in them. These investigations have, therefore, completely recorded all structures in the farming villages. Descriptions and photographs are available for twenty structures spanning a ten-year interval. In addition to the collection of architectural and artifactual data, in 1989 a number of former residents of the farming villages were interviewed about when and why they left them.

We will present the preliminary results of these studies in this paper as a means of discussing the concept of abandonment, since most observers would describe the Zuni farming villages as abandoned. First we will discuss the meaning of the term and its physical signs, some of which are accessible to the archaeologist. We will consider two specific ways to examine the material manifestations of "abandonment." One focuses on architectural consequences of the lack of use seen in longitudinal perspective; in the other we analyze the distribution of certain classes of artifacts that have been deposited or accumulated both inside and outside houses on the ground.

Abandonment

Archaeology focuses on "abandoned" places for the most part; these are abandoned in the sense that they have fallen out of use some time ago. In defining the term it is minimally clear that there is more than one type (Cordell 1984), and that some of what appears as abandonment may be related to a life-cycle stage. According to the *Oxford Universal Dictionary* (1933:2), the word means: "To cease to hold, use or practise; to give up or renounce; to give up to the control of another; to desert, leave without help." For us the key concept here is the idea of leaving or giving up something with no thought of returning to it. Also implicit in discussions of abandonment is the idea that the full-time use of a structure as a residence or work-place is the only use that counts.

As archaeologists we are familiar with this term; it is discussed particularly in areas like the American Southwest, or the Maya region where some degree of population aggregation usually preceded what is described as the abandonment of settlements. In these settings there is often an element of mystery connected to this change in the residential status of a site, and questions are raised about why the inhabitants left and where they went. Explanations usually invoke factors such as climatic alteration, warfare, and disease as agents of change.

A number of archaeologists have recently begun to discuss several types of abandonment, including a seasonal variant, in the prehistoric Southwest and elsewhere (Graham and Roberts 1986), as a long-standing behavior pattern. Our goal in this paper is to refine the concept by examining it in the present, describe a number of use and abandonment states, and identify some material expressions of these states in architectural condition and artifact patterns. We are taking an ethnoarchaeological approach, and are also concerned with understanding how the archaeological record is created. We note that changes in the way in which a settlement is used are part of the normal life-cycle of a settlement and may be reversed. The concept of abandonment appears to mask a number of behaviors related to changing use of rooms, structures, and places.

In Zuni we can answer questions about why residents left and where they went. They left first because of the federal government's policy of relocation and consolidation of farming at Zuni Pueblo in the early twentieth century (Chavez, nd; Ferguson 1985:105), and subsequently because they could no longer support themselves by farming the land, owing to degradation of the landscape and surface hydrology. During the second episode of "abandonment," Zunis left when the people who had farmed the land (the grandparents) died, and when many of the young men who might have continued trying to farm entered the military in the 1940s. For the most part, those who were left in the farming villages on a seasonal basis simply stopped moving to the villages for the summer and stayed in the main pueblo all year round. During the forty or fifty-year interval since the last episode of residential abandonment, the Zunis have not moved back to the farming villages in spite of a housing shortage which reoccupation of these structures could alleviate. The exception is the village of (Upper) Pescado which showed some renewed occupation after paved roads and utilities were installed. (In the summer of 1990 there was increased evidence of new inhabitants in that village; one new [cinder block] house was being built and major renovations on one old structure were begun.) However, while some of the older Zunis complain of the crowding, noise, and social problems in the densely settled town, the amenities of life in the main pueblo (electricity, water and sewer plumbing, cable television, and so on) are very attractive, particularly to the younger members of the tribe.

In this paper we suggest that the fact that owners of the houses in the farming villages no longer live in them does not mean that these houses are abandoned. This idea is supported by most previous occupants who, when asked whether they thought they had left these communities "for good," said that they had not. We think that the buildings in the farming villages continue to be used, but in ways that differ from their earlier use as residences. It might be more appropriate to consider the varieties of use of a structure as arrayed along a continuum.

At one end of this continuum is the status of full-time use, and at the other end is total and permanent lack of use, or abandonment, with the implication that none of the present owners or their descendants will return to the structure or the land on which it sits. In between use-states involve: (1) use for part-time living; (2) use as a place where tools, seeds, or other materials, are stored; (3) use as a source of raw materials for the construction of a new house; (4) use as a temporary dump site, especially if some of the house walls are down. And finally (5), even when the structure is not used in any of the first four ways it may serve as a very important marker of a claim to a piece of land. A man at Ojo Caliente told Barbara Mills that if at least three courses of masonry remained from a structure it was not considered by the Zuni people as residentially abandoned, that is, the land on which the house stood was not seen as available for others to build on.

There are specific physical manifestations of some of these states. For example, house exteriors that show maintenance attempts in continuing applications of plaster (Fig. 10.2), or repairs such as patches incorporating sherds or spalls (Fig. 10.3), suggest that the structure is still being used consistently. Other types of maintenance such as yard sweeping also imply use. Boarding up of windows or doors implies only intermittent use, or use for storage, but this form of maintenance implies the

Fig. 10.3   A close-up view of a house at Lower Nutria showing plaster and spalls.

Fig. 10.4   An Ojo Caliente house with boarded windows.

Fig. 10.2   An Ojo Caliente house with a fresh coat of plaster.

Fig. 10.5   Corrugated metal covering a doorway at Upper Nutria.

Fig. 10.6   *An Upper Nutria house with a vertical crack in one of its stone walls.*

Fig. 10.7   *A house at Ojo Caliente showing the erosion of a portion of the wall adjacent to the doorframe.*

Fig. 10.8   *Close-up of an eroding wall adjacent to a window frame in Ojo Caliente.*

possibility of future use (Figs. 10.4, 10.5). A missing roof, broken windows or door, or partial walls means that neither occupation nor storage is a present function of this structure, while use as a dump site or as a raw material source is usually quite evident from the exterior. Evidence of the present frequency of use of a building can be seen from its interior: the presence or absence of curtains, canned or other food on shelves or tables, clothing, and bed linens all attest to more or less recent use.

Once a structure is not being occupied or maintained, certain processes of destruction begin. One of the goals of the present research is the understanding of these processes, which seem to follow from the failure to continue to maintain fresh plaster at least every six to twelve months. Subsequent to this, cracks appear in the exterior walls, sections of adobe or stone masonry move or break off (Fig. 10.6), doors and window frames shift, and roofs collapse. We hope to understand the sequence of these events and their timing.

The major areas of difficulty seem to be at the interface of two different building materials (Figs. 10.7, 10.8), or two building episodes (Fig. 10.9). Sources of building stress may come from topography (it is hard to build a

Fig. 10.9   *An Ojo Caliente house in which a separation is developing between the two rooms of the house.*

Fig. 10.11   *Upper Nutria, the same wall of Locus 20, 1989.*

stable house on a hill), from weather (walls facing prevailing winter weather may erode more rapidly than others, and drastic temperature changes have a destructive effect), from the chemical composition of the mud (especially salt content), or from water seeping up from the ground (not as great a problem in Zuni's semidesert environment as in other places). A number of recent studies of mud brick architecture have outlined the influence of these and other variables on the longevity of this type of architecture (Bultnick 1968–9; Carter and Pagliero 1966; McIntosh 1974; Seeden 1982).

A series of structures photographed in both 1979 and

Fig. 10.12   *Upper Nutria, Locus 15, in 1979.*

Fig. 10.10   *Upper Nutria, Locus 20, in 1979.*

Fig. 10.13   *Upper Nutria, the same wall of Locus 15, in 1989.*

Fig. 10.14   *Ojo Caliente, Locus 16, in 1979.*

Fig. 10.17   *Ojo Caliente, the same wall of Locus 11, in 1989.*

Fig. 10.15   *Ojo Caliente, the same view of Locus 16, in 1989.*

1989 is seen in Figs. 10.10–10.17. We may observe a variety of changes in these four houses that are rather typical of the range of states seen in the larger sample. Figs. 10.10 and 10.11 show the east wall of a house in Upper Nutria in which a crack has developed when the plaster is no longer maintained as a coating on the wall. Figs. 10.12 and 10.13 show the collapse of a segment of the roof and east wall of another Upper Nutria house, this one made of stone in a rather atypical Zuni style. It should be noted that adobe and stone walls crack very differently; in walls constructed from the former material, a stepped crack tends to form, while stone walls break by means of a more vertical crack. The most dramatic type of change is seen in the next two photographs (Figs. 10.14 and 10.15), wherein the intact, maintained, and apparently occupied house in Ojo Caliente has completely collapsed between 1979 and 1989. Not all change observed during the ten-year interval represents deterioration. Figs. 10.16 and 10.17 show an improvement in the condition of this Ojo Caliente house, brought about by the patching and plastering seen on its west-facing wall.

The "abandonment" of artifacts

A great variety of objects are found scattered around the houses and corrals in the farming villages. These objects show wide variation in function, size, and completeness. Artifact types range from pop-tops and broken glass to stoves and refrigerators (Fig. 10.18), bed springs, and harrows. As many as 250 separate artifact types were recorded in the field. In this section we discuss some of the patterning in material culture at

Fig. 10.16   *Ojo Caliente, Locus 11, in 1979.*

Fig. 10.18   An old stove left outside a house in lower Nutria.

Table 10.1 *Artifact classes recorded inside uninhabited rooms by village.*

| Artifact class | VILLAGE | | | |
	Ojo Caliente (%)	Upper Nutria (%)	Total (%)	N
Subsistence	0.0	0.4	0.2	1
Foodstuffs	39.0	5.6	20.3	103
Indulgences	6.7	2.5	4.3	22
Personal effects	1.8	0.4	1.0	5
Domestic routine	13.0	11.2	12.0	61
Household equipment	6.3	35.4	22.6	115
Construction and maintenance	31.4	43.9	38.4	195
Transportation	1.8	0.7	1.2	6
TOTAL	100.0	100.0	100.0	
N	223	285		508
N OF ROOMS	15	19	34	

the farming villages, using data from both the 1979 and 1989 field seasons.

Since so many different artifact types were recorded in surface collections at the farming villages, we reclassified the observed objects in a classification scheme originally developed for historic artifacts at Navajo sites (Ward, Abbink, and Stein 1977). This scheme has also been applied to the analysis of historic artifacts from Zuni Pueblo (Ferguson and Mills 1982). The classification system consists of eleven major artifact categories: (1) subsistence (i.e. weapons, tools for farming and animal husbandry); (2) foodstuffs (food items or food containers); (3) indulgences (alcohol and soda containers); (4) medicinal (nothing in this category was found); (5) personal effects; (6) domestic routine (food preparation, serving, storage, and cleaning); (7) household equipment (especially furniture); (8) recreation and play; (9) construction and maintenance (tools, hardware, materials); (10) transportation (equestrian and automotive); (11) unidentified objects (unidentified bottle glass and fragments of other materials).

We use these artifact classes to address three questions important for archaeological interpretation of abandonment behavior:

(1) What artifact classes are found inside "abandoned", or uninhabited, rooms?
(2) What artifact classes are found outside structures that represent different stages of abandonment?
(3) What are the spatial patterns of artifact discard around structures at the farming villages?

The first two will be addressed using data from the 1979 season; the last will use data from 1989.

During the 1979 season, all artifacts inside uninhabited rooms were recorded at the villages of Ojo Caliente and Upper Nutria. Rooms were defined as uninhabited (or "abandoned") if they were no longer water tight; that is, they lacked window glass or doors, or their roofs had holes. This definition does not necessarily imply relinquishment of rights over the structures or the area around the structure, but does provide a measure of the structure's current status. Maintained rooms were identified in the field as structures with intact roofs and fenestration; occupied rooms are the same as maintained rooms except that they were occupied at the time of field recording for more than day-time use.

The relative frequency of artifact classes within thirty-four uninhabited rooms at Ojo Caliente and Upper Nutria is shown in Table 10.1. Category 11 was not included in the analysis here since there were so many items, and they were of limited interpretative utility for these research questions. The largest category consists of objects classified as construction or maintenance items. This result is not surprising since the class includes window frames, window glass, doors, and various pieces of hardware, and some of these would accumulate as the structure fell further and further into disrepair.

Following construction and maintenance items, two other artifact classes were also well represented in uninhabited rooms: foodstuffs and household equipment. Foodstuffs, especially empty food containers, were more

Table 10.2. *Room condition by village.*

Village	Occupied (%)	Room condition Maintained (%)	Uninhabited (%)	Total (%)	N
Ojo Caliente	15.7	28.9	55.4	100.0	83
Upper Nutria	2.6	33.3	64.1	100.0	39
Tekapo	0.0	26.3	73.7	100.0	19
TOTAL	9.9	29.8	60.3	100.0	
N	14	42	85		141

numerous in uninhabited rooms at Ojo Caliente than at Upper Nutria. These empty cans appear to be items of secondary discard, unrelated to consumption patterns within the structure before it fell into disrepair. By contrast, more household equipment was recorded in Upper Nutria uninhabited rooms (35.4 percent) than in Ojo Caliente rooms (only 6.3 percent). Aside from these differences, most other artifact classes are found in similar small percentages in uninhabited rooms at both villages.

The differences between the two villages in both the amount of household equipment and the amount of secondary refuse of food containers may be related to one major factor: the relative number of still-occupied or maintained structures at the two villages. In 1979, many more rooms were occupied or maintained at Ojo Caliente than at Upper Nutria (Table 10.2). Uninhabited rooms at Ojo Caliente appear to have been used for secondary refuse disposal by those still living in the village. At Upper Nutria only one room was occupied, by one person, and the amount of trash disposal was commensurately less.

The different pattern in proportions of household items may also be related to differences in occupancy rate. Here we suggest that reclamation processes (Schiffer 1987:99–120) are at work. Household items have relatively high salvage value and are more likely to be scavenged than, for example, the empty tin cans that make up the majority of items in the foodstuff class. Since more people were living in Ojo Caliente, more usable items were salvaged from uninhabited rooms at this village than at Upper Nutria.

The second question we address with the farming village artifact data is whether there are also differences among the artifact classes present outside of structures that may be related to different stages in structure aban-

donment. This analysis is more complex than that of interior artifacts because it is impossible to relate artifacts outside of rooms directly to particular rooms within roomblocks, and a single roomblock may contain occupied, maintained, and uninhabited rooms within it. For this analysis we grouped the exterior artifacts by loci. A locus is a spatially distinct room or set of rooms with surrounding activity areas that are generally owned and used by one extended family. In addition to occupied, maintained, and uninhabited loci, we also used two composite "conditions" of occupied/uninhabited and maintained/uninhabited so that we could incorporate those loci with more than one type of room condition.

The proportions of different artifact classes by locus condition (Table 10.3) highlight the complexity of the formation processes at the farming villages. Some artifact classes vary widely among the different locus types. For example, objects associated with construction and maintenance functions are relatively rare outside uninhabited loci, but are five times as common at loci with both uninhabited and occupied rooms. Some of these high percentages are the result of stockpiling behavior as residents dismantle unsafe structures next to ones still occupied.

Another artifact class whose occurrence varies widely among locus types is foodstuffs. About 50 percent of the artifacts surrounding loci identified as either occupied or uninhabited are foodstuffs, while this artifact class accounts for only 25 percent of the artifacts around loci that are recorded as both occupied/uninhabited. It seems likely that the pattern of using uninhabited room interiors for secondary refuse disposal is contributing to the lower percentages of foodstuffs outside of these latter loci.

What kinds of artifacts do we find outside of occupied loci that are not as well represented outside maintained or uninhabited loci? Two artifact classes stand out: personal effects and transportation items. Artifacts that are less well represented outside occupied structures include indulgences (largely because of social proscriptions), and objects of domestic routine. In the latter case we suspect that most of these items would be kept inside if usable, or placed into trash heaps if broken. Uninhabited structures offer a striking contrast with reference to items of domestic routine; they were the second most common class recorded, consisting primarily of storage containers of metal or glass that were apparently not worth scavenging.

The third type of artifact analysis was conducted with the 1989 data, and analyzes the spatial distribution of artifacts on the surface outside the houses in the villages

Table 10.3. *Table of exterior artifacts by locus condition.*

Artifact class	Occupied (%)	Maintained (%)	Unin-habited (%)	Occ./Unin. (%)	Main./Unin. (%)	Total (%)	N
				Locus condition			
Subsistence	2.9	6.2	2.2	6.9	1.9	3.1	78
Foodstuffs	49.7	33.5	51.5	24.6	41.4	42.8	1095
Indulgences	7.6	2.56	1.58	12.1	21.9	18.0	459
Personal effects	5.3	0.4	0.7	1.0	1.4	1.3	32
Domestic routine	5.9	16.5	20.0	14.8	14.7	16.2	415
Household equipment	6.4	5.4	2.9	7.2	7.4	5.5	141
Recreation	0.6	0	0	0	0.1	0.1	2
Construction and maintenance	17.5	11.2	6.1	32.5	9.5	11.7	299
Transportation	4.1	1.2	0.9	1.0	1.6	1.4	36
TOTAL	100.0	100.0	100.1	100.1	99.9	100.1	
N	171	242	923	305	916		2257
N OF LOCI	2	7	18	3	10		40

of Lower and Upper Pescado and Lower Nutria. We recorded the location of artifacts (classified in the same system) around houses in 5 m intervals from each house wall; at house corners, objects were located in quarter-circles from the adjacent corner, again in 5 m units. In analyzing the distribution of artifacts we began with the functional classification and looked at: (a) the distance of artifacts from the structure, and (b) whether they lay along a wall of the house that contains a door or a wall without a door, since behavior occurring near doors seems different than that away from them (Rothschild 1991).

In order to analyze these distributions we must recognize the existence of several dimensions of variability. The first is functional; the presence of identifiable artifacts related to specific activities will allow us in some cases to ascertain where the activities occurred around a house. These include outdoor cooking and baking, storage, and certain manufacturing and repair activities. A second dimension is structured by taphonomic processes affecting deposition and re-deposition. An aspect or subdimension of taphonomy relates to object size and the likelihood of displacement of small things from their primary use or discard area.

We have also tried to reconstruct the series of events that led to their recovery in the archaeological record. Following Schiffer (1976; 1987), we have identified a number of separate but overlapping trajectories resulting in the deposition of these items, some of which relate to artifact size.

(1) The first state results in the accumulation of objects remaining in primary use context from activities conducted outdoors. These are likely to date from the period when the houses were occupied, or when they were used sporadically.

(2) A second group represents stockpiling, the creation of piles of reusable materials. One type includes building stone or beams. These are usually composed of one type of material, but may be located in several piles near a house. A related phenomenon is the "storing" of large, whole, potentially usable items such as refrigerators and stoves or agricultural equipment. They are left because they are no longer needed (agricultural implements when a family is no longer farming, or a stove that has been replaced by a newer one), or because they are hard to move, or because it is anticipated that they may be useful in the future. One type of large object, bed parts (springs, frames, and headboards) is recycled into fence parts and gates (Fig. 10.19).

(3) A third group is remains from primary discard, disposal or dumping. In many cases this results in a cluster of one type of material or object, although there does seem to be a tendency, once a dump exists, to add other items, sometimes of a different type, to it. Objects in a dump (especially personal ones) may sometimes be burned because people fear others' taking their belongings for malevolent purposes.

(4) The act of clearing up an area – discarding "trash" and sweeping the yard – will displace several kinds of

Fig. 10.19   A view of a fence with a bed head-board used as a gate, from Lower Pescado.

items, particularly small and broken (or no longer functional) things. It will primarily affect material along the front wall of the house, often creating a cleared "arc" around the door, and it will occur during the period of the structure's occupation or intense use.

(5) The last situation involves a related process in which there is scattered discard or loss, again of small or no longer useful objects. This process may scatter artifacts according to their last use, or depending on the scattering agent (the wind, dogs, etc.), may appear more random. This process will continue after the house is no longer used and is the most difficult to model.

Artifact patterning

The artifact analysis, while preliminary, reveals a number of interesting patterns that will be taken as hypotheses for further investigation. We will discuss these in light of the five types of trajectories just outlined. First, we should note that very few, if any, items remain in their original use context. A few things relating to outdoor cooking fit this category. Several other artifacts have been recycled and have been left where they were used in this second use context (55 gallon drums for storage and old washing machine tubs used to preserve corn are good examples).

Stockpiling of architectural materials occurs all around houses and is not found at any characteristic distance nor in particular relation to the presence or absence of a door. A number of large discarded objects, although few in number, show some of the clearest spatial patterning of all artifacts examined. Old kitchen appliances are found in or close to houses (Table 10.4),

and old agricultural implements are left close to fences, or near barns or outbuildings. The latter objects decline in frequency with distance from the house, and neither large kitchen appliances nor farm tools are found close to front doors, but are often along side walls.

Dumping of trash, metal, glass, and wood is very frequent. Dumps do not show a characteristic distribution, although formal refuse disposal in occupied or frequently used houses seems to occur in front of a door, at a distance of about 10 m (Rothschild 1991). Many of the artifacts analyzed represent processes (4) and (5), above, especially if they consist of small items. Six classes of artifacts that occur in relatively high frequencies can be examined.

Foodstuffs consist here mainly of small to medium-sized mammal and chicken bone fragments. These are mostly located in the 15–25 m strip around the houses, and along walls without doors. A single structure, Lower Nutria 14, is the exception, with foodstuffs occurring mostly between 5 and 10 m from the house walls.

Personal items consist mostly of clothing and shoe parts. These tend to be found close to houses, which is probably the result of displacement from the house interiors by dogs, wind, or other natural forces.

Items of domestic routine, in this case, are mainly broken pottery. They are distributed in a pattern that is similar to that of foodstuffs, which is not altogether surprising since both often relate to food consumption. Here too we find most sherds lying at a distance of 15–25 m from the house walls, although for this artifact class there is little differentiation with respect to the location of doors. Again Lower Nutria 14 is distinctive, having the greatest frequency of items in this class between 5 and 10 m from its walls.

The category of construction and maintenance includes many nails, fragments of window glass, pieces of wallboard and tar paper, etc. The objects in this class are found close to houses, and along walls with doors in them, indicating a closer connection with the house. As the deposition of these things may reflect building decay as well as maintenance we cannot be clear as to their significance. However, Lower Nutria 14 again displays a contrasting pattern to most other structures, with fewer objects in this class near house walls.

Indulgences at the Zuni farming villages are composed mostly of soda and beer cans and bottles. There is no pattern visible in Table 10.4 because many of these items were clustered in dumps rather than being spread across the landscape. Some of these artifacts may have accumulated after the period of the structures' occupation or maintenance.

Table 10.4. *Distribution of artifact types around structures (mean number of items per location, distances in meters).*

Structure		subsistence	foodstuffs	indulgences	personal
Upper Pescado 1	walls + door	0	5	22	1
	walls − door	2	2.5	4.3	1
	0–5	1	5	7	10
	5–10	1	2	20	6
	10–15	1	7	42	5
	15–25	1	10	48	11
Upper Pescado 5	walls + door	0	2	0	1
	walls − door	0	3	10.3	1.7
	0–5	1	0	36	7
	5–10	0	1	24	2
	10–15	0	2	18	1
	15–25	0	2	7	2
Lower Pescado 10	walls + door	0	0	10	0
	walls − door	5	1	13	1.5
	0–5	2	3	25	2
	5–10	3	4	10	2
	10–15	3	11	14	0
	15–25	0	13	11	4
Lower Nutria 1	walls + door	1	1	9	3
	walls − door	0	6	8	3
	0–5	1	3	18	9
	5–10	0	2	10	3
	10–15	0	0	10	2
	15–25	0	16	3	2
Lower Nutria 4	walls + door	0.5	1.5	21	3.5
	walls − door	0	11.5	6.5	4.5
	0–5	0	2	22	4
	5–10	1	9	21	5
	10–15	2	8	48	10
	15–25	0	45	45	8
Lower Nutria 6	walls + door	2	3	6	2
	walls − door	1	9	14.25	1
	0–5	2	7	27	4
	5–10	2	15	6	2
	10–15	0	9	9	1
	15–25	3	10	30	2
Lower Nutria 14	wall + door	0	8	1	0
	walls − door	10	3.3	5.75	0.75
	0–5	3	11	3	2
	5–10	6	31	8	0
	10–15	0	12	12	1
	15–25	3	2	12	0

Table 10.4. (*cont.*)

		domestic routine	household equipment	construction/ maintenance	transport
Upper Pescado 1	walls + door	13	14	150	4
	walls − door	11.7	0.3	27	0.7
	0–5	32	7	169	4
	5–10	53	5	160	2
	10–15	116	6	68	1
	15–25	185	11	33	3
Upper Pescado 5	walls + door	4	8	24.3	2
	walls − door	3	2.3	31	0.3
	0–5	19	11	103	2
	5–10	15	8	34	2
	10–15	14	3	22	0
	15–25	15	2	18	0
Lower Pescado 10	walls + door	20.5	0	42.5	0.5
	walls − door	1.51	1	39	0.5
	0–5	9	3	122	1
	5–10	18	4	45	0
	10–15	23	4	29	0
	15–25	38	2	34	1
Lower Nutria 1	walls + door	1.5	2	12	0
	walls − door	25.5	2	23	1
	0–5	30	7	48	0
	5–10	8	0	22	0
	10–15	5	0	12	2
	15–25	9	4	15	0
Lower Nutria 4	walls + door	22	4	47.5	0
	walls − door	10.5	3	51.5	0
	0–5	19	2	354	0
	5–10	75	3	34	0
	10–15	42	11	98	1
	15–25	107	0	28	0
Lower Nutria 6	walls + door	23	2	3	2
	walls − door	14.7	0	18.3	0
	0–5	17	0	70	2
	5–10	12	1	24	0
	10–15	15	0	36	0
	15–25	24	2	18	0
Lower Nutria 14	wall + door	1	0	3	0
	walls − door	9.7	8.7	41.25	0.25
	0–5	8	4	48	0
	5–10	15	10	71	4
	10–15	5	11	60	0
	15–25	8	8	52	0

Table 10.4. (*cont.*)

		recreation	unidentified glass
Upper Pescado 1	walls + door	1	13
	walls − door	0	42
	0–5	1	155
	5–10	0	36
	10–15	0	99
	15–25	1	220
Upper Pescado 5	walls + door	0	15
	walls − door	0.75	15
	0–5	3	65
	5–10	2	181
	10–15	1	20
	15–25	0	4
Lower Pescado 10	walls + door	0.5	7.5
	walls − door	1	6.5
	0–5	1	4
	5–10	0	21
	10–15	2	32
	15–25	0	14
Lower Nutria 1	walls + door	0	15
	walls − door	0.3	148
	0–5	1	211
	5–10	0	40
	10–15	0	60
	15–25	0	39
Lower Nutria 4	walls + door	0	70.5
	walls − door	0.5	37.5
	0–5	0	111
	5–10	1	93
	10–15	1	293
	15–25	0	270
Lower Nutria 6	walls + door	1	100
	walls − door	0	87.75
	0–5	0	108
	5–10	0	90
	10–15	0	74
	15–25	1	210
Lower Nutria 14	wall + door	0	7
	walls − door	0.75	27
	0–5	2	49
	5–10	3	68
	10–15	1	66
	15–25	0	40

Unlike the analysis above, here we will look at the unidentified class because it contains mainly broken glass. What is most interesting about the distribution of this type of artifact is that it is not related in its patterning to the indulgences group, nor is it clearly patterned at all. The one significant observation to be made here is that there is less glass near doors, especially at Lower Nutria 14, indicating that it has been cleared away by some means.

The single structure (Lower Nutria 14) that offered a contrast to the others in several artifact category distributions represents the one house, among those analyzed here, that was in continual use. The husband was herding and farming and came daily; his wife and he both used the house at weekends. The distribution patterns of refuse from this structure may serve as a model in which artifacts related to construction and maintenance and food stuffs may signal occupation or its absence.

Conclusion

In this paper we have proposed that the concept of abandonment must be refined, and is perhaps best seen as a continuum ranging from full-time residential occupation to complete and irreversible abandonment. It is important that we, as archaeologists, try to understand the material correlates of the various elements of the continuum in order to recognize them in the archaeological record. We have observed some architectural manifestations of the various use-states, but we need to understand the elements affecting rates of structure deterioration better.

Artifactual signatures of these states have also been examined. There is variability in the frequency of certain classes of items left inside and outside rooms, and in the spatial distribution of these items outside of houses. These seem closely tied to patterns of refuse disposal and dislocation, including scavenging. We have suggested a number of processes affecting the ultimate recovery of artifacts in the archaeological record. While the artifacts associated with these processes will vary in other contexts, patterns should be visible, relating to activities performed, artifacts used, and the forces of disturbance or redeposition.

When archaeologists recover material from what is (or was) a surface, the assemblage is often assumed to represent a relatively brief moment, or slice, of time. What we have demonstrated here is that a surface collection may derive from several different types of use, and several record-creating processes, even within a relatively brief

period. We know from subsequent excavations at one of the farming villages (Lower Pescado) that historic-period middens may be vertically accumulated in the same way that prehistoric middens were. What we have observed in the present analysis is a kind of horizontal "stratigraphy" in which several processes have produced their own particular patterns of material remains, yielding a complex palimpsest.

It is too soon to identify clearly the kinds of change that are correlated with specific material traces, although our preliminary observations suggest that several patterns of architectural condition and artifact distribution relate to behaviors associated with varying uses of structures. Aspects such as replastering or roof and window maintenance indicate building use for part or full-time residence or storage.

It appears that the study of artifact distribution both inside and outside structures can inform us as to where on the "use-abandonment" continuum the structure lies. The significant variables include distribution (random vs. clustered), diversity, density, and size of materials. Density of construction debris seems related to the use state of the structure. As the structure deteriorates, hardware and parts accumulate inside. Stockpiling of building materials produces a different spatial pattern, with piles of like materials (building stone, planks, etc.) concentrated rather than scattered outside the structure. Use of a room for dumping also seems to produce a unique pattern of mixed materials. The likelihood of redeposition of small artifacts from various kinds of disturbance makes them rather unreliable indicators of use. The surface scatter of somewhat larger objects, in contrast to their collection in refuse piles, is an indicator of the lack of maintenance of an area.

Finally, we can say that the patterns of use, neglect, and reuse of the farming village houses that are emerging from this analysis appear to be characteristic of Southwestern behavior over a very long period. These patterns are undoubtedly found in other places as well, both in prehistoric and historic eras. If we can use archaeologically visible traits to identify different conditions along the continuum we will be in a much stronger position to understand the reality of life in the past.

Acknowledgments

The initial Farming Village Study (1979) was funded by the National Endowment for the Humanities. The authors would like to acknowledge the assistance of a number of individuals: The Zuni Tribal Council and the Zuni People, for allowing us to conduct research; the Zuni Archaeology Program, directed by Roger Anyon, for many kinds of support; Christine Goetze and Christina Koizumi who did all the laborious data entry; and Lee Horne, Mike Schiffer, and Glenn Stone for useful comments on the manuscript. None of these, of course, is responsible for any problems with the final product.

References

Bultnick, Gilbert
  1968–9 Contributions to the Study of the Preservation of Mud-Brick Structures. *Mesopotamia* 5 (3–4):445–73.
Carter, Theresa H. and Roberto Pagliero
  1966 Notes on Mud-Brick Preservation. *Sumer* 22:65–76.
Chavez, Lorenzo
  n.d. Autobiography of Lorenzo Chavez. Transcript prepared by George Mills. Unpublished manuscript on file at the Zuni Archaeology Program, Pueblo of Zuni.
Cordell, Linda S.
  1984 *Prehistory of the Southwest*. Academic Press, Orlando.
Ferguson, T. J.
  1985 Patterns of Land-Use and Environmental Change on the Zuni Reservation, 1846–1985: Ethnohistorical and Archaeological Evidence. Expert testimony submitted to US Claims Court, Zuni Indian Tribe V. United States Docket no. 327–81L. (CT.CL, filed 12 May 1981).
  1989 The Impact of Federal Policy on Zuni Land Use. In *Seasons of the Kachina*, edited by Lowell J. Bean, Proceedings of the California State University Conferences on the Western Pueblos, pp. 89–131. Ballena Press Anthropological Papers No. 34.
Ferguson, T. J. and Barbara Mills
  1982 Archaeological Investigations at Zuni Pueblo, NM, 1977–80. *Zuni Archaeology Program Report* No. 183, Pueblo of Zuni.
Graham, Martha and Alexandra Roberts
  1986 Residentially Constrained Mobility: A Preliminary Investigation of Variation in Settlement Organization, *Haliksa'I*, UNM Contributions to Anthropology, 5 (5):104–15.
Hart, E. Richard
  1991 The Zuni Land Conservation Act of 1990. In *Zuni History, Victories in the 1990s*, Sec. 2, edited by E. Richard Hart and T. J. Ferguson. Institute of the North American West, Seattle.
Holmes, Barbara E. and Andrew Fowler
  1980 The Alternate Dams Survey. An Archaeological Sample Survey and Evaluation of the Burned Timber and Coalmine Dams, Zuni Indian Reservation, McKinley County, New Mexico. *Zuni Archaeology Program Report* 65, Zuni Pueblo.
Kintigh, Keith W.
  1985 *Settlement, Subsistence, and Society in Late Zuni Prehistory*. University of Arizona Anthropological Paper 44. University of Arizona Press, Tucson.
McIntosh, Roderick
  1974 Archaeology and Mud Wall Decay in a West African Village. *World Archaeology* 6:154–61.
Mills, Barbara J. and T. J. Ferguson
  1980 Processes of Architectural Change: Examples From the Zuni Farming Villages. Presented at the 45th Annual Meeting, Society for American Archaeology, Philadelphia.
Mills, Barbara J., Barbara E. Holmes, and T. J. Ferguson
  1982 An Architectural and Ethnohistorical Study of the Zuni Farming Villages. Performance Report, Zuni Archaeology Program.
Oxford Universal Dictionary
  1933 Third edition. The Clarendon Press, Oxford.
Rothschild, Nan A.
  1991 Incorporating the Outdoors as Living Space: Ethnoarchaeology at Zuni Pueblo, NM. *Expedition* 33(1):24–32.
Schiffer, Michael B.
  1976 *Behavioral Archaeology*. Academic Press, New York.
  1987 *Formation Processes of the Archaeological Record*. University of New Mexico Press, Albuquerque.
Seeden, Helga
  1982 Ethnoarchaeological Reconstruction of Halafian Occupational Units at Shams-ed-Din Tannira. *Berytus* 5 (30):55–96.
Ward, Albert E., Emily K. Abbink, and John R. Stein
  1977 Ethnohistorical and Chronological Basis of the Navajo Material Culture. In *Settlement and Subsistence Along the Lower Chaco River, the CGP Survey*, edited by C. A. Reher, pp. 217–78. University of New Mexico Press, Albuquerque.

11
Abandonment and the production of archaeological variability at domestic sites

ARTHUR A. JOYCE and SISSEL
JOHANNESSEN

Introduction

Since the pioneering work of Robert Ascher (1961, 1968), archaeologists have stressed the importance of studying archaeological formation processes for understanding human behavior in the past (Binford 1981a, 1981b; Schiffer 1972, 1976, 1983, 1987; Wood and Johnson 1978). A systematic understanding of archaeological formation processes provides the inferential bridge between static patterns of the archaeological record and dynamic patterns of ongoing behavior. This provides a method by which human behavior in the past can be inferred from the material patterns remaining from that behavior. At domestic sites, ignorance of archaeological formation processes has often limited the ability of archaeologists to make informed inferences concerning the activities represented by material patterning in and around house-floors (Lange and Rydberg 1972; Schiffer 1985; Stanislawski 1973). However, recent research on formation processes of domestic sites is beginning to provide the middle-range linkages needed to infer the processes responsible for the composition of domestic site assemblages (Siegal 1990; Deal 1985; Hayden and Cannon 1983, 1984; Lange and Rydberg 1972; Moore and Gasco 1990; Savelle 1984; Schiffer 1985, 1987; Stevenson 1991). Abandonment processes have been shown to be especially significant in the formation of archaeological assemblages at domestic sites (Bonnichsen 1973; Cameron 1991; Lange and Rydberg 1972; Longacre and Ayers 1968; Robbins 1973; Schiffer 1972, 1976; Stevenson 1982).

This study examines how processes of site abandonment affected material patterns at the site of La Concha, an abandoned single-family household compound in rural Mexico. By using interviews with informants the material patterns observed at the site are compared to the activities performed during site use and abandonment. The study focuses on the variable effects of site abandonment on material patterns even within a relatively small domestic site like La Concha. Several general factors are discussed that led to differential treatment of various parts of the site during abandonment and which resulted in variation in material patterning.

Abandonment and the formation of domestic sites

Previous research has shown that material patterning at domestic sites results in large part from human refuse disposal during site use, abandonment, and postabandonment (Cameron 1991; Deal 1985; Hayden and Cannon 1983; Lange and Rydberg 1972; Savelle 1984; Schiffer 1976, 1985, 1987; Stevenson 1982, 1991). Archaeologists have identified several types of refuse disposal that transfer materials from behavioral to archaeological contexts including primary refuse disposal, secondary refuse disposal, abandonment refuse disposal, and *de facto* refuse disposal. Primary and secondary refuse disposal involve the intentional discard of items at or near the end of their use-life (Schiffer 1972, 1976, 1987). Primary refuse disposal is the discard of material at its location of use. Secondary refuse disposal involves the discard of refuse in a location other than where it was used. Abandonment refuse is a special case of primary and secondary refuse disposal occurring prior to and during gradual site abandonment. Gradual abandonment causes individuals to relax their standards of cleanliness and begin to deposit materials in areas not normally used for discard within houses or other enclosed living areas (Schiffer 1985:25; Stevenson 1982). *De facto* refuse disposal (Schiffer 1987:89) involves the transfer of materials retaining some functional or other value to the archaeological record during site abandonment without being discarded (e.g. leaving functional items at an abandoned site because of inability to transport the object, haste of site abandonment, or caching activities; see below). This section discusses previous research on refuse disposal at domestic sites, especially during site abandonment, to provide a framework for examining the data from La Concha.

Disposal of secondary refuse is often the dominant mode through which materials enter the archaeological record during site occupation, while primary refuse disposal appears usually to be a relatively insignificant process. Secondary refuse disposal during site occupation has been systematically examined by Hayden and Cannon (1983:154) at four highland Maya communities (see also Deal 1985). Hayden and Cannon argue that the underlying structure of refuse disposal patterns for these communities results primarily from several principles including economy of effort, temporary retention of potentially recyclable materials, and hindrance minimization. Refuse with hindrance potential and little value, termed "casual refuse," such as plant remains, bones, ashes, and small inorganic remains, is usually discarded in the "toft" area. The "toft" is located just outside the structure and patio; it is used for maintenance-storage activities and discard of refuse (Hayden and Cannon 1983:126; Hurst 1971:116; Lewis 1976:105). Secondary refuse is often deposited in the toft area as a result of the sweeping of house-floors. House sweepings also accumulate along the walls of structures especially in artifact traps such as drainage ditches. Secondary refuse with some potential value (e.g. broken ceramic vessels, broken axeheads) or hindrance potential (typically larger items) are often provisionally discarded until the material is either reused or taken to a permanent dumping location. Provisional discard locations are usually in out-of-the-way places such as along walls, fences, under beds, or in the toft area. Provisionally discarded refuse has a high probability of being left at sites after abandonment. Final discard of refuse is usually at discrete locations such as household or community dumps. Particularly dangerous material such as glass is often buried in pits.

The disposal of abandonment and *de facto* refuse occurs by definition during site abandonment (Schiffer 1987). Abandonment processes that variably affect refuse disposal include: the manner by which sites are abandoned (i.e. gradual/planned or rapid/unplanned), whether or not return is planned, means of transportation, distance to the next site, and season of abandonment (Bonnichsen 1973; Cameron 1991; Lange and Rydberg 1972; Longacre and Ayers 1968; Robbins 1973; Schiffer 1972, 1976; Stevenson 1982). Stevenson systematically examined site abandonment processes at historic mining camps in the Yukon in relation to two major variables of abandonment behavior, the manner in which sites are abandoned and whether or not return is planned. In sites where abandonment was planned and gradual he found little *de facto* refuse, low associations between this type of material and activity areas, and few normally curated items. However, at sites which were rapidly abandoned, *de facto* refuse, including items normally curated, was abundant and highly correlated with intended areas of use. These patterns occurred because planned abandonment allowed individuals to remove most items that retained some value, while during rapid abandonment many valuable items could not be transported. However, when abandonment was planned with anticipated return to the site, considerable quantities of *de facto* refuse were found (Stevenson 1982:252–5; see also Deal 1985:269; Schiffer 1985:26). When return was anticipated *de facto* refuse was cached to protect it for reuse upon return to the site. This caching behavior often resulted in the clustering of *de facto* refuse relative to rapid abandonment conditions as well as a decline in the direct association of *de facto* refuse with activity loci. Stevenson (1982:248) also found that abandonment refuse was more abundant and clustered at sites where abandonment was gradual and planned, rather than rapid and unplanned. In the next section, these principles of refuse disposal (Deal 1985; Hayden and Cannon 1983; Schiffer 1985; Stevenson 1982) are used as a framework to examine the effects of site abandonment on material patterning at La Concha.

Site description and methodology

The site of La Concha lies on a small rocky hill several meters south of the Pacific coastal highway (Mexico 200) approximately 5 km east of the village of Santa Rosa in the *municipio* of Tututepec, Oaxaca (Fig. 11.1). The La Concha hill is one of a series of similar rocky hills in the area. The four thatch huts that made up the household compound were built on the hilltop which is a relatively flat area of about 900 sq m. The hill drops down steeply from this area approximately 10 m to the surrounding plain. A small seasonal stream lies approximately 350 m west of La Concha. Settlement in the general vicinity of the site is relatively sparse and limited to similar types of dispersed household compounds.

La Concha consists of four abandoned thatch houses (Fig. 11.2) and the materials left scattered by the former occupants in and around those structures. Outside the buildings, the site can be divided into three areas: paths, patio, and toft. The patio is the open, central area between Structures 1, 2, and 3 where many day-to-day activities would have taken place and which in occupied sites is generally kept clean of debris to allow for ease of movement. The toft area encloses the patio and includes a portion of the flat surface on top of the hill, primarily south and east of Structure 1 and the area surrounding Structure 4, as well as the slopes of the La Concha hill. There were two paths leading up to the structures. One led up from the highway and joined the patio area

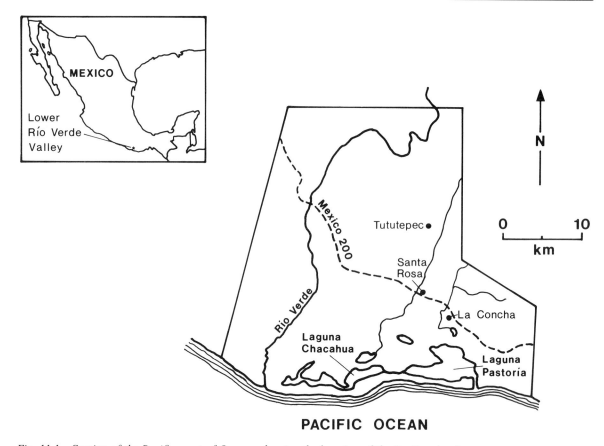

Fig. 11.1   Section of the Pacific coast of Oaxaca showing the location of the La Concha site.

several meters east of Structure 3. The other was located west of Structure 4 and linked La Concha to a house compound on a similar hill about 50 m to the west. La Concha is now generally brush covered even within the patio and paths. A few trees and many economically useful plants grow around the site.

Ethnoarchaeological research at La Concha was carried out during June and July of 1986. The work consisted of the identification and mapping of the four buildings and all materials left in these structures and the patio area including trash middens and economically useful plants. Samples were taken from trash middens and floral material was recovered using flotation techniques. Much of the toft area was heavily overgrown with brush and could not be systematically mapped so that only a general impressionistic description of the area could be achieved.

While it would have been preferable to have observed actual preabandonment and abandonment behavior at the site, a number of local informants were questioned

briefly on several occasions concerning those activities. Informants provided information on the identity of the former occupants, duration of occupation, time elapsed since site abandonment, reasons for site abandonment, and the functions of the structures and particular items abandoned at the site. Informants included the family living in the adjacent household as well as a cousin of one of the former occupants of La Concha who was periodically checking the site. The informants reported that the site had been occupied for about ten years by a family of six or seven individuals including a husband and wife, their 20-year-old son and an 18-year-old daughter, as well as two or three younger children of undetermined age. The site had been abandoned six months before the study because the family had the opportunity to move to a better piece of land. While at the site, informants reported that among the four buildings (Fig. 11.2), Structure 1 had been a kitchen, Structures 2 and 3 living and sleeping quarters, and Structure 4 a house for the eldest son. All structures were reported

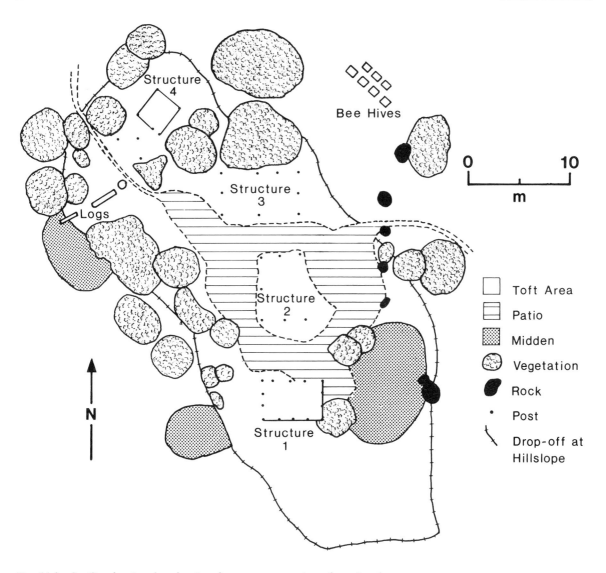

Fig. 11.2   La Concha site plan showing the structures, patio, toft, and paths.

to have been occupied simultaneously and were similarly constructed of pole frames and thatch roofs and walls (Fig. 11.3). Informants reported that site abandonment had been planned and gradual. The family was apparently considering a return to the site, but the impression left by the informants was that return was uncertain and would depend on general living conditions at the new location. It was unclear exactly where the family had moved, but it was obvious that it involved a considerable distance. Available means of transportation from La Concha to the new site included walking, horseback,

and, at least along the coastal highway, buses and trucks.

Material patterning at La Concha

Materials mapped within the four structures as well as in the patio area are listed in Tables 11.1–11.5, respectively (Table 11.4, listing the materials in Structure 4, also includes a short list of the material in the toft area immediately surrounding the building which was mapped in detail). Items are grouped into twelve general functional categories: furniture, cooking vessels, serving

Fig. 11.3   Front of La Concha Structure 1 showing the open (northern and western) sides of the building.

Fig. 11.4   Interior of Structure 1 showing the raised adobe hearth (right background) and kitchen furniture, including wooden table and bench.

vessels, utensils, containers, kitchen accessories, clothing, agricultural implements, pastoral implements (generally horse-riding equipment), religious paraphernalia, food/food refuse, and other items. Construction elements of each structure are not included in the tables unless they were being cached after having been scavenged from another structure. The distribution of items within and adjacent to the buildings at La Concha are discussed below in relation to their probable means of disposal.

Structure 1 had been built to be open on its northern and western sides, and remained in excellent condition (Fig. 11.3). From its material remains, an archaeologist would certainly have defined Structure 1 as a kitchen

(Fig. 11.4). In fact, many of the items associated with Structure 1 were apparently *de facto* refuse intimately associated with their use areas (Table 11.1). This material included kitchen furniture (e.g. raised adobe hearth, wooden table, and bench), containers, serving vessels, and kitchen utensils. A granite mano and metate and a split tire which may have been used as a water trough were discovered in the patio 2 m east of Structure 1, but were undoubtedly associated with kitchen activities. All of this material is typically found in fully functioning native kitchens observed in the area.

Table 11.1. *Items within Structure 1.*

Item	Quantity
Furniture	
wooden shelves	4
raised adobe hearth	1
burned chunks of clay (probably pieces broken off hearth)	5
wooden "dining" table (145 × 80 × 78 cm)	1
wooden storage table (100 × 32 × 85 cm)	1
wooden bench	1
wooden chair (missing one leg)	1
metal shelf frame without shelf	1
metal box (100 × 52 × 48 cm) used as a table	1
Cooking vessels	
metal pot	1
Serving vessels	
metal plate	1
plastic cup	1
glass jar	1
soda bottle (355 ml)	1
Utensils	
chocolate frother	2
double-edged razor blade	1
steel knife blade	1
home-made brush (sponge tied to the end of a stick)	1
Containers	
burlap sack (filled with 20 cornhusks)	1
gourd water container	1
gourd container	1
plastic containers	2
plastic bag (containing 8 peach seeds)	1
plastic bag (containing gourd seeds)	1
ceramic jars (*ollas*)	2

piece of a wooden crate (29 × 29 × 5 cm)   1

Kitchen accessories
plastic rings made from bottles   2
straw brushes   3
glass cooking-oil jar   3
wire-mesh screen probably used for cooking   1
wooden board or lid (30 × 25 × 2 cm)   1

Agricultural implements
burned and rusted machete blade   1

Food/food refuse
corn husks   25
corn cobs   8
peach seeds   8
desiccated lime rinds   4
seeds (taxon unknown)   5
chicken bone   1

Other items
gourd seeds   approx. 12
metal hooks possibly for hanging items on   26
   wall
metal rings (approx. 10 cm dia.)   3
metal container with bottom cut out   1
metal gear (9 cm diameter)   1
burned potsherd   1
unburned potsherds   11
adobe brick   1
burned pebbles   4
burned granite slab   1
unburned pebbles   2
pieces of cloth   1
leather straps   4
pieces of rope   9
rolls of cordage   2
empty cigarette pack   1
wooden beams (possibly removed from   2
   Structure 2)
wooden planks   2
pieces of plastic   2
pieces of glass   3
matchbox   1

Few items of primary or secondary refuse appeared to be directly associated with Structure 1. For example, several glass bottles and a metal cylindrical container with the bottom removed were placed along the east wall inside Structure 1 and may represent refuse in provisional discard locations, but could also be *de facto*

Fig. 11.5   *La Concha Structure 2, looking west across the patio.*

refuse (see Hayden and Cannon 1983). A tin can, glass jar, and iron bar along the outside east wall are probably provisional discard (see Deal 1985). Several meters northeast of Structure 1 was a provisional discard area containing a variety of ceramic, plastic, glass, and tin containers; all of the ceramic vessels were broken. House sweepings were noted along the walls of Structure 1 and consisted almost solely of small unobtrusive objects such as maize cobs, pottery sherds, pieces of glass, and chicken bones. Primary refuse was generally found embedded in the floor and consisted of seeds, burned clay, and pottery sherds.

Table 11.2. *Items within Structure 2.*

Item	Quantity
Serving vessels	
glass cup	1
Clothing	
sandal	1
Other items	
piece of a metal drill	1
metal bar	1
flat piece of metal	1
D-batteries	4
packages of medical tablets (Diyodohidroxi Quinoleina)	2
matchbox	1
pieces of cloth	2
pieces of rope	3
plastic netting	1

In contrast to Structure 1, Structure 2 had been almost entirely dismantled with the exception of some of its pole frames (Fig. 11.5). Few items remained that provided any clues as to the preabandonment activities associated with this building (Table 11.2). Building materials (e.g. roofing tiles, poles) lay around the area of Structure 2, although the amount of material was far less than would have been present when it was intact. The presence of several postholes in the area of Structure 2 as well as a stack of poles cached in Structure 1 suggest that the former was being systematically scavenged, probably for building materials or firewood. Other than building materials, objects found lying in and around the floor of Structure 2 appeared to have been primarily abandonment refuse (e.g. battery plates, part of a metal drill, D-battery, iron bar, sandal). A variety of economically useful plants were growing in and around Structure 2, including sesame, watermelon, squash, bean, tomato, *tomatillo*, amaranth, and *purslane*. These are probably the result of seeds having been dropped onto the house-floor (i.e. primary refuse).

Table 11.3. *Items within Structure 3.*

Item	Quantity
Furniture	
plastic baby seat	1
wooden cabinet drawer	1
wooden shelf	1
wood-log seats	2
Cooking vessels	
ceramic cooking bowl	1
Utensils	
clothes iron	1
Containers	
empty wooden crate	1
wooden crate (containing crate panel, straw sack, cloth, leather, and one sandal)	1
empty straw sacks	2
straw sack (containing grain)	1
bottle gourd (containing pieces of cloth)	1
plastic shoulder bag (containing 2 bottles of disinfectant, 1 bottle emulsion, a 50 ml syringe and needle, plastic bags, small metal chain, cosmetics jar)	1
plastic market-bag (containing dried plants and glass vase)	1
empty plastic market-bag	1
Clothing	
pair of sandals	1
hat	1
leather belt	1
Agricultural tools	
metal hoe blade	1
wooden digging stick	1
Pastoral implements	
horse-hair animal tether	1
Food/food refuse	
corn husks	4
corn cobs	2
grain	?
dried plants (unknown taxon)	?
seeds (unknown taxa)	8
pig mandibles	2
Other items	
metal rodent trap	1
barbed wire (1.5 m in length)	1
piece of metal	1
metal handle	1
bent metal rod	1
piece of wire	1
metal chains	2
broken ceramic grater bowl	1
potsherds	8
plastic clamp	1
plastic cushion	1
plastic bags	4
wooden crate panel	1
piece of wood	1
wooden hanger	1
pieces of cloth	11
cloth netting	1
pieces of rope	9
pieces of leather	5
bottle with skull-and-crossbones on label (poison)	1
battery plates	5
matchbox	2
bottles of disinfectant	2
bottle of emulsion	1
50 ml syringe and needle	1
cosmetics jar	1
glass vase	1

*Fig. 11.6   La Concha Structure 3, looking to the
northwest with Structure 4 in the background.*

*Fig. 11.7   Front of La Concha Structure 4 showing the
roofed porch.*

The nature of material patterning for Structure 3 (Fig.
11.6) was similar to that observed at Structure 2. While
the roof of Structure 3 was largely intact, a variety of
building materials (e.g. wooden beams, door assembly)
were strewn around the house-floor, indicating that the
walls had been dismantled. Much of the material left in
and around Structure 3 (Table 11.3) appeared to be *de
facto* refuse, although some items might be better
classified as abandonment refuse thrown into the building during abandonment. These items included furniture, containers, and clothing which were generally consistent with a variety of domestic activities of men,
women, and children. Agricultural and pastoral tools
were also present which would have been used for activities performed away from the site.

A smaller inventory of items in Structure 3 is more
clearly abandonment, primary, and secondary refuse.
Abandonment refuse probably included materials such
as an iron handle, batteries, an empty poison bottle, a
broken grater bowl, and a bent metal rod. House sweepings included two pig jaws and some maize husks, while
small potsherds ground into the floor were probably
primary refuse.

Table 11.4. *Items associated with Structure 4.*

Item	Quantity
Items within Structure 4 (including porch area):	
Furniture	
wooden platform (bed or table)	1
wooden shelf (a reused cabinet drawer suspended on wall)	1
wooden door-jam	1
wooden crate suspended as a shelf (containing 3 straw sacks, 4 pieces of cloth, 1 piece of leather)	1
wooden table-top	1
Cooking vessels	
ceramic cooking griddle	1
Serving vessels	
empty tequila bottle	1
glass jar	1
Utensils	
sponge	1
Containers	
straw bag (containing plastic bag with seeds, 2 metal rings, gourd)	1
straw sacks	3
straw sack (containing 20 corn husks)	1
basket	1
gourds	7
ceramic jar	2
cardboard box (containing 2 gourds, 1 basket, 1 tin can)	1
cardboard box (containing 2 gourds, 3 pairs of pants, 1 shirt)	1
wooden crate (containing iron cylinder and plastic bag)	1
metal buckets	2
tin cans	2
powdered-milk can	1

Table 11.4. (*cont.*)

plastic bags (containing several coffee beans)	2
plastic flower pot	1
plastic market-bag (containing metal tool, wrench, gears)	1
empty plastic market-bag	1
plastic chlorox bottle	1
plastic container with oil residue	1
plastic container (containing plastic repair-kit and glue)	1
empty plastic container	1
plastic bag (containing nuts, bolts, screws, and ball-bearings)	1
empty plastic bags	3
plastic water jug	1

Clothing
pairs of pants	3
shirt	1
crushed straw hat	1
leather belts	2
sole of sandal	1
pair of sandals	1

Agricultural implements
digging sticks	3

Pastoral implements
iron animal brand	1
horse bit	1
leather horse tether	1

Religious paraphernalia
wooden house-altar	1
religious shrine (cabinet with glass door containing figure of a saint)	1
picture of Saint Joseph and baby Jesus	1
candle	1

Food/food refuse
seeds (unknown taxon)	?
coffee beans	?
plum (*ciruela*) pits	24
corn husks	29
corn cobs	1
desiccated orange peel	1

Other items
metal rings	3
flat pieces of metal	1
pieces of wire	3
metal street sign	1
metal tools	2

wrench	1
metal gears	3
metal hooks	3
metal pipe	1
nuts	approx. 6
bolts	6
screws	6
ball-bearings	6
metal bar	1
metal cylinder	1
roll of barbed wire (3 m length)	1
piece of metal clamp	1
metal clamp	1
metal bucket with bottom cut out	1
20 centavo coin	1
50 centavo coin	1
wooden board	5
panel from a wooden crate	1
logs	5
wooden hook	1
plastic lid	1
plastic patches	1
piece of plastic	1
pieces of leather	6
piece of cardboard	2
pieces of cloth	11
pieces of rubber	5
pieces of rope	8
piece of straw sack	1
worn petate	1
medicine bottle containing fragrant substance	1
panel from a wooden crate	1
broom head	1
potsherds	5
tube of glue	1
D-batteries	2
matchbox	1

Items in toft area near Structure 4:
Furniture
wooden footstand (?)	1

Food/food refuse
corn husk	2

Other items
cover to a metal box	1
metal hubcaps	2
metal grater on a wooden frame	1
metal wire	1
metal bolt	1
wire and cord hanger	1

back to a wooden chair	1
wooden hanger	1
pieces of cloth	3
matchbox	2
straw sack	1
potsherds	9

Structure 4, like Structure 1, was largely intact and in excellent condition (Fig. 11.7). Structure 4 contained an area fully enclosed by walls with a single door which could be tied shut as well as a small roofed porch. Structure 4 contained the greatest quantity of material relative to the other structures at La Concha (Table 11.4). Many of the items in Structure 4 appeared to be cached *de facto* refuse. A variety of bags, boxes, and crates were found in Structure 4 containing numerous items such as cloths, gourds, baskets, and tools. Other items of *de facto* refuse hanging on walls and piled within the structure included various tools and gears, a wooden bed frame, gourds, wood, a ceramic jar and cooking griddle, and a metal bucket. Materials probably in provisional discard locations included a glass jar, a plastic chlorox bottle, and a dilapidated petate (woven straw sleeping-mat). The only primary refuse appeared to be a few plum (*ciruela*) pits on the house-floor.

An altar stood along the southeast wall (Fig. 11.8). Lying on top of the altar was a religious shrine, a religious picture, an empty tequila bottle, a candle, a plastic bag full of coffee beans, a medicinal bottle containing a fragrant substance, a sponge, and 70 centavos. Since most of these objects are commonly used in tradi-

tional house-rituals in the region (Greenberg 1981), and since the altar appears to have been a fixture in Structure 4, it is probable that the religious paraphernalia belonged in the building even during site-use. The shrine was removed shortly after our meeting with the relative of the family who had lived at La Concha. Since no other objects were removed during the course of our work at La Concha, it appears that the shrine had a special value to the family which they chose not to risk, given the presence of strangers at the site, even though they did not appear to object to our work there. The reason that the shrine was not removed earlier may be that its installation in a new house requires fairly elaborate ritual preparation including a religious ceremony (Greenberg 1981).

A wide variety of material was also found in the roofed porch area and along the outside walls of Structure 4. *De facto* refuse in the porch included a plastic bag containing nuts, bolts, screws, and ball-bearings; two digging sticks; a horse bit; a straw hat; a ceramic jar; a roll of barbed wire; batteries; and various pieces of leather, rope, and wire. *De facto* refuse along the outside walls of Structure 4 included plastic containers, a wooden chair, and a metal grater. Materials probably in provisional discard in the porch included a table or bed top, a wooden crate panel, an oil-covered rag, and a sandal sole, while provisionally discarded items along the walls of the building included a piece of metal, wire, and two hubcaps. A scatter of potsherds and maize husks on the ground just outside the porch area may have been the result of house sweepings.

The patio area and paths were generally free of refuse (see Table 11.5). In addition to the provisional and *de facto* refuse associated with Structure 1, there were a few candles, probably abandonment refuse, lying several meters west of Structure 2. A small dumping area (approximately 80 cm in diameter) containing charcoal, burned potsherds, and glass was noted 3 m southwest of Structure 3 at the boundary between the patio and toft areas. It probably represents abandonment or postabandonment refuse as it would have presented a health hazard during site use. A few small potsherds, both modern and prehispanic, were also found scattered throughout the patio and on the two paths.

The toft area was generally covered with refuse. The slopes of the hill seemed to be an area where secondary refuse was tossed (see Hayden and Cannon 1983), especially household items such as potsherds, ash, tin cans, glass, food refuse, and pieces of cloth and wood. Several beehives were located in the toft area approximately 8 m northeast of Structure 3 on the upper slope of

Fig. 11.8   Wooden altar inside La Concha Structure 4 showing the religious shrine (center) and other religious paraphernalia.

Table 11.5. *Items within patio area.*

Item	Quantity
Cooking vessels	
metal pot	1
Serving vessels	
glass jar	1
drinking glass	1
plastic baby-bottle	1
plastic bowl	1
Containers	
metal bucket	1
tin can	1
piece of wooden crate	1
broken wooden box	1
plastic jug (containing 4 corn cobs)	1
plastic bucket	2
plastic market-bag	1
broken ceramic jars	2
glass bottle	1
Kitchen accessories	
stone mano (grinding stone)	1
stone metate (grinding basin)	1
Religious paraphernalia	
broken ceramic incense burner	1
Food/food refuse	
corn cobs	11
Other items	
iron bar	1
metal jar cap	1
flat pieces of metal	2
battery plates	15
5-volt battery	1
rubber tire split lengthwise (possibly used as a water basin)	2
piece of cloth	2
piece of rope	1
pieces of glass	approx. 6
potsherds	approx. 12
broken sandal	1
pieces of plastic	2
tin container (Vicks Vapo-Rub)	1

the hill (Fig. 11.2). Hanging in a tree several meters east of Structure 4 were two pairs of sandals, a horse bit, and leather and rubber straps that appeared to be *de facto* refuse.

Two major middens were located around the perimeter of the hilltop to the east and west of Structure 1 (Fig. 11.2). The material in these middens appeared to be primarily ash and food refuse, undoubtedly the result of cooking activities in Structure 1. Food refuse included large amounts of acacia bean pods (*guaje*), maize cobs, and squash seeds, as well as plum pits, peanut shells, and seeds of papaya, chile, and mango. These middens were covered with a dense growth of cucurbits, indicating that some of the seeds had sprouted. Pieces of wood, cloth, paper, plastic, pottery, bits of rock and adobe, and a plastic doll's head were also observed in these middens. Preliminary results of flotation samples taken from the midden west of Structure 1 are presented in Table 11.6.

A third midden containing animal feces was located 8 m south of Structure 4. The horse-riding paraphernalia associated with Structure 4 suggests the presence of horses in the area. This midden was not sampled, although cucurbits growing on the surface suggest that it was also used for deposition of kitchen refuse.

A wide variety of economically useful plants were also observed growing around the site including *guaje*, *nopal*, *ciruela*, castor bean, and marigolds. Many of these plants would not naturally be found in this setting, indicating that their presence was the result of intentional and/or unintentional human interference in the local habitat.

Site abandonment and material patterning at La Concha

Site abandonment at La Concha appears to have created a complex pattern of material remains. This complexity was largely the result of the differential treatment of the four structures during site abandonment which resulted in significant variability in the composition and density of artifacts associated with each structure. This section examines the distribution of artifacts at La Concha as a function of site abandonment. The patterns observed at La Concha are compared to the expectations proposed by Stevenson (1982) in relation to variables of site abandonment.

The majority of *de facto* refuse at La Concha was concentrated in Structure 4, and at least some was stored in boxes and bags. This pattern is consistent with Stevenson's (1982) prediction that considerable amounts of *de facto* refuse should be clustered in caches generally away from use locations when abandonment is gradual and

Table 11.6. *Flotation data*

Original sample size: 10 liters
Total weight of flotation material (> 2 mm): 44.6 gm
Summary of flotation material:

	weight (gm)	% of total
Uncharred materials:		
Fresh wood and stems:	20.0	44.8
Legume pods and "conglomerate" (possibly feces):	15.0	33.6
Maize:	2.6	5.8
"Seeds" (e.g. squash, papaya, mango, chile):	1.2	2.7
Non-edibles (e.g. cloth, paper, plastic):	1.2	2.7
Peanut shells:	0.2	0.4
Charred material:		
(primarily wood with some maize and small seeds):	4.4	9.9

planned with the possibility of return. The absence of abandonment refuse in Structure 4 is also consistent with this hypothesis. Storage of materials in Structure 4 probably occurred because the building was fully enclosed and more secure than the others. The presence of agricultural and pastoral tools in Structure 4 (Table 11.4) are consistent with the building having been the residence of an adult male as reported by the informants. However, the large quantity of materials piled within Structure 4 indicates caching of items that had been used throughout the site during its occupation. Items were apparently cached in Structure 4 as the result of delayed curation where stored objects such as the religious shrine are gradually removed between a site's last occupation and its permanent abandonment (Tomka, this volume).

Materials found in Structure 1 were also primarily *de facto* refuse and they were intimately associated with their use location (i.e. the kitchen). In fact, material patterning at this structure approximated "Pompeii premise" conditions where the everyday functioning of a site is interrupted and items are left where they "drop" (Binford 1981b). This is a pattern that Stevenson (1982) predicted for conditions of rapid unplanned abandonment. The lack of abandonment refuse would be consistent with these conditions.

Material patterns associated with Structures 2 and 3 were relatively similar and involved patterns that Stevenson found for sites where abandonment was planned and gradual without anticipation of return. There was no effort made to preserve Structures 2 and 3 for reuse in case of return to the site. These were the only structures with evidence of abandonment refuse, although more

abandonment refuse might have been left if the permanent dumping location was not so close at hand. Other than collapsed building material, few items were found in Structure 2, and these consisted almost entirely of abandonment refuse. Structure 3 contained more refuse than Structure 2, including both *de facto* and abandonment refuse. While there was a considerable amount of *de facto* refuse in Structure 3, much of this material was either immobile or appeared to have had low use value relative to *de facto* refuse in Structures 1 and 4. Some of the material characterized as *de facto* refuse in Structure 3 might more accurately be classified as abandonment refuse.

Construction materials from both Structures 2 and 3 were obviously being scavenged either for incorporation into other houses or for firewood. That only Structures 2 and 3 were being disassembled suggests that it was being done either by the former occupants or under their direction. It seems unlikely that scavengers would focus solely on these structures while ignoring the building materials and valuable *de facto* refuse in the others.

Considered as a whole, material patterns at La Concha resemble the patterns predicted by Stevenson (1982). *De facto* refuse, especially cached materials, were concentrated in one area of the site (Structure 4), while abandonment refuse was concentrated in other areas (Structures 2 and 3). The large amount of *de facto* refuse associated with use locations (especially Structure 1), may relate to the site's isolation and the presence of friendly neighbors and relatives who could guard the site. These factors may have caused the former occupants to feel more secure about leaving seemingly valuable items unprotected. Many of the objects in Structure 1 (e.g. furniture, pottery) were also made from locally available materials. Tomka (this volume) has shown that items made from local materials are more likely to be left at permanently abandoned sites as *de facto* refuse than are items made from non-local materials. In addition, much of the *de facto* refuse throughout the site consisted of heavy and unwieldy items such as large ollas, furniture, and the religious shrine. This is expected, given that the new site was at a considerable distance (Deal 1985:270; Stevenson 1979, 1982).

The data from La Concha demonstrate that abandonment of multistructure sites can result in differential treatment of structures creating complex patterning in the archaeological record. At La Concha, only Structure 4 exhibited patterns that reflected the process of abandonment at the site as a whole. Examination of any other structure would have led one to conclude that a different set of processes had been responsible for site formation. It should be recognized that when multiple structures are involved in abandonment, some may be singled out for storage purposes, others for disposal of abandonment refuse, some might be dismantled, and others might be actively occupied with few changes in associated activities right up to the time of actual abandonment (see Rothschild *et al.*, this volume). The probability of differential treatment of structures appears to be greatest when abandonment is gradual and planned with anticipated return. However, as conditions of abandonment become more rapid and unplanned, differential treatment of structures resulting from abandonment processes are less probable, and material patterning will more closely resemble those present during site use.

Differential treatment of structures during site abandonment at La Concha can be related to several factors. Structure 1 seems to have been left intact because of its specialized function and associated large or immobile items. Thus, the amount of effort required to rebuild the kitchen if the family did return to the site undoubtedly outweighed the immediate benefits of dismantling it for firewood or building materials. The concentration of stored *de facto* refuse in Structure 4 probably resulted in part from its being somewhat protected from the elements and potential looters. In addition, the presence of the religious shrine in Structure 4 suggests that this building may also have had a special religious significance for the family who had occupied the site. The preservation of both Structure 1 and 4 suggest that buildings which performed specialized functions in the economic, social, or religious life of a community should

have a higher probability of being left intact and relatively unaffected by abandonment processes.

Structures 2 and 3 appear to have been dismantled because they were neither secure nor retained sufficient value to make their preservation worthwhile. Abandonment of these two residences would have decreased their visibility in the archaeological record relative to the other buildings. In fact, the removal of material from Structure 2 during abandonment probably would have made it nearly invisible archaeologically after only a few years of decay.

Processes of site abandonment at La Concha differentially altered the relationship between material patterning and preabandonment behavior at the site. It is the ongoing set of behaviors that occurred during site use that most archaeologists are interested in reconstructing (Binford 1981b). Only if all activities were suddenly stopped because of some catastrophe and materials remained "frozen" where they fell could archaeologists reliably reconstruct the behavior of the ongoing community without reference to abandonment and postabandonment processes. At La Concha, Structure 1 exhibited material patterns most closely related to those expected to have been present during site use. Structure 4 also seemed to retain some items that would have been associated with it during use, although these patterns were complicated by caching activities. Structures 2 and 3 were dramatically altered as a result of abandonment, leaving few material clues suggesting their function.

The type of material that was least altered by abandonment was primary and secondary refuse, including materials in provisional discard locations. Patterns of primary and secondary refuse disposal at La Concha largely conform to the principles set forth by Hayden and Cannon (1983:154) in their study of refuse disposal in the Maya Highlands (see also Deal 1985). Refuse disposal at La Concha was simplified by the location of the site on a hill. Tossing materials down the side of the hill seemed to be the method of final discard for most materials. Because of the ease of final discard at La Concha, the majority of provisionally discarded materials were items that retained some value, as useless items could simply be dropped over the side of the hill. Locations of provisional discard were usually along walls and in out-of-the-way locations of the toft area (see Deal 1985; Hayden and Cannon 1983). Floor sweepings were observed along house walls. The two middens associated with Structure 1 appeared to be the location of disposal for floor sweepings, ash, and food refuse from the kitchen. House-floors also contained a few items of primary refuse that were ground into the floor or were small and probably missed during sweeping. Thus, pre-abandonment behaviors most directly reflected in the archaeological record would seem to be those involving refuse disposal (also see Deal 1985; Hayden and Cannon 1983; Schiffer 1976). If not for the large amount of *de facto* refuse left at the site owing to the possibility of return, it is likely that the majority of items associated with house-floors would have been provisionally discarded refuse (see Hayden and Cannon 1983:133).

Conclusions

When interpreting the material remains at domestic sites, it is crucial for archaeologists to consider the nature of site abandonment. Stevenson (1982) has shown that material patterning at sites with evidence for rapid, unplanned abandonment should closely reflect the activities performed during site use. However, the research at La Concha suggests that gradual abandonment, especially when reoccupation is a probability, has a much more variable effect on material patterning at domestic sites. The research suggests that specialized structures and associated materials in domestic sites are often less affected by gradual abandonment than simple residences. Therefore, when specialized structures such as public buildings or kitchens are isolated in the archaeological record, associated materials may be more useful for inferring behaviors that occurred in those structures during use. Conversely, houses may often be expected to yield relatively few artifacts, and site abandonment should be considered as a key process in the formation of house-floor assemblages. Artifacts remaining on house-floors of gradually abandoned sites should consist mostly of primary and abandonment refuse as well as items in provisional discard. The data also suggest that unspecialized houses, which are the most common structures in villages of contemporary and prehispanic Mesoamerica (Ashmore and Willey 1981:6; Haviland 1966; Manzanilla 1986; Thompson 1892; Wilk and Ashmore 1988), may be more difficult to detect in the archaeological record relative to specialized structures and are therefore often under-represented. Of all the materials remaining at domestic sites, however, primary and secondary refuse appears to be least affected by abandonment and therefore most closely related to the ongoing behaviors that occur at these sites during occupation (also see Hayden and Cannon 1983).

Delayed curation is an additional factor resulting from the gradual abandonment of sites that will complicate the archaeological record (also see Tomka, this volume). As exemplified by Structure 4 at La Concha,

some buildings will have been locations of caching activities resulting from delayed curation. If the removal of cached items during delayed curation is incomplete then these buildings should have concentrations of *de facto* refuse that are significantly greater than in other structures. These loci of cached materials resulting from delayed curation may mimic structures used as formal storage facilities during site occupation. Therefore, the evidence from Structure 4 suggests that archaeologists should be particularly cautious when inferring storage functions for buildings based solely on the presence of dense concentrations of artifacts.

The La Concha research suggests that broad areal sampling at archaeological sites is crucial to control for abandonment processes. Sampling of multiple structures is important since, as this study has shown, site abandonment can result in differential treatment of buildings. Differential treatment can occur when an entire site is abandoned or when multistructure households are abandoned during the occupation of a larger settlement (see Rothschild *et al.*, this volume). Extremely complex patterns might result when families own several structures that are widely dispersed throughout a settlement, as in the Middle East (Horne 1982). Even in communities where families occupy only one structure, abandonment can be complicated by cooperation between families. This is especially likely for traditional societies where related families live in close proximity to one another (see Hayden and Cannon 1982). Unique patterns might also be expected for societies such as the Iroquois where numerous nuclear families live in the same structure. Thus, the scale of abandonment must also be considered when examining material patterning in the archaeological record.

In conclusion, the ethnoarchaeological research at La Concha provides archaeologists with additional middle-range linkages at domestic sites. The research confirms that site abandonment is one of the most significant processes that transfer materials from the behavioral to the archaeological realm (Schiffer 1972, 1976). By describing and explaining some of the variability that results from site abandonment, this study has added to the growing body of research on archaeological formation processes, providing more precise linkages between human behavior and the material patterns in the archaeological record.

Acknowledgments
The research at La Concha was conducted in conjunction with the Río Verde Archaeological Project (RVAP) which was funded by the National Geographic Society.

We would like to thank the directors of the RVAP: Raul Arana, Susan Gillespie, David Grove, and Marcus Winter. We would also like to thank Fran Ahern, Wendy Ashmore, Robert Blumenschine, Cathy Cameron, Scott O'Mack, Anne Pyburn, and Steve Tomka for their input during the course of the research and preparation of this article. An earlier version of this article was presented at the 1987 annual meeting of the Society for American Archaeology (Toronto, Ontario).

References

Ascher, R.
  1961 Experimental Archaeology. *American Anthropologist* 63:793–816.
  1968 Time's Arrow and the Archaeology of a Contemporary Community. In *Settlement Archaeology*, edited by K. C. Chang, pp. 43–52. National Press Books, Palo Alto.
Ashmore, W. and G. R. Willey
  1981 A Historical Introduction to the Study of Lowland Maya Settlement Patterns. In *Lowland Maya Settlement Patterns*, edited by W. Ashmore, pp. 3–18. University of New Mexico Press, Albuquerque.
Binford, L. R.
  1981a *Bones: Ancient Men and Modern Myths.* Academic Press, New York.
  1981b Behavioral Archaeology and the "Pompeii Premise." *Journal of Archaeological Research* 37:195–208.
Bonnichsen, R.
  1973 Millie's Camp: An Experiment in Archaeology. *World Archaeology* 4:277–91.
Cameron, C. M.
  1991 Structure Abandonment in Villages. In *Archaeological Method and Theory*, edited by M. B. Schiffer, Vol. III, pp. 155–94. University of Arizona Press, Tucson.
Deal, M.
  1985 Household Pottery Disposal in the Maya Highlands: An Ethnoarchaeological Interpretation. *Journal of Anthropological Archaeology* 4:243–91.
Greenberg, J. B.
  1981 *Santiago's Sword: Chatino Peasant Religion and Economics.* University of California Press, Berkeley.
Haviland, W. A.
  1966 Maya Settlement Patterns: A Critical Review. In *Archaeological Studies in Middle America*, edited by M. A. Harrison and R. Wauchope, pp. 21–47.

Middle American Research Institute Publication 26. Tulane University, New Orleans.
Hayden, B. and A. Cannon
  1982 The Corporate Group as an Archaeological Unit. *Journal of Anthropological Archaeology* 1:132–58.
  1983 Where the Garbage Goes: Refuse Disposal in the Maya Highlands. *Journal of Anthropological Archaeology* 2:117–63.
  1984 *The Structure of Material Systems: Ethnoarchaeology in the Maya Highlands.* SAA Papers No. 3. Society for American Archaeology, Washington, DC.
Horne, L.
  1982 The Household in Space: Dispersed Holdings in an Iranian Village. In *Archaeology of the Household*, edited by R. R. Wilk and W. L. Rathje. *American Behavioral Scientist* 25(6):677–86.
Hurst, J.
  1971 A Review of Archaeological Research. In *Deserted Medieval Villages*, edited by M. Beresford and J. Hurst, pp. 76–144. Lutterworth Press, London.
Lange, F. and C. Rydberg
  1972 Abandonment and Post-abandonment Behavior at a Rural Central American House Site. *American Antiquity* 37:419–32.
Lewis, K.
  1976 Camden: A Frontier Town. *Anthropological Studies 2.* Institute of Archaeology and Anthropology, University of South Carolina, Columbia.
Longacre, W. A. and J. A. Ayers
  1968 Archaeological Lessons from an Apache Wickiup. In *New Perspectives in Archaeology*, edited by S. R. Binford and L. R. Binford, pp. 151–9. Aldine Press, Chicago.
Manzanilla, L., ed.
  1986 *Unidades Habitacionales Mesoamericanas y sus Areas de Actividad.* Instituto de Investigaciones Antropológicas, Serie Antropológica 76. Universidad Nacional Autónoma de México, Mexico City.
Moore, J. D. and J. L. Gasco
  1990 Perishable Structures and Serial Dwellings from Coastal Chiapas: Implications for the Archaeology of Households. *Ancient Mesoamerica* 1(2):205–12.
Robbins, L. H.
  1973 Turkana Material Culture Viewed from an Archaeological Perspective. *World Archaeology* 5:209–14.
Savelle, J. M.
  1984 Cultural and Natural Formation Processes of a

Historic Inuit Snow Dwelling Site, Somerset Island, Arctic Canada. *American Antiquity* 49(3):508–24.

Schiffer, M. B.

1972 Archaeological Context and Systemic Context. *American Antiquity* 37: 156–65.

1976 *Behavioral Archaeology*. Academic Press, New York.

1983 Toward the Identification of Formation Processes. *American Antiquity* 48(4):675–706.

1985 Is There a "Pompeii Premise" in Archaeology. *Journal of Anthropological Research* 41:18–41.

1987 *Formation Processes of the Archaeological Record*. University of New Mexico Press, Albuquerque.

Siegel, P. E.

1990 Demographic and Architectural Retrodiction: An Ethnoarchaeological Case Study in the South American Tropical Lowlands. *Latin American Antiquity* 1(4):319–46.

Stanislawski, M. B.

1973 Ethnoarchaeology and Settlement Archaeology. *Ethnohistory* 20(4):275–393.

Stevenson, M. G.

1979 *Looking for Gold. Historic Sites Survey of Kluane National Park, Southwest Yukon*. Masters thesis, Department of Archaeology, Simon Fraser University.

1982 Toward an Understanding of Site Abandonment Behavior: Evidence from Historic Mining Camps in the Southwest Yukon. *Journal of Anthropological Archaeology* 1(3):237–65.

1991 Beyond the Formation of Hearth-Associated Artifact Assemblages. In *The Interpretation of Archaeological Spatial Patterning*, edited by E. M. Kroll and T. D. Price, pp. 269–99. Plenum Press, New York.

Thompson, E. H.

1892 The Ancient Structures of Yucatan not Communal Dwellings. *Proceedings of the American Antiquarian Society* n.s., 8(2):262–9.

Wilk , R. R. and W. Ashmore, eds.

1988 *Household and Community in the Mesoamerican Past*. University of New Mexico Press, Albuquerque.

Wood, W. R. and D. L. Johnson

1978 A Survey of Disturbance Processes in Archaeological Site Formation. In *Advances in Archaeological Method and Theory*, edited by M. B. Schiffer, Vol. I, pp. 315–81. Academic Press, New York.

PART V

Abandonment processes within sites: archaeological cases

12
Ceramic analysis as a tool for discovering processes of pueblo abandonment

BARBARA KLIE MONTGOMERY

Recent investigations into abandonment processes have relied heavily on ethnoarchaeological studies of abandonment at the household and community levels. Archaeologists have turned toward ethnographic observation as a tool for recognizing behaviors associated with the abandonment of individual houses or entire villages (e.g. Lange and Rydberg 1972; Rothschild *et al.*, this volume; Stevenson 1982). Although the study of abandonment in living societies provides the archaeologist with an array of behavioral possibilities, these accounts must be tested against specific prehistoric cases. In some instances, the events, activities, or behaviors associated with past abandonments may not be repeated by contemporary societies and, therefore, can only be attained through the investigation of archaeological remains. A major problem lies in identifying abandonment processes from material remains that have been subsequently affected by a variety of natural or cultural disturbances.

In order to identify abandonment behaviors, archaeologists need techniques for measuring variability in the prehistoric record. Variability due to natural or cultural disturbances must be distinguished from patterns produced by abandonment behaviors. One technique, the Relative Room Abandonment Measure (Reid 1973), looks at variability in the spatial distribution of ceramic remains at pueblo sites. Two analytical units – whole pots on room floors and sherd density in room fill – are compared to determine the sequence of room abandonment.

The Relative Room Abandonment Measure (Reid 1973, 1978, 1985; Reid, Schiffer, and Neff 1975; Reid

and Shimada 1982) was originally developed as a relative dating technique for distinguishing early abandoned from late abandoned rooms at Grasshopper, a 500-room pueblo occupied during the AD 1300s in the mountains of Arizona. This paper illustrates the additional utility of the measure to identify unexpected behaviors associated with the abandonment of Chodistaas, an eighteen-room pueblo occupied during the late AD 1200s in the Grasshopper Region (Fig. 12.1).

After introducing the Room Abandonment Measure as it was originally applied at Grasshopper, the basic analytical units are borrowed and slightly restructured for the analysis of other pueblo abandonments. The comparison of floor pots to fill sherds not only measures temporal variability in *room abandonment*, but also enables the discovery of processes related to *pueblo abandonment*.

The Relative Room Abandonment Measure

The Relative Room Abandonment Measure orders excavated pueblo rooms at Grasshopper according to when they were abandoned as measured by a cross-plot of whole pots on room floors against the density of sherds in the fill (Fig. 12.2).

According to the model, the following processes are assumed to have operated at Grasshopper (Reid 1973;

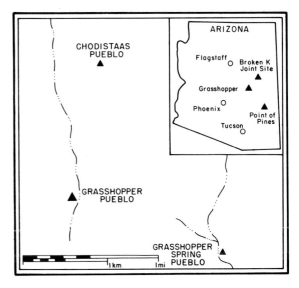

Fig. 12.1 The location of relevant archaeological sites in Arizona.

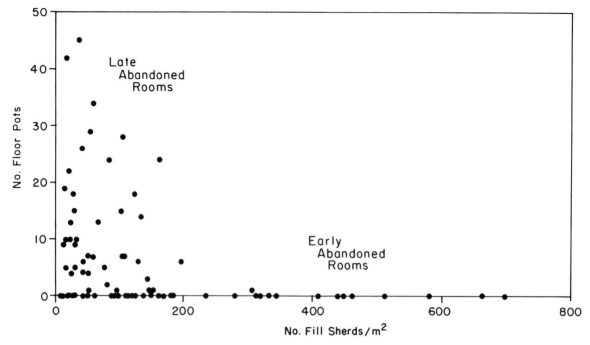

Fig. 12.2   The Relative Room Abandonment Measure as applied to Grasshopper Pueblo (after Reid 1973:116). (Note: Fill-sherd density is expressed in square meters rather than cubic meters because the abandonment measure addresses sherd deposition in two-dimensional space [Reid 1973:115], the only feasible approach to pueblo rooms where trash levels vary greatly in depth within and between rooms.)

Reid, Schiffer, and Neff 1975:217; cf. Ciolek-Torrello 1978):

1. When a habitation room is abandoned while the pueblo is still occupied, usable objects will be retained [curated] in moving to another nearby habitation room.
2. Even if all usable objects are not retained, habitation room floors abandoned while the pueblo is still occupied maintain a high probability of being scavenged for usable items.
3. Abandoned habitation rooms may be used for secondary refuse disposal.
4. The last habitation rooms abandoned will not be scavenged or used as dumps (Reid 1985:22).

The Room Abandonment Measure is based on the normal operation of curation, scavenging, and trash disposal behaviors associated with room abandonment. These behaviors produce recognizable patterns in the ceramic remains, which provide a relative measure of the sequence of room abandonment.

1. Rooms abandoned while the pueblo was still occupied contain little or no *de facto* refuse on the last utilized habitation floor but may contain a high density of secondary refuse in the room fill above the floor.
2. Rooms abandoned at or near the time of pueblo abandonment have a high density of *de facto* refuse on the last utilized habitation floor and a low density of secondary refuse in the room fill above the floor (Reid 1985:22).

These two variables, secondary refuse as measured by the density of fill sherds and *de facto* refuse as measured by the number of floor pots, "were plotted as a scattergram (Figure 2) . . . The distribution confirms the assumption that rooms with a high sherd density have no ceramic vessels on the floor and that rooms with high de facto refuse have a low sherd density in the fill" (Reid 1973:115).

The abandonment measure can be restructured into a four-cell matrix to analyze floor and fill remains from a slightly different perspective:

		No. of floor pots	
		Low	High
Fill-sherd density	Low	A	B
	High	C	D

When individual rooms are assigned to the appropriate category, patterns emerge that not only provide information on the sequence of room abandonment, but also lead to the *discovery* of abandonment behaviors. With this restructuring, the Room Abandonment Measure is adapted for comparing processes of *pueblo abandonment*.

Reid's application of the abandonment measure identifies rooms that fall within group B, or late abandoned rooms, and group C, those rooms abandoned early in the sequence. Ciolek-Torrello's (1978) research on defining room function leads to the identification of rooms belonging to group A. Many rooms with few pots on the floor and a low density of fill sherds were ceremonial or limited-activity rooms abandoned late in the occupation. Activities in these rooms involved few pots, unlike storage or habitation rooms (See Ciolek-Torrello 1985 and Reid and Whittlesey 1982 for room function typologies).

Although this matrix produces categorical data, data sets will fall along a continuum that cross-cuts these categories. Only the extreme cases fall neatly into one of the four groups. Grasshopper, for example, contains rooms that range from many floor pots with very low densities of fill to no floor pots and high densities of fill, with rooms falling between these two extremes (Fig. 12.2). The division of rooms into four groups simplifies the data while highlighting patterns in the ceramic remains.

Analyses of abandonment at Grasshopper have identified late abandoned rooms that fall within groups A and B, and early abandoned rooms belonging to group C. The Room Abandonment Measure, based on a limited set of expected processes of site formation, would predict the absence of rooms with both a large number of floor pots and a high density of fill sherds. It is not surprising, therefore, that rooms at Grasshopper have not been assigned to group D.

Pueblo abandonment beyond the Grasshopper region

The Room Abandonment Measure has also been applied at Broken K Pueblo (Schiffer 1989) and at the Joint Site (Schiffer 1976). These applications attest the viability of the abandonment categories at sites outside the Grasshopper region (see Fig. 12.1). Conveniently, these sites are also particularly suited for comparison with Grasshopper and Chodistaas. The ninety-five-room pueblo of Broken K (Hill 1970) and the Joint Site, with thirty-six rooms, bridge the size gap between the 500-room pueblo of Grasshopper and the eighteen-room

settlement at Chodistaas. Furthermore, the occupations of Broken K (AD 1150–1300) and the Joint Site (AD 1220–70) overlap with the occupation of Chodistaas (AD 1263–90s).

Schiffer (1976:129–33) uses the Room Abandonment Measure as a relative dating technique at the Joint Site where he compares the density of floor sherds with the density of sherds in the room fill to distinguish between early and late abandoned rooms. The number of floor sherds is used as a proxy measure of the number of floor pots because vessels were not reconstructed. Schiffer (1989:40–1) also uses this technique to distinguish between trash-filled rooms and late abandoned rooms at Broken K Pueblo.

Room abandonment at these two pueblos follows a pattern similar to Grasshopper (See Schiffer 1976:131, 1989:40). Again we find rooms that fall within groups A, B, and C. These similarities suggest that these three groups, when found together within pueblo sites, may be representative of behaviors associated with pueblo abandonments throughout much of east-central Arizona.

The absence of rooms that fall within group D is not surprising given our understanding of site formation. Under normal abandonment circumstances, rooms with *large numbers of floor vessels* would not be expected also to contain *high densities of fill sherds*. Expectations are crushed when we return to the Grasshopper region to look at Chodistaas Pueblo. Many of the rooms at Chodistaas fall into group D.

Abandonment at Chodistaas Pueblo

Tree-ring dates securely place the construction of Chodistaas between AD 1263 and 1288. The entire pueblo burned during the 1290s, leaving a rich archaeological record of household ceramic assemblages intact on room floors (Montgomery 1992; Montgomery and Reid 1990; Reid 1989).

Following patterns seen at Grasshopper, Broken K, and the Joint Site, rooms with large numbers of floor vessels would be expected to contain low densities of sherds in the fill (group B). Contrary to expectations, many rooms at Chodistaas with large numbers of floor vessels also contain high densities of fill sherds, placing them in group D.

Fig. 12.3 provides a comparison of ceramic remains from Grasshopper, Chodistaas, and Grasshopper Spring, a nearby pueblo contemporaneous with Chodistaas. The plot of floor pots versus fill-sherd densities for rooms from each site has been overlain by a grid representing the four abandonment categories. Rooms with at

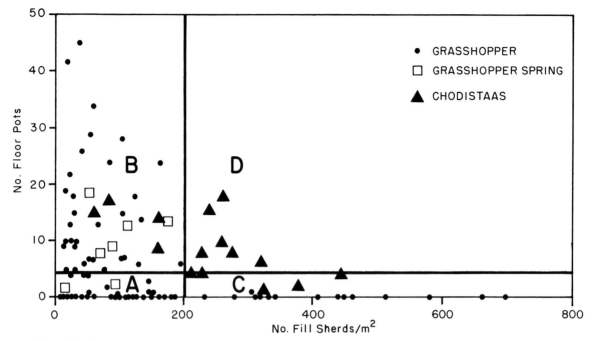

Fig. 12.3   Abandonment groups at Grasshopper, Grasshopper Spring, and Chodistaas pueblos.

least four vessels are defined as having a large number of floor pots. A total greater than 200 sherds/sq m was defined by Ciolek-Torrello (1978:85) as representing early abandoned rooms and is defined here as "high" fill density.

Fig. 12.3 emphasizes the similarities between Grasshopper and Grasshopper Spring and the very different pattern seen in the Chodistaas ceramics. Group D stands out as unique to Chodistaas, a discovery that alerts us to the possibility of previously unrecognized abandonment behaviors.

Formation processes and fill-sherd density

Before we can be confident that these fill deposits are the product of abandonment activities, other cultural and natural processes must be eliminated as possible contributors to ceramic variability (see Montgomery 1992; Montgomery and Reid 1990:91–4).

Slope wash, often a major source of room fill, is not responsible for high densities of sherds in rooms at Chodistaas. These above-ground masonry rooms are located on the highest point of a bluff. The densest area of surface artifacts is found downslope to the east of the pueblo (see Montgomery and Reid 1990:fig. 2).

Another process partially attributable to natural causes, the collapse of walls and roofs, was not likely to produce thousands of fill sherds. The size of roof beams at Chodistaas, where the average diameter measures 10 cm and the largest beam is only 16.4 cm, suggests that roofs were not activity areas that could support large numbers of pots. For comparison, beams from Canyon Creek cliff dwelling that supported roofs used as activity areas measure up to 35 cm in diameter. Furthermore, roof beams at Chodistaas spanned the length of the rooms, which in many cases are twice the length of rooms at Canyon Creek. Although a few pots may have been stored on roofs at Chodistaas, these pots could not have produced an average of more than 6000 sherds in the fill of each room. Clearly, large numbers of fill sherds were not deposited by natural processes at Chodistaas. Next, we turn to cultural processes.

Examples of intentional filling of rooms for reoccupation have been reported for some pueblo sites. At Point of Pines (Haury 1958; see Fig. 12.1), for example, a portion of the main pueblo was burned and then filled with trash to prepare the area for rebuilding and reoccupation. Although two rooms at Chodistaas have prehistoric features built on room fill (a wall across one room and a hearth in the center of another), this temporary reoccupation hardly required the filling of other rooms (Montgomery and Reid 1990:94). The fact remains that most of the rooms at Chodistaas have a high density of fill sherds and no evidence of reoccupation.

In some instances the archaeologist may be responsible for high density counts when sherds from floor vessels are included as part of room fill (see Schiffer 1989), but at Chodistaas broken floor vessels were carefully separated from fill materials in the field and again in the lab after cleaning.

Temporal variation

The striking difference between Chodistaas (AD 1263–90s) and Grasshopper (AD 1300–1400) raises the possibility of temporal differences in abandonment behaviors within the Grasshopper region. A look at patterns in the ceramic remains of Grasshopper Spring, a nine-room pueblo occupied and abandoned around the same time as Chodistaas, reveals that Chodistaas is indeed an anomalous case.

Chodistaas and Grasshopper Spring are located less than two miles apart (Fig. 12.1). Tree-rings date the beginning of construction to the AD 1270s, slightly later than Chodistaas. Grasshopper Spring also burned during the 1290s when the entire pueblo was abandoned. Ceramic assemblages resting on room floors appear to be complete sets of household vessels and contain the same types of pottery as at Chodistaas.

As expected from the large numbers of floor vessels, rooms at Grasshopper Spring contain low densities of fill sherds and fit neatly into group A or B (Fig. 12.3). In spite of the many characteristics shared by Chodistaas and Grasshopper Spring, patterns in the ceramic remains of room fill indicate that different activities were associated with the abandonment of these two pueblos. Differences in abandonment behaviors, therefore, are not the result of temporal variation in cultural practices.

Ritual burial of structures at Chodistaas

The most reasonable explanation for the presence of rooms at Chodistaas with both large numbers of floor pots and high densities of fill sherds is that rooms were intentionally filled with deposits from middens surrounding the pueblo (Montgomery and Reid 1990:94). The intentional filling of rooms probably occurred soon after the burning of the pueblo. This abandonment behavior is interpreted as a ritual act associated with the "death" of the pueblo and subsequent burial of household belongings.

That household belongings at Chodistaas were buried and those at Grasshopper Spring, which also burned, were not is probably related to ethnic differences between the two communities. Evidence for two ethnic

groups includes major differences in projectile point morphology (Lorentzen 1991), architectural layout, and types of thermal features (Lowell 1991). Thermal features at Chodistaas include both firepits and slab-lined hearths, while only firepits are found at Grasshopper Spring. Differential treatment of homes at the time of their destruction can be added to the evidence supporting the presence of two ethnic groups living side by side on the Grasshopper plateau during the late AD 1200s.

Intentional filling of structures for reoccupation is an activity that has been recognized sporadically at prehistoric sites throughout the Southwest. Burned rooms at the mountain pueblo of Point of Pines, as discussed earlier, were intentionally filled for reoccupation (Haury 1958).

Ritual intentions are more difficult to document and usually involve the burning of structures and the archaeological recovery of human remains (e.g. Wilshusen 1986). The Duckfoot Site (AD 850s–880) in southwestern Colorado provides one example of the burning of pit structures after several individuals died and were placed on the floors of these structures (Lightfoot 1992; Varien and Lightfoot 1989). Examples of ethnographic groups in the Southwest who burned one or more structures after the death of an individual include the Western Apache (Bushkirk 1986:107; Gifford 1940:68; Goodwin 1969:518–21), the Havasupai (Iliff 1954:124; Spier 1928:234, 292), the Papago (Tohono Oodam) (Beals 1934:17; Drucker 1941:147; Underhill 1941:46), and Pima (Drucker 1941:147; Ezell 1961:93; Grossman 1873:415), and the Mohave (Drucker 1941:146–7; Allen 1891:615). Although the burned rooms at Chodistaas are probably not associated with the death of individuals (no human remains were found on the room floors), the Room Abandonment Measure indicates an uncommon abandonment situation that, at least provisionally, is best characterized as ritual behavior.

Conclusion

Application of the Relative Room Abandonment Measure to look at variability in ceramic remains at pueblo sites enables the archaeologist to distinguish between early and late abandoned rooms. The restructuring of this abandonment measure into four groups reveals patterns in pueblo abandonment as well as in the abandonment of individual rooms. Previously unrecognized abandonment behaviors were identified at Chodistaas.

Comparison of floor and fill remains is essential for building a complete and accurate picture of abandonment processes. The seemingly unusual events surrounding the abandonment of Chodistaas would have gone undetected, and possibly misconstrued, without consideration of both variables.

This abandonment measure should be applied to other pueblo sites, and perhaps earlier pithouse villages (see Wheat 1954:168–72 and Whittlesey 1986:120–3), so that variability in abandonment behaviors can be identified and compared throughout the Southwest. It is especially important that we watch for rooms that contain both large numbers of floor vessels and a high density of fill sherds (group D). Analysis of the ceramic remains from Chodistaas suggests that this technique may be capable of identifying instances of ritual behavior associated with prehistoric abandonments, a rare opportunity in the archaeological record.

Another implication of this study is the vital role that ritual behavior may have played in the formation of the archaeological record. The deposition of artifacts in the fill of rooms at Chodistaas appears to be directly related to a ritual event and not the result of processes that occurred subsequent to abandonment.

Accounting for the unanticipated combination of floor and fill ceramics at Chodistaas provides an excellent example of the symbiotic relation between ethnoarchaeology, experimental archaeology, and prehistory. Curation, scavenging, and trash disposal behaviors are better understood because of ethnoarchaeological studies (e.g. Deal 1985; Hayden and Cannon 1983). Experiments inform on many aspects of site formation, ranging from the effects of trampling on size distributions of artifacts (Nielsen 1991) to the effects of erosion and depositional processes (Skibo 1987). But information derived from studies of contemporary peoples or from experiments must be used in conjunction with prehistoric data to gain a complete picture of the past (see Montgomery and Reid 1990:95–6; Reid 1985:12–13).

Abandonment at Chodistaas illustrates the importance of analyzing prehistoric behavior on a case-by-case basis. Unexpected events, related to abandonment, were discovered at Chodistaas, which can only be accounted for by analyzing the formation of the archaeological record at this particular site. The ritual burial of pueblo rooms and household assemblages may have been a relatively common activity that has gone unnoticed and its effects on the formation of the archaeological record unappreciated. The question of how artifacts are deposited in the fill of pueblo rooms needs to be examined closely, using prehistoric as well as ethnographic and experimental data, and may lead to further discovery of past behaviors rarely, if ever, observed in present-day societies.

Acknowledgments
The information for this analysis was collected by the University of Arizona Archaeological Field School at Grasshopper with permission from the White Mountain Apache Tribe. An earlier version of this paper was presented at the 55th Annual Meeting of the Society for American Archaeology held in Las Vegas, Nevada. Travel funds for these meetings were provided by the Department of Anthropology at the University of Arizona. I would like to thank J. Jefferson Reid, Michael Schiffer, Catherine Cameron, Sarah Schlanger, Ricky Lightfoot, Steve Tomka, and members of the Department of Anthropology Writers Group, each of whom provided valuable comments on early versions of the manuscript.

References

Allen, G. A.
1891 Manners and Customs of the Mohaves. *Smithsonian Institution Annual Report* (1890), pp. 615–16. Washington, DC.

Beals, R. L.
1934 *Material Culture of the Pima, Papago, and Western Apache.* US Department of the Interior, National Park Service, Berkeley.

Bushkirk, W.
1986 *The Western Apache.* University of Oklahoma Press, Norman and London.

Ciolek-Torrello, R. S.
1978 A Statistical Analysis of Activity Organization: Grasshopper Pueblo, Arizona. Unpublished PhD dissertation, University of Arizona, Tucson. University Microfilms, Ann Arbor.
1985 A typology of room function at Grasshopper Pueblo, Arizona. *Journal of Field Archaeology* 12: 41–63.

Deal, M.
1985 Household Pottery Disposal in the Maya Highlands: An Ethnoarchaeological Interpretation. *Journal of Anthropological Archaeology* 4:243–91.

Drucker, P.
1941 *Culture Element Distributions: XVII Yuman-Piman.* Anthropological Records 6(3), University of California Press, Berkeley and Los Angeles.

Ezell, P. H.
1961 The Hispanic Acculturation of the Gila River Pimas, *American Anthropological Association* 5(2). Menasha, WI.

Gifford, E. W.
1940 *Culture Element Distributions: XII. Apache-Pueblo*, Anthropological Records 4(1), University of California Press, Berkeley and Los Angeles.

Goodwin, G.
1969 *The Social Organization of the Western Apache*, The University of Arizona Press, Tucson.

Grossman, F. E.
1873 *The Pima Indians of Arizona*, Smithsonian Report for 1871, Washington, DC.

Haury, E. W.
1958 Evidence at Point of Pines for a Prehistoric Migration from Northern Arizona. In *Migrations in New World Culture History*, edited by R. H. Thompson, pp. 1–7. University of Arizona Press, Tucson.

Hayden, B. and A. Cannon
1983 Where the Garbage Goes: Refuse Disposal in the Maya Highlands. *Journal of Anthropological Archaeology* 2:117–63.

Hill, J. N.
1970 *Broken K Pueblo: Prehistoric Social Organization in the American Southwest*. University of Arizona Anthropological Papers 18, Tucson.

Iliff, F. G.
1954 *People of the Blue Water*. Harper and Brothers, New York.

Lange, F. W. and C. R. Rydberg
1972 Abandonment and Post-Abandonment Behavior at a Rural Central American House-Site. *American Antiquity* 37:419–32.

Lightfoot, R.
1992 Archaeology of the House and Household: A Case Study of Assemblage Formation and Household Organization in the American Southwest. Unpublished PhD dissertation, Washington State University, Pullman.

Lorentzen, L. H.
1991 Change in Projectile Point Form and Function. Paper presented at the meetings of the Southwest Anthropological Association, Tucson.

Lowell, J. C.
1991 Illuminating Fire Feature Variability in the Grasshopper Region of Arizona. Paper presented at the 56th Annual Meeting of the Society for American Archaeology, New Orleans.

Martin, P. S., W. A. Longacre, and J. N. Hill
1967 Chapters in the Prehistory of Eastern Arizona, III'. *Fieldiana: Anthropology* 57.

Montgomery, B. K.
1992 Understanding the Formation of the Archaeological Record: Ceramic Variability at Chodistaas Pueblo, Arizona. Unpublished PhD dissertation, University of Arizona, Tucson. University Microfilms, Ann Arbor.

Montgomery, B. K. and J. J. Reid
1990 An Instance of Rapid Ceramic Change in the American Southwest. *American Antiquity* 55:88–97.

Nielsen, A. E.
1991 Trampling the Archaeological Record: an Experimental Study, *American Antiquity* 56:483–503.

Reid, J. J.
1973 Growth and Response to Stress at Grasshopper Pueblo, Arizona. Unpublished PhD dissertation, University of Arizona, Tucson. University Microfilms, Ann Arbor.
1978 Response to Stress at Grasshopper Pueblo, Arizona. In *Discovering Past Behavior: Experiments in the Archaeology of the American Southwest*, edited by P. F. Grebinger, pp. 195–213. Gordon and Breach, London.
1985 Formation Processes for the Practical Prehistorian: An Example from the Southeast. In *Structure and Process in Southeastern Archaeology*, edited by R. S. Dickens, Jr. and H. T. Ward, pp. 11–33. The University of Alabama Press, University, Alabama.
1989 A Grasshopper Perspective on the Mogollon of the Arizona Mountains. In *Dynamics of Southwest Prehistory*, edited by L. S. Cordell and G. J. Gumerman, pp. 65–97. Smithsonian Institution Press, Washington, DC.

Reid, J. J., M. B. Schiffer, and J. M. Neff
1975 Archaeological Considerations of Intrasite Sampling. In *Sampling in Archaeology*, edited by J. W. Mueller, pp. 209–24. University of Arizona Press, Tucson.

Reid, J. J. and I. Shimada
1982 Pueblo Growth at Grasshopper: Methods and Models. In *Multidisciplinary Research at Grasshopper Pueblo, Arizona*, edited by W. A. Longacre, S. J. Holbrook, and M. W. Graves, pp. 12–18. University of Arizona Anthropological Papers No. 40, University of Arizona Press, Tucson.

Reid, J. J. and S. M. Whittlesey
1982 Households at Grasshopper Pueblo. *American Behavioral Scientist* 25(6): 687–703.

Schiffer, M. B.

1976 *Behavioral Archeology*. Academic Press, New York.

1989 Formation Processes of Broken K Pueblo: Some Hypotheses. In *Quantifying Diversity in Archaeology*, edited by R. D. Leonard and G. T. Jones, pp. 37–58. Cambridge University Press, Cambridge.

Skibo, J. M.

1987 Fluvial Sherd Abrasion and the Interpretation of Surface Remains on Southwestern Bajadas. *North American Archaeologist* 8(2): 125–41.

Spier, L.

1928 *Havasupai Ethnography*, Anthropological Papers No. 3, American Museum of Natural History, New York.

Stevenson, M. G.

1982 Toward an Understanding of Site Abandonment Behavior: Evidence from Historic Mining Camps in the Southwest Yukon. *Journal of Anthropological Archaeology* 1: 237–65.

Underhill, R.

1941 *The Papago Indians of Arizona and Their Relatives the Pima*. US Department of the Interior, Bureau of Indian Affairs, Washington, DC.

Varien, M. D. and R. Lightfoot

1989 Ritual and Nonritual Activities in Mesa Verde Region Pit Structures. In *The Architecture of Social Integration in Prehistoric Pueblos*, edited by W. D. Lipe and M. Hegmon, pp. 73–87. Occasional Paper No. 1, Crow Canyon Archaeological Center, Cortez, Colorado.

Wheat, J. B.

1954 Crooked Ridge Village (Arizona W:10:15) *University of Arizona Bulletin* 25(3), *Social Science Bulletin* 24, University of Arizona, Tucson.

Whittlesey, S. M.

1986 The Ceramic Assemblage. In *The 1985 Excavations at the Hodges Site, Pima County, Arizona*, edited by R. W. Layhe, pp. 61–126. Arizona State Museum Archaeological Series No. 170, University of Arizona, Tucson.

Wilshusen, R. H.

1986 The Relationship between Abandonment Mode and Ritual Use in Pueblo I Anasazi Protokivas. *Journal of Field Archaeology* 13:245–54.

13
Abandonment processes in prehistoric pueblos

RICKY R. LIGHTFOOT

Introduction

This paper presents a discussion of site abandonment processes and applies a simulation approach in a case study of abandonment of a ninth-century pueblo in the American Southwest. The general questions addressed are: (1) To what extent can one use archaeological assemblages to explain both abandonment and preabandonment activities and processes? (2) How can one tell what was removed from or added to the systemic assemblage at the time of abandonment? (3) What can intrasite variability in abandonment assemblages tell us about abandonment processes and behavior?

There is an ongoing and sometimes heated debate in archaeology over what kind of record the archaeological record is, and how we should legitimately use it to learn about the past (Ascher 1961; Binford 1981; Schiffer 1976, 1985). Specifically, there have been many accusations that other archaeologists are misusing the archaeological record by falsely assuming a "Pompeii premise," the term coined by Ascher to refer to a perception of archaeological deposits as "the remains of a once living community, stopped as it were in time" (Ascher 1961:324). Schiffer (1985) criticized Southwestern archaeologists for failing to evaluate adequately the effects of formation processes in creating floor assemblages. He argued that: "The real Pompeii premise is that archaeologists can treat house-floor assemblages at any site as if they were Pompeii-like systemic inventories" (Schiffer 1985:18). Schiffer advocated one alternative which was to evaluate *de facto* refuse depletions, which are reductions from the basic systemic artifact inventory. Cordell, Upham and Brock (1987:573) criticized this

approach because Schiffer had offered no means of scientifically evaluating his results. They concluded that "we can discern no strategy for determining or even evaluating how many of what kinds of objects should be found in any location or context" (p. 574). This paper offers one method of addressing the problem.

To evaluate the content of floor assemblages, archaeologists need independent means of estimating the expected systemic inventory and evaluating the effects of abandonment and postabandonment processes on the archaeological assemblage (Schiffer 1985; Cordell, Upham and Brock 1987; Reid *et al.* 1989). I use the discard assemblage from the Duckfoot Site in southwestern Colorado (Fig. 13.1) to simulate the content of the systemic ceramic inventory. I then compare this expected systemic inventory with the contents of structure floors and evaluate abandonment behavior at the Duckfoot Site.

Abandonment processes

The study of abandonment behavior is important to archaeologists because abandonment processes influence the form and content of archaeological assemblages. Archaeologists are often interested in interpreting behavior and organization based on activities represented by artifact assemblages on floors. Two types of behavior that are uniquely associated with

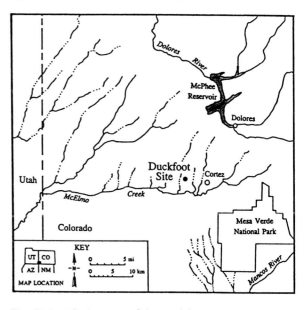

Fig. 13.1 The location of the Duckfoot Site in southwestern Colorado.

abandonment are *de facto* refuse deposition and curate behavior. *De facto refuse* (Schiffer 1972, 1976, 1987) consists of the tools, facilities, and other cultural materials that, although still usable, are abandoned within an activity area. By definition then, *de facto* refuse deposition only occurs at the time of abandonment. *Curate behavior* (Binford 1973, 1979, 1983) is the process of removing and transporting still-usable or repairable items from an abandoned activity area for continued use elsewhere. Schiffer (1985) discusses four other processes that deplete or alter *de facto* refuse assemblages, especially at the time of structure or settlement abandonment. *Lateral cycling* (Schiffer 1972, 1976, 1985) involved the transfer (e.g. giving, selling) of objects from one user to another. *Draw down* (Schiffer 1985, 1987) refers to the tendency for people not to replace worn or broken items when they know they are about to move. *Scavenging* (Schiffer 1972, 1985) refers to removal of *de facto* refuse from an abandoned structure by people still living in the settlement. *Collecting* and *looting* (Schiffer 1976, 1985, 1987) refer to both prehistoric and modern removal of artifacts by non-residents after abandonment of a settlement. It is worth noting that while curate behavior, lateral cycling, scavenging, and looting deplete the *de facto* refuse inventory of one structure or settlement, they also enrich the systemic inventory of another structure or settlement.

Stevenson (1982) studied patterns of abandonment refuse in historic mining settlements in the Yukon Territory. He contrasted assemblages of sites that differed in their abandonment mode with respect to two variables, "degree of prior planning" and "anticipation of returning." Degree of prior planning, which I equate with rate of abandonment, recognizes that abandonment is not a moment in time but a process that takes place over a period of time. Thus, the rate of abandonment refers to the length of the period after which the residents of a settlement or structure know that they are going to leave.

Rate of abandonment

Under conditions of rapid abandonment, Stevenson (1982) found: (1) evidence of manufacture or maintenance in progress; (2) abundant *de facto* refuse; (3) an abundance of items that would normally be curated; (4) *de facto* refuse abandoned in its activity loci; (5) little secondary refuse in living areas. Under conditions of gradual abandonment Stevenson found the opposite of each of these conditions to be generally true.

What Stevenson refers to as "secondary refuse in the living areas" (number 5 above) should more appro-

priately be called "abandonment refuse" (*sensu* Schiffer 1985:27). Abandonment refuse refers to trash that is allowed to accumulate in an activity area when people know the area is soon to be abandoned. Stevenson's expectation that there will be little evidence of manufacturing of artifacts and facilities in progress when abandonment is gradual is similar to Schiffer's (1985) concept of draw down.

Anticipation of return

Where abandonment was rapid and return *was* anticipated, Stevenson (1982) found that there was a particularly strong association between *de facto* refuse and activity loci, and that there was little clustering, or caching, of valuable items away from their use locations. Where departure was rapid and return *not* anticipated items of personal value were more likely to be curated than abandoned, and there was a greater tendency to abandon common, replaceable, utility items in favor of curating personal items.

Under conditions of gradual abandonment, where the residents anticipated returning, Stevenson (1982) found that caching, or clustering of valuable items away from activity loci, was common and that little *de facto* refuse occurred in association with activity loci in living areas. Finally, in gradual abandonments where return was *not* expected, Stevenson (1982) found that there was no caching of valuables and that trash was abundant and in concentrated arrangements within living areas. He also noted one settlement where buildings and mining facilities were dismantled in order to salvage the materials. This salvage activity took place under planned conditions without anticipated return, though it also required a different set of access and transportation conditions than were met by the other mining camps Stevenson studied.

Access

Access refers to the accessibility of a site to postabandonment processes that would deplete its archaeological assemblages (Schlanger 1989, 1991). Access would take into account the distance to the new settlement, the transport capability of the departing population, and the proximity of neighbors who might scavenge to collect materials from the abandoned settlement. If the distance to the new site is great, the transport capability is limited, and the number of return trips to the abandoned site are limited, then the occupants must prioritize what to carry and what to leave behind. If the new settlement is near the abandoned settlement, then one would expect the ease of access to result in abundant curate behavior

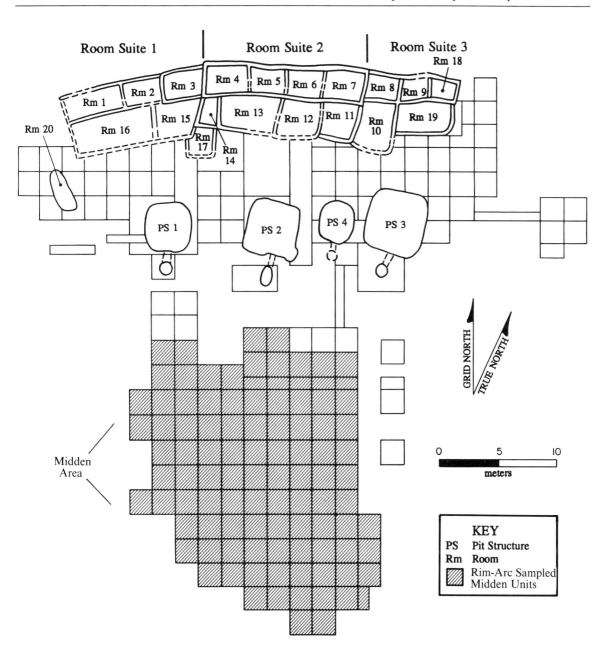

Fig. 13.2　Duckfoot site architecture and excavated areas.

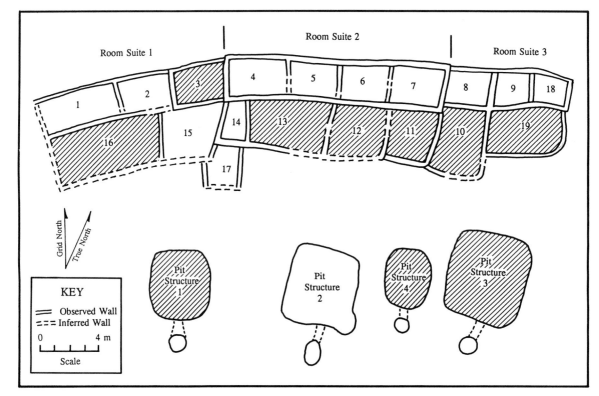

Fig. 13.3   Duckfoot site architecture showing burned (shaded) versus unburned structures.

and reflect a gradual abandonment pattern regardless of the abruptness of initial departure.

Abandonment ritual

There may be circumstances in which ritual activities are important in determining abandonment behavior and material culture content. There are several ethnographic accounts in which the content and structure of the abandonment assemblage was strongly influenced by ritual practices (Brooks 1990; Kent 1984:139–41; Deal 1985:275; DeBoer 1990).

Wilshusen (1986) demonstrated a significant association between the occurrence of "ritual features" in structures and both deliberate destruction of roofs and human interments in late ninth-century Anasazi pit structures at Dolores. Several researchers (Glennie 1983, Glennie and Lipe 1984; Wilshusen 1985, 1986) have shown that it is unlikely that Pueblo I earthen structures burned accidentally as they would be difficult to ignite and slow to burn (cf. Seymour and Schiffer 1987). It is more likely that structures were burned intentionally at the time of abandonment, perhaps as a part of an abandonment ritual.

The archaeological data

The general principles and concepts of assemblage formation discussed above provide a framework for understanding archaeological abandonment assemblages. This study applies these concepts in a case study of an archaeological assemblage from the Duckfoot Site (Fig. 13.2). The Duckfoot Site is a small, well-preserved Pueblo I period (AD 750–900) Anasazi ruin (Lightfoot 1987, 1992a, 1992b; Lightfoot and Varien 1988; Varien and Lightfoot 1989). Based on details of architecture and construction technique, three architectural suites may be inferred (Fig. 13.2). Each suite consists of a block of living rooms, storage rooms, and a pit structure. A fourth pit structure was added late in the sequence.

Length of occupation

Several of the analytic techniques used in this study have been applied recently in evaluating archaeological site use life and continuity of occupation (e.g. Pauketat 1989). One of the main strengths of the Duckfoot data set is the precision of dating afforded by 375 dated tree-ring specimens, with over half being cutting dates. The dates include clusters of cutting and non-cutting dates in the mid AD 850s, the mid 860s, and the early 870s when Pit Structure 4 was added. The latest date from the site is 876. Based on these distributions and a detailed analysis of dates from individual structures, a total occupation span of twenty-five years is inferred, beginning in the mid AD 850s and ending by 880 (Lightfoot 1992b).

Burning of structures

At the Duckfoot Site three of the four pit structures, six of seven front rooms, and one of ten back rooms were burned at the time of abandonment (Fig. 13.3). The burned roof material lay directly on the floors of these structures, with no intervening layer of naturally deposited sediment. Pit Structure 2 was the only pit structure that did not burn. A mound of sediment in the center of the structure and cultural fill within postholes suggest that Pit Structure 2 was deliberately dismantled and filled. Pit Structure 2 was also the only one in which the floor was covered with abandonment refuse and lacked complete or nearly complete reconstructible vessels.

The burning and deliberate destruction of architectural facilities at the site suggests that return to the settlement was not anticipated. The fact that Pit Structure 2 was unburned suggests that it may have been abandoned before the other structures, so that building materials could be salvaged.

Funerary ritual

During the occupation at Duckfoot, the remains of six humans were buried in shallow pits in the southeastern portion of the midden. In addition, at the time of abandonment, seven individuals were placed on the floors of pit structures. Skeletons from both the midden and the pit structure floors include males, females, adults, adolescents, and children. All but one of the adults interred on structure floors were full articulated skeletons. The exception was an adult male on the floor of Pit Structure 2, represented only by a skull and torso. I interpret these interments as deliberate and not accidental catastrophes, though the deaths may have been catastrophic.

The abandonment vessel assemblage

Many of the structures contain *de facto* refuse, including grinding tools, axes, chipped stone tools, and ceramic vessels. Obvious *de facto* refuse includes thirty-six complete or nearly complete vessels, forty-three partial vessels, and forty-eight sherd containers (large sherds that have been recycled for use as shallow bowls or platters).

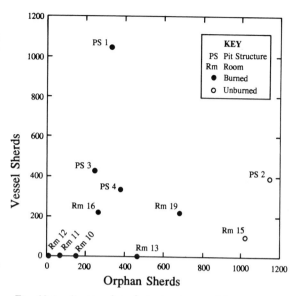

Fig. 13.4   Scatterplot of pit structure and front room floor sherd assemblages showing quantity of orphan sherds compared to sherds in reconstructible vessels.

Fig. 13.4 illustrates differences in structure abandonment assemblages by comparing the frequency of floor sherds accounted for by reconstructible vessels to the frequency of orphan sherds that were not part of reconstructible vessels. This essentially depicts *de facto* refuse along the vertical axis compared to primary, secondary, and abandonment refuse along the horizontal axis. Pit Structure 1 is in a class by itself with 75 percent of its 1375 floor sherds accounted for by reconstructible vessels. Pit Structure 2 is at the opposite extreme, with only 25 percent of its 1540 floor sherds accounted for by vessels. Room 15 is an unburned front room with a large number of orphan sherds but few sherds that refit to form reconstructible vessels. Pit Structure 3 has approximately two-thirds of its floor sherds that formed parts of reconstructible vessels, while Pit Structure 4 and Room 16 fall into an intermediate range with about equal numbers of orphan sherds and reconstructible vessel sherds. The cluster of dots in the lower left corner represents rooms with few sherds and no reconstructible ceramic vessels. While they are similar in appearance, the graph in Fig. 13.4 is different from Reid's "Relative Room Abandonment Measure" as used by Montgomery (1990 and this volume). Fig. 13.4 only includes floor sherds, whereas the Relative Room Abandonment Measure compares the abundance of sherds on floors with their abundance in postabandonment fill of the same structure.

Summary of abandonment context

The interment of human bodies in each pit structure at the time of abandonment suggests there may have been some catastrophic circumstance that stimulated a rapid, unplanned abandonment. The intentional destruction of all pit structures and living rooms implies that there was no anticipation of return. The destruction of the structures meant there was no intent to reuse the same facilities, and the absence of caching meant the *de facto* refuse was irretrievable. Survey data in the locality surrounding Duckfoot indicate a hiatus in occupation of more than 100 years after the abandonment of the dozen or so Pueblo I habitations in the locality.

Discard processes

Midden deposits at the Duckfoot site are south of the pit structures and cover an estimated 400 sq m. The boundaries of the midden were determined by excavating a contiguous block of squares to a point at which artifact frequency diminished sharply. Only in the southeastern corner of the midden did excavations fail to reach this limit, but excavation coverage does include an estimated 96 percent of the midden deposits. Other artifacts occur on the modern ground surface, in structure fills, in postabandonment deposits above the courtyard, and so forth. These artifacts are treated as part of the discard assemblage in this study. Also, the miscellaneous floor sherds that do not contribute to restorable vessels are considered to be part of the discard assemblage and these probably represent abandonment refuse.

Postabandonment processes

Postabandonment access to the Duckfoot Site was limited by distance, destruction of facilities, limited transport capability, and perhaps by taboos associated with funerary and abandonment rituals. None of the structures contained abundant refuse in their post-occupational fill, which supports an argument for simultaneous abandonment of structures in this small pueblo. If there was postabandonment looting and collecting at the Duckfoot Site, it was not likely to affect the pit structure floor assemblages where the massive roofs collapsed and sealed the floors. The rooms did not burn as intensely as the pit structures and their fill is much shallower. The bones of woodrats (*Neotoma* sp.) are common in room fills, and while some may have been food for the Anasazi, others could have been postabandonment residents of the decaying room block. This would further suggest a more gradual collapse of the room block. If the rooms were collapsing gradually it would mean that the contents of the rooms would have

been accessible to some postabandonment collecting soon after abandonment. Postabandonment sherd collecting from the midden deposits for use as pottery temper also remains a possibility that cannot be ruled out.

Recovery processes

The completeness of recovery of the archaeological discard assemblage affects the results of this study because the expected systemic inventory is derived from the discard assemblage. All the rooms, pit structures, and courtyard areas were excavated as well as an estimated 96 percent of the midden deposits. All excavated deposits except the natural, upper fill of pit structures were screened through quarter inch mesh. An estimated 4 percent of the midden deposits remain unexcavated, as well as a "halo" of low-artifact-density deposits beyond the excavated portion of the site. The recovered assemblage is estimated to include more than 90 percent of the artifacts at the site, and it is expected to be representative of the total population of artifacts in the archaeological assemblage.

What was the systemic inventory?

The remainder of this paper discusses an approach to assessing the content and context of the abandonment assemblage independently, focusing on ceramics. This approach uses the archaeological discard assemblage, which includes midden deposits, fill contexts, and miscellaneous floor sherds, to infer the content of the systemic inventory. The abandonment floor assemblages are then compared to this expected systemic inventory to evaluate the effects of cultural formation processes.

Simulation of vessel breakage and discard

I developed a program that used a Monte Carlo process (Aldenderfer 1978:14) to simulate the total vessel discard assemblage produced by a user-defined systemic inventory and occupation span. The simulation models the same variables used in the general discard equation (cf. Schiffer 1976:60; 1987:54):

$$\text{Total discard} = \frac{(\text{Systemic frequency}) \times (\text{Length of occupation})}{\text{Artifact use life}}$$

Which may be transformed to solve for systemic frequency:

$$\text{Systemic frequency} = \frac{(\text{Artifact use life}) \times (\text{Total discard})}{\text{Length of occupation}}$$

Using this formula, if one can calculate or estimate artifact use life, total discard, and length of occupation, then it is possible to estimate the frequency of an artifact type in the systemic inventory. The simulation introduces a stochastic element by comparing the breakage probability of each vessel in the systemic inventory to a random number (e.g. the Monte Carlo process) on an annual basis. The inverse of each vessel-class use life represents an annual probability of breakage. The simulation model assumes that the initial systemic vessel inventory was restored annually to its starting values and that all broken vessels are discarded at the site. Based on the interpretation of Duckfoot tree-ring dates (Lightfoot 1992b), the breakage and discard simulation was run with a twenty-five-year occupation duration.

The simulation only accounts for manufactured vessel forms, which excludes sherd containers, sherd scoops, and other modified form classes. Reuse of sherds as tools should not affect the outcome as long as the sherds are eventually discarded at the site. The results would, however, be altered if significant numbers of sherds were ground for use as pottery temper. During the period of occupation at Duckfoot, local pottery contains predominantly crushed rock temper, though later occupants of the area did use crushed sherd temper. The model assumes little about the location of vessel manufacture or trade, only that vessels used at the site were broken and discarded there. The results are also heavily dependent on the assumption that most of the discard assemblage has been recovered through excavations in structures, courtyards, and midden areas, and that the discard assemblage has been minimally altered by postabandonment processes, such as looting, collecting, and erosion.

Estimating vessel use life
Ethnoarchaeological studies offer a source of information on use life of earthenware pottery (David 1972; David and Hennig 1972; DeBoer 1974; DeBoer and Lathrop 1979; Foster 1960; Longacre 1985; Mills 1989; Pastron 1974). DeBoer (1985) also demonstrated that there is a relationship between vessel use life and vessel weight, though his generalization does not account for differences in manufacturing and replacement cost of decorated versus undecorated vessels.

First, average use life values were derived for four functional categories of vessels summarized by Mills (1989:Table 4) from ethnoarchaeological literature. Cooking vessels have an average use life of 2.2 years, which appears inflated by the long use lives (4.5 years) of Kalinga cooking vessels. Without the Kalinga vessels, the average use life of cooking vessels is 1.5 years. More recent studies of Kalinga vessel use life suggest that these early figure were too high, and revised estimates of

Table 13.1. *Inferred use lives of early Anasazi vessels.*

Vessel Form	Inferred Use Life (yrs)
Small cooking jars	1.2 years
Medium cooking jars	1.5 years
Bowls	1.5 years
Large cooking jars	3.0 years
Large storage jars (ollas)	5.4 years
Other (eg. decorated jars)	6.4 years

cooking vessel use life are more consistent with the other cross-cultural averages (pers. comm., James Skibo 1992). In all cases the use lives of serving vessels is approximately the same as for cooking vessels, or about 1.5 years. Storage vessels have a cross-cultural average use life of 5.4 years, and other vessel forms have an average use life of 6.4 years. These four functional categories do not take into account variations in breakage rate due to differences in vessel size. This factor is incorporated into the values used in the simulation, as at least plausible breakage rates for early Anasazi vessels (Table 13.1).

Estimating total discard of gray ware vessels
While the content and structure of floor assemblages is strongly influenced by the final use and abandonment activities in the individual structure, the midden represents an accumulation of secondary refuse from the entire occupation of the site. To estimate the number of discarded gray ware vessels by size and form class, the rim sherds were analyzed to estimate the parent vessel form, rim diameter, and portion of the rim present (Egloff 1973). The estimated portions of rim arc were summed and divided by 360 degrees to estimate the minimum number of discarded vessels from each form class. Where radius values were not available, the sherds were assigned to a form class alone and the sum of lengths in each class was divided by the mean rim circumference for whole vessels in that class. This method produced additional vessel estimates without size subgroups.

The ability to estimate vessel size based on rim diameter is dependent on vessel form and is contingent on there being a significant relationship between the two variables (Blinman 1988; Fitting and Halsey 1966; Whallon 1969). Rim diameter is strongly correlated with vessel volume in some vessel forms (e.g. bowls, wide mouth jars) but not in others (e.g. ollas). The relationship between rim diameter and effective volume (volume of a jar when filled to the base of the neck, as opposed to

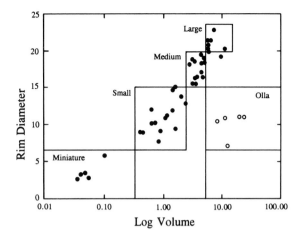

Fig. 13.5   Scatterplot of gray ware jar rim diameter (in centimeters) versus the effective volume (filled to the point of inflection, in liters). The x-axis shows effective volume on a logarithmic scale.

Table 13.2. *Estimated number of vessels in the Duckfoot Site total discard assemblage, which includes midden, other fills, modern ground surface, and miscellaneous sherds, from structure floors that were not part of restorable vessels.*

Vessel form	Total discard
Gray ware olla	46
Large gray ware jar	45
Medium gray ware jar	114
Small gray ware jar	125
Bowl	82
Other	27
Total	**439**

total volume when filled to the rim) of wide-mouth jars in the Duckfoot assemblage is effectively linear when a logarithmic transformation is applied to the effective volume (Fig. 13.5).

Midden deposits at the Duckfoot Site cover approximately 400 sq m and are 20 to 30 cm thick over that area (Fig. 13.2). Gray ware ceramics from 384 sq m of excavated midden and surrounding deposits were included in the rim arc analysis. The excavation units in this sample account for more than 65,000 sherds including more than 57,700 gray wares, 3616 of which are rim sherds. The total discard assemblage includes the sherds in the midden and in all other contexts except sherds that are parts of reconstructible vessels in structures. Sherds from rim-arc-sampled contexts represent 53 percent of the total ceramic discard assemblage by weight. This sample should be adequate to estimate accurately the relative proportion of vessel forms in the sherd assemblage. Rim arc sample results were used to transform the remaining gray ware sherd discard assemblage into vessel estimates by form and size classes on the basis of weight (Table 13.2). A correction factor of 10 percent was added to the total weight of sherds outside the rim arc sample to account for sherds not recovered from the unexcavated periphery of the site.

The combined category of red ware and white ware sherds at Duckfoot represents 7 percent of the sherd assemblage by weight and 10 percent by count. I use relative sherd frequencies to estimate the proportion of

bowls, jars, and other forms. This proportion was then multiplied by total sherd weight and divided by average vessel weight for each form class. The calculations for estimating decorated vessels in the discard assemblage are less precise than those used for gray ware vessels, and therefore the decorated vessel estimates are more suspect than those of gray wares.

Results of the simulation

The vessel assemblage values that produced the best simulation of the Duckfoot discard assemblage consist of six small jars, seven medium jars, five large jars, ten ollas, five bowls, and seven other vessel forms (such as decorated jars, seed jars, and miniature jars). These values represent the estimated average momentary population of vessels in use for the entire settlement.

Site systemic inventory
What can the difference between the archaeological vessel assemblage and the simulated systemic inventory tell us about abandonment behavior? Fig. 13.6 compares the actual assemblage of complete or nearly complete vessels from the floors of all Duckfoot structures with the expected assemblage. Medium jars are very near their expected frequency of occurrence, while small cooking jars and other vessel forms are about a third more abundant than expected. Large jars, ollas, and bowls are much less common than expected.

The vessel categories that are depleted are the most valuable in terms of replacement costs. Large gray ware cooking jars and ollas are expensive because their size requires more time and materials than smaller vessels. Decorated vessels, though small, have a high production

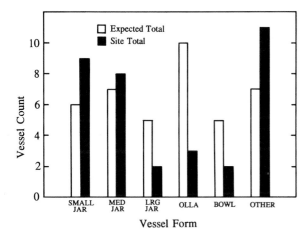

Fig. 13.6   Histogram showing the whole vessel assemblage from structure floors at Duckfoot compared to a simulated systemic vessel inventory.

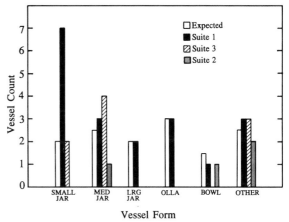

Fig. 13.7   Histogram showing Duckfoot site architectural suite vessel assemblages compared to a simulated systemic vessel inventory.

cost because of the manufacturing steps of polishing, preparing paint, and painting designs. Additionally, the decorated vessels may have had greater personal value because the design communicated a more complicated message than undecorated gray ware vessels. Thus relative costs would seem to be a reasonably good explanation of what was curated versus abandoned when Duckfoot was evacuated.

If abandonment was rapid, then surplus vessels may have been curated and moved to the new site on an immediate priority basis. The data illustrated in Fig. 13.6 suggest that if the simulated assemblage accurately portrays the systemic assemblage at Duckfoot, then large cooking jars, large storage jars (ollas), and bowls were prioritized for curation and transport to the new habitation site.

Architectural suite systemic inventory

What do the abandonment assemblages of individual architectural suites tell us about abandonment behavior? The three architectural suites at Duckfoot may be treated as separate household units. The expected systemic inventory for each household group is modeled as one third of the whole site inventory, though some variation is expected. Do individual architectural suites have abandonment assemblages in the archaeological context that approximate the simulated household systemic inventory? Fig. 13.7 shows the abandonment vessel assemblage for each architectural suite compared to the simulated household vessel inventory.

The vessel forms that appeared depleted in the whole site comparison only appear depleted in Architectural Suites 2 and 3. Architectural Suite 1 has an abandonment vessel inventory that closely approximates the expected inventory with two exceptions: small jars are more than three times more abundant than expected, and miniature jars are absent.

Architectural Suite 3 had restorable vessels in Pit Structure 3 and in Room 19. The architectural suite as a whole contained approximately the expected number of small and medium cooking jars, though it lacked large cooking jars, ollas, bowls, and decorated jars. Two miniature jars are represented in the "other" category, bringing it near its expected level for the architectural suite (Fig. 13.7).

Architectural Suite 2 is unique in having an unburned pit structure (Pit Structure 2) that lacks whole vessels, except for two miniature jars. Approximately ten to fifteen years after the completion of Architectural Suites 2 and 3, Pit Structure 4 was added between them. It is not clear which architectural suite Pit Structure 4 was associated with, but for this comparison its assemblage was grouped with Architectural Suite 2. Pit Structure 4 burned at abandonment with an apparently depleted vessel assemblage consisting of one medium cooking jar and one decorated bowl on the floor. In spite of the fact that it consists of the largest number of structures, Architectural Suite 2 has the most depleted vessel assemblage on its floors.

The simulated vessel inventory, derived from the discard assemblage, provides a standard for comparing and evaluating how many vessels to expect in a systemic inventory for the site as a whole or for an individual suite of structures. The diversity of abandonment assemblages probably reflects differences in abandonment processes between architectural suites. The abandonment inventory of Architectural Suite 1 approximates the expected systemic assemblage, though its small-jar frequency may have been enriched by lateral cycling, scavenging from the other architectural suites, or abandonment ritual. Architectural Suite 2 has a depleted vessel inventory which suggests that its systemic inventory may have been depleted by curation, scavenging, or lateral cycling. Pit Structure 2 with its unburned roof would have been more susceptible to scavenging than the other pit structures.

Architectural Suites 1 and 3 meet many of the expectations of rapid abandonment: abundant *de facto* refuse in the living area, presence of "normally curated" items, and little secondary refuse (or abandonment refuse) in the living area. Architectural Suite 2, and Pit Structure 2 in particular, fits the material conditions expected for a more gradual abandonment; the suite contains abundant abandonment refuse (*sensu* Schiffer 1985) on floors, few "normally curated" items, and no artifact manufacturing in progress.

Abandonment assemblage enrichment?

Most of the processes that result in depletion of *de facto* refuse inventories may also result in the enrichment of assemblages in other structures and sites. Of particular concern at the Duckfoot Site was the impact of funerary ritual on the content and distribution of pit structure floor assemblages. It is common to find vessels and other funerary offerings in graves. Therefore, because pit structures at Duckfoot were used as tombs at the time of abandonment, there is a possibility that the floor assemblages were enriched as a part of the funerary events associated with the abandonment of the pit structures. While *de facto* refuse is more abundant in the pit structures than in rooms, the simulated assemblage comparisons at the architectural suite level show little evidence of enrichment of the *de facto* refuse assemblages. It seems reasonable to infer that the abandonment vessel inventory at the Duckfoot Site reflects more typical activities in the systemic context and not just the funerary events associated with abandonment.

The only evidence of inventory enrichment associated with abandonment is the larger than expected number of small jars in Pit Structure 1. Small jars are not more abundant than expected for the site as a whole, but they are more concentrated than expected in a single room

suite. Taken together, these results could be interpreted as indicating that small jars have been modeled incorrectly in the expected assemblage, or that there was lateral cycling of small jars (such as gifts, items of exchange, or funerary goods) from the residents of other architectural suites at the time of abandonment. The only vessel category in Architectural Suite 1 that is significantly under-represented is miniature vessels, which are absent entirely. Therefore, it is reasonable to interpret the abandonment vessel inventory in Architectural Suite 1 as equivalent to the expected systemic vessel inventory with the exception of small and miniature jars.

Architectural Suite 3 has an assemblage that is depleted in all vessel categories except small jars, medium jars, and miniature jars. Small jars occur in their expected frequency, while small and miniature jars are slightly more abundant than expected though probably within a normal range of variation. Architectural Suite 2 is the most depleted, in spite of the fact that in the current groupings it contains the largest number of domestic rooms (three) as well as two pit structures (Pit Structures 2 and 4). The single medium jar and olla are below their expected value; the decorated bowl is equal to its expected value, while miniature jars are more abundant than expected. With the exception of small jars, the assemblages do not appear enriched at the level of the architectural suite.

I interpret the assemblage differences between architectural suites to be largely the result of abandonment processes. For example, depletion of the *de facto* refuse vessel assemblages could be due to curation of vessels or to a failure to replace broken vessels during the final period of occupation when abandonment was anticipated.

Conclusion

This study applies general principles of site formation and abandonment to explain abandonment behavior in a prehistoric site context. Some approaches to the study of formation processes have been criticized because they do not go far enough in attempting to evaluate "how many of what kinds of objects should be found in any location or context" (Cordell, Upham, and Brock 1987:574). Archaeologists often equate a rich floor assemblage in a burned structure with a complete systemic inventory (e.g. Montgomery and Reid 1990:93–4; Pauketat 1989:299–300). This type of inference is tempting, and in some cases may be justified, but it is rarely tested. This paper experiments with an approach that uses discard assemblages as a means of estimating the systemic inventory. There is a quantitative relationship between item use and items discarded in the systemic context. This paper uses only the ceramic assemblage, but the approach could easily be expanded to other material categories. The methods and results of this study also contribute to an increasing literature in archaeology of attempts to monitor population size and duration of occupation for archaeological sites based on the types and frequencies of refuse they contain (Kohler and Blinman 1987; Pauketat 1989; Schlanger 1991; Varien 1990).

One weakness of this method is its reliance on empirical generalizations derived from ethnoarchaeological research for calibrating discard rates for various tool and vessel forms and uses. Some variability exists in ethnogeographically derived ceramic vessel breakage and discard rates. This variability may result from differences in materials (e.g. clay and temper), technology (e.g. firing temperature), or use (e.g. whether cooking cornmeal mush is the equivalent of cooking rice). At this time, however, ethnoarchaeological data provide the best source for deriving an estimate of vessel use lives (Mills 1989).

By modeling abandonment as a distinct period in the depositional history of sites, we are better able to filter out its effects on the content and organization of refuse we find in structures and activity areas. Separating the effects of abandonment processes from those of pre-abandonment processes on the formation of archaeological assemblages may strengthen our ability to evaluate other inferences about social organization and cultural behavior (Lightfoot 1992a; Varien and Lightfoot 1989). This study introduces some methods and approaches that may be useful in evaluating abandonment assemblages and processes.

Acknowledgments
I thank William D. Lipe and Mark D. Varien for challenging me to worry more about what produced the floor assemblages at Duckfoot and helping me to conceptualize ways to evaluate them. I appreciate the useful comments I received on previous versions of the manuscript from Catherine M. Cameron, Melissa Gould, Kristin A. Kuckelman, A'ndrea Elyse Messer, Barbara K. Montgomery, Michael B. Schiffer, and Sarah H. Schlanger. I appreciate the continuing support of the Crow Canyon Archaeological Center. A grant from the Wenner-Gren Foundation for Anthropological Research supported ceramic refitting studies which made vessel reconstruction possible and contributed to a much better understanding of abandonment processes at Duckfoot.

References

Aldenderfer, Mark S.
1978 Computer Simulation for Archaeology: An Introductory Essay. In *Simulations in Archaeology*, edited by Jeremy Sabloff, pp. 11–49. Smithsonian, Washington, DC.

Ascher, Robert
1961 Analogy in Archaeological Interpretation. *Southwestern Journal of Anthropology* 17:317–25.

Binford, Lewis R.
1973 Interassemblage Variability–The Mousterian and the "Functional Argument." In *The Explanation of Culture Change: Models in Prehistory*, edited by C. Renfrew, pp. 227–53. Duckworth, London.
1979 Organization and Formation Processes: Looking at Curated Technologies. *Journal of Anthropological Research* 35:255–73.
1981 Behavioral Archaeology and the "Pompeii Premise." *Journal of Anthropological Research* 37:195–208.
1983 Forty-Seven Trips: A Case Study in the Character of Archaeological Formation Process. In *Working at Archaeology*, edited by L. R. Binford, pp. 243–68. Academic Press, New York.

Blinman, Eric
1988 The Interpretation of Ceramic Variability: A Case Study from the Dolores Anasazi. PhD dissertation, Washington State University. University Microfilms, Ann Arbor.

Brooks, Robert
1990 Household Abandonment Among Sedentary Plains Societies: Behavioral Sequences in Interpretation of the Archaeological Record. Paper presented at the 55th Annual Meeting of the Society for American Archaeology, Las Vegas, Nevada.

Cordell, Linda S., Steadman Upham, and Sharon L. Brock
1987 Obscuring Cultural Patterns in the Archaeological Record: A Discussion from Southwestern Archaeology. *American Antiquity* 52:565–77.

David, Nicolas
1972 On the Lifespan of Pottery, Type Frequencies, and Archaeological Inference. *American Antiquity* 37:141–2.

David, Nicolas and Hilke Hennig
1972 *The Ethnography of Pottery: A Fulani Case Seen in Archaeological Perspective*. Addison-Wesley Module 21, Reading, MA.

Deal, Michael
1985 Household Pottery Disposal in the Maya High-

lands: An Ethnoarchaeological Interpretation. *Journal of Anthropological Archaeology* 4:243–91.

DeBoer, Warren R.
1974 Ceramic Longevity and Archaeological Interpretation. *American Antiquity* 39:335–443.
1985 Pots and Pans Do Not Speak, Nor Do They Lie: The Case of Occasional Reductionism. In *Decoding Prehistoric Ceramics*, edited by Ben A. Nelson, pp. 347–57. Southern Illinois University Press, Carbondale.
1990 Abandoned Homes and Better Gardens: A Case Study From the Tropical Rainforests of Ecuador. Paper presented at the 55th Annual Meeting of the Society for American Archaeology, Las Vegas, NV.

DeBoer, Warren R. and Donald W. Lathrap
1979 The Making and Breaking of Shipbo-Conibo Ceramics. In *Ethnoarchaeology: Implications of Ethnography for Archaeology*, edited by C. Kramer, pp. 102–38. Columbia University Press, New York.

Egloff, B. J.
1973 A Method for Counting Ceramic Rim Sherds. *American Antiquity* 38:351–3.

Fitting, James E. and John R. Halsey
1966 Rim Diameter and Vessel Size in Wayne Ware Vessels. *Wisconsin Archaeologist* 47:208–11.

Foster, George M.
1960 Life expectancy of Utilitarian Pottery in Tzintzuntzan, Michoacan, Mexico. *American Antiquity* 25:606–9.

Glennie, Gilbert D.
1983 Replication of an A.D. 800 Anasazi Pithouse in Southwestern Colorado. Unpublished MA thesis, Washington State University, Pullman.

Glennie, Gilbert D. and William D. Lipe
1984 Replication of an Early Anasazi Pithouse. Paper presented at the 49th Annual Meeting of the Society for American Archaeology, Portland, OR.

Kent, Susan
1984 *Analyzing Activity Areas: An Ethnoarchaeological Study of the Use of Space.* University of New Mexico Press, Albuquerque.

Kohler, Timothy A. and Eric Blinman
1987 Solving Mixture Problems in Archaeology: Analysis of Ceramic Materials for Dating and Demographic Reconstruction. *Journal of Anthropological Archaeology* 6:1–28.

Lightfoot, Ricky R.
1987 *Annual Report of Investigations at the Duckfoot Site (5MT3868), Montezuma County, Colorado.* Crow Canyon Archaeological Center, Cortez, CO.
1992a Archaeology of the House and Household: A Case Study of Assemblage Formation and Household Organization in the American Southwest. PhD dissertation, Washington State University. University Microfilms, Ann Arbor.
1992b Architecture and Tree-Ring Dating at the Duckfoot Site in Southwestern Colorado. *Kiva* 57:213–36.

Lightfoot, Ricky R. and Mark D. Varien
1988 *Report of 1987 Archaeological Investigations at the Duckfoot Site (5MT3868), Montezuma County, Colorado.* Crow Canyon Archaeological Center, Cortez CO.

Longacre, William A.
1985 Pottery Use-Life Among the Kalinga, Northern Luzon, the Philippines. In *Decoding Prehistoric Ceramics*, edited by Ben A. Nelson, pp. 334–46. Southern Illinois University Press, Carbondale.

Mills, Barbara J.
1989 Integrating Functional Analyses of Vessels and Sherds Through Models of Ceramic Assemblage Formation. *World Archaeology* 21:133–47.

Montgomery, Barbara K.
1990 Ceramic Analysis as a Tool for Discovering Processes of Pueblo Abandonment. Paper presented at the 55th Annual Meeting of the Society for American Archaeology, Las Vegas, NV.

Montgomery, Barbara K. and J. Jefferson Reid
1990 An Instance of Rapid Ceramic Change in the American Southwest. *American Antiquity* 55:88–97.

Pastron, A. G.
1974 Preliminary Ethnoarchaeological Investigations Among the Tarahumara. In *Ethnoarchaeology*, edited by C. B. Donnan and C. W. Clewlow, Jr, pp. 93–116. Archaeological Survey Monograph IV, Institute of Archaeology, University of California, Los Angeles.

Pauketat, Timothy R.
1989 Monitoring Mississippian Homestead Occupation Span and Economy Using Ceramic Refuse. *American Antiquity* 54:288–310.

Reid, J. Jefferson, Michael B. Schiffer, Stephanie M. Whittlesey, Madeleine J. Hinkes, Alan P. Sullivan II, Christian E. Downum, William A. Longacre, and H. David Tuggle
1989 Perception and Interpretation in Contemporary Southwestern Archaeology: Comments on Cordell, Upham, and Brock. *American Antiquity* 54:802–14.

Schiffer, Michael B.
1972 Archaeological Context and Systemic Context. *American Antiquity* 37:156–65.
1976 *Behavioral Archaeology.* Academic Press, New York.

1985 Is There a "Pompeii Premise" in Archaeology? *Journal of Anthropological Research* 41:18–41.

1987 *Formation Processes of the Archaeological Record.* University of New Mexico Press, Albuquerque.

Schlanger, Sarah H.

1989 The Effects of Site Formation Processes on the Character of Ground Stone Tool Assemblages. Paper presented at the 54th Annual Meeting of the Society for American Archaeology, Atlanta.

1991 On Manos, Metates, and the History of Site Occupation. *American Antiquity* 53:460–73.

Seymour, Deni and Michael B. Schiffer

1987 A Preliminary Analysis of Pithouse Assemblages from Snaketown, Arizona. In *Method and Theory for Activity Area Research: An Ethnoarchaeological Approach*, edited by Susan Kent, pp. 549–603. Columbia University Press, New York.

Stevenson, Marc G.

1982 Toward an Understanding of Site Abandonment Behavior: Evidence from Historic Mining Camps in the Southwest Yukon. *Journal of Anthropological Archaeology* 1:237–65.

Varien, Mark D.

1990 Measuring Site Use Life: Accumulation Rate Studies. Paper presented at the 55th Annual Meeting of the Society of American Archaeology, Las Vegas, NV.

Varien Mark D. and Ricky R. Lightfoot

1989 Ritual and Non-Ritual Activities in Mesa Verde Region Pit Structures. In *The Architecture of Social Integration in Prehistoric Pueblos*, edited by W. D. Lipe and M. Hegmon, pp. 73–88. Occasional Paper No. 1. Crow Canyon Archaeological Center, Cortez, CO.

Whallon, Robert, Jr

1969 Rim Diameter, Vessel Volume, and Economic Prehistory. *Michigan Academician* 2(2):89–98.

Wilshusen, Richard H.

1985 The Relationship Between Abandonment Mode and Feature Assemblage in Pueblo I Anasazi Protokivas. Paper presented at the 50th Annual Meeting of the Society for American Archaeology, Denver.

1986 The Relationship Between Abandonment Mode and Ritual Use in Pueblo I Anasazi Protokivas. *Journal of Field Archaeology* 13:245–54.

14

Household abandonment among sedentary Plains societies: behavioral sequences and consequences in the interpretation of the archaeological record

ROBERT L. BROOKS

Introduction

Since at least the early 1970s, archaeologists have studied abandonment processes and their effect on the archaeological record (Schiffer 1976:88). Initially, concerns were with *de facto* refuse and curation practices as part of the abandonment process. More recently, archaeology has witnessed an intensification and diversification in the study of this phenomenon. Archaeological investigations have been directed at differences in planned vs. unplanned abandonment (Brooks 1989) and utilization of sites from initial occupation to abandonment (Binford 1982; Stevenson 1982), while ethnoarchaeological research has focused on the nature of the abandonment process (cf. Kent 1988; Stevenson 1985; Tomka 1989).

Three fundamental concepts regarding abandonment have arisen from this research. First, differences can be drawn in the nature of the abandonment process; Tomka (1989) has distinguished between episodic, seasonal, and permanent abandonment. Second, abandonment processes operate at the settlement, aggregate, and individual household level. Third, abandonment activities do not always represent orderly planned events; they may be unplanned because of either natural or cultural forces. These considerations can be viewed as a matrix of abandonment functions (Fig. 14.1)

From another perspective the process of abandonment cannot be viewed as a separate, static event. It is always dynamically linked to other events through a structure of behavioral activities. For example, abandonment of an individual household because of deterioration is usually tied in some fashion to construction of a new residence.

This paper explores household abandonment processes found among sedentary Native American societies in the Great Plains region of the United States. Because of the rapid and extensive acculturation of their material culture and architectural patterns, ethnoarchaeological studies are impractical. Instead, it has been necessary to consult ethnohistorical and ethnographic studies. From these accounts, a sequence of abandonment and associated practices has been constructed. In turn, findings from this research are evaluated through comparison with archaeological data from a fourteenth-century Plains Village settlement on the Southern Plains.

The Great Plains region

During late prehistoric and early historic times, the Great Plains region was occupied by a number of semi-sedentary to sedentary village farming societies referred to as Plains Villagers (Wedel 1959). These include the Caddoan-speaking Wichitas, Pawnees, and Arikaras and the Siouan-speaking Omaha, Ponca, Kaw/Kansa, and Mandan (Fig. 14.2). These groups maintained an agricultural existence supplemented principally by bison hunting. The actual percentage of meat vs. corn in the diet, however, varied considerably from group to group. More southerly groups such as the Wichita appear to have been more intensively growing crops, whereas more northerly groups focused greater attention on bison hunting.

These Plains Villagers lived in settlements of seventy-

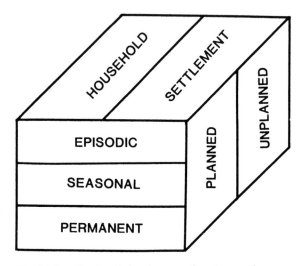

Fig. 14.1   Matrix of abandonment functions and processes.

Fig. 14.2 Geographic distribution of Plains Village societies referenced in this chapter.

five to as many as 2500 individuals strategically located on fertile terraces of the principal streams and rivers. On the Southern Plains, residences took the form of large beehive houses made of cane and thatch (e.g. those of the Wichita). Farther north, earthlodges were constructed by the Pawnees, Mandans, and Hidatsa. From late prehistoric to historic times, there is increasing aggregation into larger village complexes, principally caused by conflicts with surrounding groups. In many instances the villages have palisades and other defensive fortifications. Despite increased aggregation into larger groups, social organization remained at an egalitarian level although some evidence of greater social complexity and ascribed status is thought to occur among Caddoan-speaking groups such as the Arikara and Wichita (cf. Holder 1970; Wedel 1972).

Household abandonment

A review of the ethnohistoric and ethnographic literature on these societies has yielded data on various components in the matrix of abandonment functions. Plains Villagers practiced abandonment at the household and community levels and on an episodic, seasonal, and permanent basis. In this study the concern is

with permanent household abandonment. Permanent abandonment took a number of forms on the Plains and is related to planned and unplanned activities. The most common reason for abandonment of residences was generalized deterioration of the structure. Particularly in the central and northern Plains, an earthlodge would last for roughly seven to ten years before it required replacement (Wilson 1934; Weltfish 1965; Fletcher and LaFlesche 1911). Because of the long period of use and the energy investment required for construction of a new lodge, the abandonment process was carefully planned, sometimes as much as two years in advance (Weltfish 1965:88). Planned abandonment of the old lodge was also procedurally linked in most cases to the construction of the new residence. On the southern Plains, grass dwellings such as those of the Wichita were constructed (cf. Newcomb 1961). Because of their less rugged construction, Wichita houses' use-lives were somewhat shorter than those of earthlodges, averaging less than five years without major rehabilitation. However, the reduced structural integrity also resulted in less preconstruction planning. There are no indications that the Wichita had to develop long-range plans for their house construction. Across the Plains though, the process of house construction and abandonment was closely linked to the overall life-cycle of the residence. As derived from ethnographic and ethnohistoric data, the three basic processes of the residence's life-cycle were construction, use and maintenance, and abandonment. These can be structurally arranged in a sequence of events.

(1) An existing house is periodically evaluated in terms of condition and need for replacement.

(2) If it is determined that replacement rather than repair is necessary, then the household unit begins working on obtaining the necessary materials and organizing kin and non-kin groups to aid in demolition of the old residence and construction of the new house. Construction refers to acquisition of raw materials, selection of the construction site and necessary land alteration activities (e.g. digging of the floor area, leveling of the house area, clearing away scrub growth, etc.). In the case of the Hidatsa, the floor area is cleared to a depth of 0.5 m or greater (Wilson 1934:361). If the location represented the setting of an existing house, then work efforts also consisted of demolition of the deteriorated structure. No estimates are available on the length of time required for razing of the existing house. Erection of the structural elements of the house included wall and support posts, walls, and the roof. Floor preparation (plastering with mud), and placement of the hearth and other internal features (e.g. storage pits,

benches, sleeping platforms, windscreens, etc.) concluded the construction work. The acquisition period for materials can be from several months to as much as two years (as in the case of the Pawnee; Weltfish 1965). Construction might take from a few days to a few weeks depending on the type of dwelling and the season of the year. The archaeological consequences of the activities can potentially include the remains of structural elements and evidence of internal features.

A number of aspects of planned abandonment bear further discussion. First, building materials might not necessarily be scavenged from the existing house. The Pawnee were inclined to rebuild totally, using all new materials (Weltfish 1965), whereas the Hidatsa would often reuse major support posts (Wilson 1934:362). This was principally determined by the scarcity of wood and whether the group wished to risk the use of potentially damaged posts. Thus, scavenging of existing dwellings (e.g. retrieval of posts) might not necessarily be present nor would recycling necessarily reflect scarcity conditions. If the Pawnees needed to plan up to two years in advance to obtain the necessary materials, scarcity was a concern – but not to the extent that reuse of existing building materials was considered.

Second, because of the long-range planning of abandonment and new-house construction, and the short length of time (comparatively) required for construction, there is little evidence that goods were stockpiled for interruptions in the normal acquisition of food and other supplies. The one exception is the materials necessary for building of the new residence. Apparently, household members stayed with kin groups during the interim between old-house demolition and new-house completion. An archaeologist would be unlikely to encounter stockpiled goods in a house. If such did occur, it was probably unrelated to this type of abandonment procedure.

Third, if the new residence was to be constructed on the location of the existing structure, or at the location of another demolished residence, excavation to a solid floor could result in the destruction of the archaeological context of the abandoned dwelling. This type of churning and mixing of multiple house plans is characteristic of Plains Village sites (Wood 1969).

(3) Use refers to basic domestic activities such as cooking, plant and animal processing, tool and clothing manufacture and repair, sleeping, and a variety of other domestic, economic, and/or ritual activities. Many of these activities produce finished items and/or by-products which are discarded on the house-floor. These tools and refuse have the potential for entering the archaeological record as a portion of the house-floor context, as discard within an interior refuse pit, or they may be removed from the residence for some reason. Assuming that some tasks and activities are spatially isolated, the patterns in the discard of these remains have considerable potential for interpreting the economic, social, and religious behavior of the house's inhabitants.

(4) The alternate aspect of this process in the house's life-cycle, maintenance, can result in distortion of discarded materials. Although rebuilding or structural additions to houses undoubtedly cause considerable mixing of house-floors, the principal distortions introduced by maintenance activities are thought to be a product of periodic episodes of sweeping and cleaning of the house-floor. Sweeping or cleaning not only removes the by-products and finished items from their initial discard locations but probably results in most trash being periodically removed from the house. Most importantly, items are no longer where they were initially discarded. Instead of primary or *de facto* refuse, we have secondary refuse. Thus, the remains found on house-floors by archaeologists interested in household analysis represent an unqualified distortion.

(5) The final household life-cycle process, abandonment, is critical to the theme of this paper. Abandonment refers to the time when, for a variety of reasons, the inhabitants move from the house. Depending on the nature of the abandonment, the archaeological context may be significantly affected.

In planned abandonment, either the structure has reached the end of its use life-cycle or some other factor is stimulating a move. One example might be the shift to a new village location. The result is that the structure probably will be scavenged for high-reproduction-cost goods or other valued items. In areas where wood may be at a premium, the support posts may be removed and transported to the new house site as documented for the Hidatsa. After abandonment, additional disturbance results from activities such as scavenging of the house remains by other members of the village or burning and clearing of the house area. Scavenging occurs when other families in the village find materials within the abandoned structure that can be reused (much as we laterally recycle goods today). Burning of the dwelling takes place as a ritual associated with abandonment of the residence or perhaps to rid the area of vermin (rats and fleas). These factors further distort the integrity of the remaining house-floor. Such activities, however, represent a normal sequence of events in the life-cycle of the structure.

In unplanned abandonment, something quite different

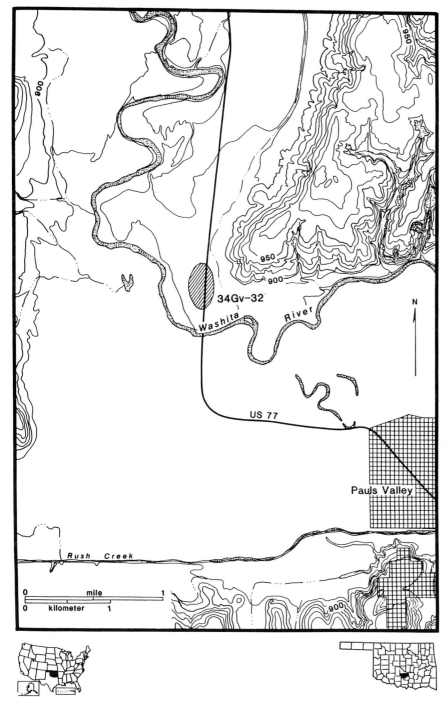

Fig. 14.3 Location of the Arthur site, Garvin County, Oklahoma.

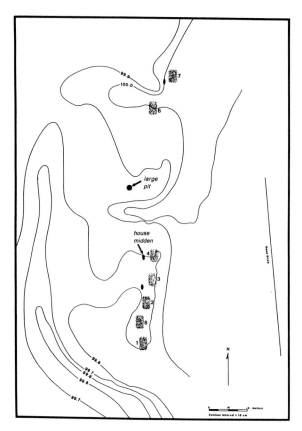

*Fig. 14.4   Settlement pattern of houses and house
middens at the Arthur site.*

occurs. Here, a natural or cultural event disrupts or
interrupts the normal sequence of the house life-cycle.
These events range from the house unexpectedly catch-
ing fire (e.g. Wichita grass houses; Caddoan wattle and
daub houses) to the death of a resident (e.g. the situation
among the Pawnee as well as some other Caddoan language speaking groups). Such natural and/or cultural
events punctuate the normal processes of house use and
maintenance with one outcome being interruption of the
cleaning episodes and final scavenging prior to abandonment. In these cases, the house-floor has greater
numbers of finished items and by-products and contains
artifacts in their primary discard locations. Thus, the
nature of the abandonment process results in house-
floors with greater integrity for analysis of spatial patterns bearing on household activities.

The Arthur site data

During 1982, the Oklahoma Archeological Survey excavated five houses at the Arthur site, a Washita River

phase village in south-central Oklahoma (Figs. 14.3 and
14.4). The Washita River phase represents the southern
expression of the Plains Village tradition culture pattern
(Bell 1984; Brooks 1987). Houses of the Washita River
phase are wattle and daub structures approximately
6.5 m × 4.5 m with two or four central support posts and
a central hearth. Residences have numerous intra-mural
features such as storage/trash pits, benches, and platforms. The archaeological consequences of the distinction between planned versus unplanned abandonment
became apparent during analysis of remains found on
the occupational surfaces of the five houses at the site.

Excavation of the houses at the Arthur site involved
identifying discrete feature concentrations and clearing
these areas until the structural pattern was revealed.
Remains found *in situ* on house-floors were plotted for
point-specific provenience with all five houses excavated
in a standardized fashion. Dated radiocarbon and
archaeomagnetic samples from the five houses place the
range of the site between AD 1300 and 1377 (Table 14.1).
On the basis of overlap in sigma values for the dates and
evidence of differential craft specialization within individual houses, it appears that the houses represent contemporaneous occupations within the village.

House abandonment sequences at the Arthur site

Examination of cultural remains and architectural characteristics revealed significant differences in the content
and context of the various dwellings at the site. Only
House 7 contained evidence that the structure burned.
The other four houses exhibited patterns in their structural context and artifact content which are interpreted as
representing a normal or planned abandonment
sequence. Houses 1–4 contain few finished artifacts on
the floor and no refit sequences (although refit sequences
are present within intra-mural pits). These houses also
appear to have been scavenged prior to final abandonment; many of the wall postholes, as well as the
central support posts, were filled with alluvial sediments
rather than the typical organic stain resulting from post
decomposition. This situation attests to the fact that the
posts were pulled and the holes subsequently filled from
one or more sedimentation episodes.

Although Houses 1–4 display similar contexts and
contents, House 3 was selected to illustrate best the
characteristics of the normally abandoned house (Fig.
14.5). Two central hearths are present in the house and
some evidence for remodeling of the west wall is notice-
able in the posthole pattern. As previously discussed,
postholes for House 3 are filled with orange-brown,

Table 14.1. *Chronometric dates for houses at the Arthur site.*

House	Provenience	Date	Lab no.	Corrected MASCA midpoint
1	Pit 1	665 ± 75 B.P.	Beta 4712	AD 1317
2	Pit 2	550 ± 90 B.P.	Beta 4713	AD 1377
3*	Sq hearth	660 ± 30 B.P.	ART 1–20–82	AD 1290
3*	Cir hearth	640 ± 15 B.P.	ART 1–15–82	AD 1310
4	Center post	580 ± 60 B.P.	Beta 4714	AD 1350
7	Center post	680 ± 70 B.P.	Beta 4407	AD 1312

* These dates represent archaeomagnetic samples.

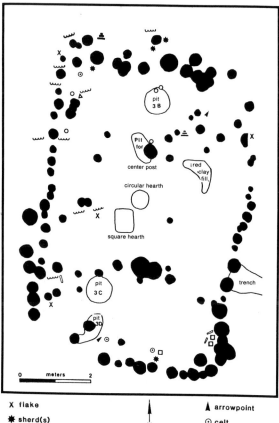

Fig. 14.5 Distribution of features and artifacts where planned abandonment has occurred, House 3, Arthur site.

water-borne sediments. The distribution of artifacts on the floor of House 3 provides further supportive data for normalized abandonment. Thirty-seven items were found on the house floor (excluding refuse pits surfaces). There are a number of significant facts pertaining to these pieces and their spatial distribution. First, few of the approximately forty artifacts are large items. Most are relatively small or are fragments of once larger items (e.g. manos or grinding basins). The absence of refit sequences among these items is of particular significance. If the house represented an uninterrupted sequence of use and discard activities, then refit items should be anticipated. This absence of refit sequences is highly indicative of disruptive activities such as sweeping. A second attribute specific to these items is their spatial distribution. Most materials are either around the perimeter of the house adjacent to the exterior wall or in the vicinity of internal postholes (reflecting supports for benches, sleeping platforms, etc.). This pattern might be anticipated if the house had been swept some time prior to abandonment. This is an apparent contrast to the data presented by Stevenson (1982) indicating that sweeping and maintenance activities are relaxed immediately prior to abandonment. Artifacts are not randomly distributed within the house, nor are they clustered in what could be identified as work areas. Instead, they are in locations where they might be missed during house-cleaning activities. Analysis of these remains in regard to social activities, work areas, or as a basis for spatial partitions in the sexual division of labor would be misleading. The primary behavioral activities accurately reflected in the spatial distribution of remains in House 3 are housekeeping and maintenance functions.

A much different context exists for House 7, the burned dwelling (Fig. 14.6). In uncovering House 7, burned posts were found in place with considerable

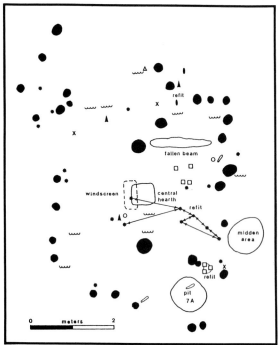

x	flake(s)	△ gary point
✳	sherd(s)	▲ arrowpoint
■	metate fragment	○ hammerstone
□	mano	ƒ bone or
●	sandstone abrader	shell scatter
ℓ	bone tool	

Fig. 14.6 Distribution of features and artifacts where unplanned abandonment has taken place, House 7, Arthur site.

roof-fall overlying the house-floor. Over 100 artifacts were present on the house-floor. Some of these were large items such as a complete bison metatarsal, a windscreen, and a grinding basin (Table 14.2). Refit sequences were established for four artifact categories: a pottery vessel, a sandstone abrader, a windscreen, and the previously mentioned grinding basin. Refit sequences for the sherds are extensive, with over fifty sherds rejoined to comprise one almost complete vessel. The spatial distributions of artifacts within House 7 are also noticeably different from those present in House 3. Some artifacts are randomly dispersed as would be the case in a house prior to a sweeping episode whereas others are concentrated, illustrating probable work areas.

Based on these findings, House 7 experienced an event

Table 14.2. *Distribution of artifacts residing on house floors with length or width dimensions greater than 10 cm.*

Category	House 3	%	House 7	%	Total
Hammerstones	1	50	1	50	2
Manos	1	17	5	83	6
Abraders	1	33	2	67	3
Grinding basins	0	0	1	100	1
Windscreen	0	0	1	100	1
Pottery vessel	0	0	1	100	1
Bone pin or awl	1	50	1	50	2
Bison metatarsal	0	0	1	100	1
Total	4		13		17

which interrupted the normal sequence of maintenance and abandonment. This interruption was undoubtedly a fire. However, it cannot be determined whether the fire was accidental or intentional. A partial child burial (*c.* 2 years of age) was found in the refuse pit of House 7 and could be causally related to the burning. Depending on the nature of the death, the house could have been hastily abandoned and then intentionally burned. Whatever the case, the critical factor is the occurrence of an event which disrupted the normal behavioral sequence. This led to a better contextual record of materials and spatial patterning of activities within the house. Archaeologists relying on information from features at House 7 would undoubtedly discern some of the patterned behavior but the spatial context and pattern to the material remains is what has permitted a fuller interpretation.

Spatial divisions of labor in work activities can be discerned from these materials and their patterns (see Fig. 14.6). The southeast quadrant surrounding the refuse pit appears to be where food processing was conducted. Refitted fragments of a grinding basin as well as several manos were found within or immediately adjacent to the pit. The pit also contained charred corn. It is interesting that hammerstones were found within this activity set. These were possibly used in the manufacture of manos and grinding basins as well as in the processing of corn. If dry corn was being ground into meal, breaking up the kernels prior to grinding would facilitate processing. Sandstone abraders were found in this quadrant as well as in the northeast quadrant. The abraders were probably used in the resharpening of bone tools used in hide working (awls) and agricultural field maintenance (bone hoes and digging sticks). Review of the distribution of functionally related artifacts suggests that the southeast quadrant or perhaps the eastern half of the house was used for women's work activities. The north-central portion of the house contains the bison metatarsal, flaking debris, and chipped stone tools (a Washita arrowpoint and Gary dart point). It is not known whether the bison metatarsal was a tool preform or not, although the presence of tools normally associated with men's work activities attests to this area being associated with male members of the household. The pattern of the pottery refit sequence is also noteworthy. Sherds for this sequence are scattered over roughly one quarter of the house floor with the epicenter being directly over the central hearth. Because of the higher density of sherds in this area, it is suspected that the pot was sitting on one of the cross beam supports for the center posts. A fall from this height would account for the broad dispersal of sherds.

In summary, the unplanned abandonment of House 7 provided an unusual opportunity to obtain a house-floor with a high degree of contextual integrity. The greater integrity permitted a much more exacting interpretation of work areas within House 7 and processes of use and abandonment.

Criteria for determination of house-floor integrity

Comparisons of House 3 and House 7 revealed a number of criteria which can be used to identify the nature of the abandonment process. Determination of whether a house represents planned or unplanned abandonment can aid in defining the correspondence between the house's contextual integrity and remains on the house floor. These criteria are termed floor correspondence measures, and they pertain to the characteristics and spatial distribution of architectural features and items found on the house-floor.

Architectural correspondence measures
Two attributes of the structural characteristics of the house provide clues as to the nature of the abandonment process.

(1) *Posthole characteristics.* It is possible to detect whether posts were left in place or pulled. If postholes with organic stains attesting to decomposition in place or charred posts are present, then potential evidence for unplanned abandonment exists. If, however, postholes are filled with non-organic sediments indicative of post removal, then a case can be presented for a planned abandonment sequence. This is not to say that all (or

even most) charred or organically decomposed posts reflect unplanned abandonment processes. There are undoubtedly many more cases where burned posts are indicative of normal abandonment processes than ones where unplanned activities are manifest.

(2) *Spatial distribution of structural elements.* If burned posts have not been displaced and intact post sections are present, then it is doubtful that scavenging has taken place and evidence exists for unplanned abandonment. This is also true for large segments of daub or roof fall residing above the house-floor. If, however, the context of wall posts and roof fall have been disturbed, it is unlikely that the house-floor has the integrity found in an unplanned abandonment. This measure must be used with some caution. There are undoubtedly many cases where house abandonment is a planned event with the final sequence of the abandonment process being intentional burning of the empty dwelling. Based strictly on architectural evidence, this pattern might be erroneously identified as unplanned abandonment.

Artifact correspondence measures
Three attributes related to artifacts or items present on the house-floor bear on the nature of the abandonment process.

(1) *The size effect.* Larger items left on the floor are thought to reflect unplanned abandonment. This is because larger items usually have considerable energy investment and would be curated if normal abandonment of the house was being undertaken. Large items would be scavenged from the house with only small specimens or fragments of large items remaining. The presence of large items or a refit sequence for a large item is suggestive of unplanned abandonment where consideration was not given to planned removal of high-cost (or value) artifacts. This was supported by a t-test significant at the 0.002 probability level regarding size difference between artifacts on the floors of Houses 3 and House 7.

(2) *Refit sequences.* One of the more significant correspondence measures for identifying unplanned abandonment is the number of refit sequences found on house-floors. In the case of normalized abandonment, it is anticipated that curation, sweeping, and scavenging activities would leave few artifact refit sequences. The greater the number of artifact classes with refit sequences and the more complete the sequence, the more likely the potential for unplanned abandonment and increased contextual integrity of the occupational surface.

(3) *Spatial distribution of items on the house-floor.* In this study, it has been observed that artifacts on the

house-floor tend to exhibit a more uniform distribution when their discard locations have not been distorted by planned abandonment procedures. On the other hand, in cases where planned abandonment is operating, spatial distributions of artifacts tend to be more biased, with many items spatially restricted to the periphery of the house wall or internal post area.

No single correspondence measure is adequate for determining the nature of the abandonment process or the contextual integrity of the house-floor. Instead, some combinations of these measures must be used to determine the overall characteristics of the house and its potential for ascertaining planned versus unplanned abandonment. In situations where it is more likely that planned abandonment is the rule, it is recommended that no attempts be made to discern spatial distributions of materials as they relate to work areas or divisions within the house. In cases where abandonment processes appear to be unplanned, then distortions in the patterns of items on the house-floor may be diminished, thus permitting more productive spatial analysis.

Summary

The focus of this paper has been abandonment processes as derived from ethnohistoric and ethnographic sources. Data from various Plains Village societies demonstrate that the activities of house use and maintenance and subsequent abandonment are critical to comprehension of spatial patterns of remains on the floors of dwellings. The use of data from a fourteenth-century Plains Village community illustrated the archaeological consequences of these processes, especially as they pertain to differentiating between planned and unplanned abandonment. From the study of the cultural processes of use, maintenance, and abandonment and their linkages to the archaeological record, a number of criteria have been identified which can aid in formally defining the type of abandonment and the contextual integrity of the house-floor. The correspondence measures developed during the course of this work also provide a set of procedures for determining the abandonment process operating. Where the archaeologist is dealing with single-room residential structures, these measures can aid in establishing the nature of the abandonment, the type of abandonment (planned or unplanned) and the integrity in spatial patterning of artifacts on the house floor.

Recent interest has focused on the archaeology of the household in sedentary societies (cf. Wilk and Rathje 1984; Netting, Wilk, and Arnould 1982). These studies have yielded substantive information on the social, economic, and religious aspects of family life at the household level. However, without consideration of the factors which distort the contextual integrity of the house-floor (use, maintenance, and abandonment), the use of archaeological data for meaningful interpretation will be minimal. Results from this research suggest that the interruption in the normal house life-cycle that occurs in unplanned abandonment provides a much better context for the study of household activities.

References

Bell, Robert E.
1984 The Plains Villagers: The Washita River. In *Prehistory of Oklahoma*, edited by Robert E. Bell. Academic Press, New York.

Binford, L. R.
1982 The Archaeology of Place. *Journal of Anthropological Archaeology* 1:5–31.

Brooks, Robert L.
1987 *The Arthur Site: Settlement and Subsistence Structure at a Washita River Phase Village.* Oklahoma Archeological Survey, Studies in Oklahoma's Past 15.
1989 Planned Versus Unplanned Abandonment of Dwellings: Impacts on the Context of House Floors. Paper presented at the 54th Annual Meeting of the Society for American Archaeology, Atlanta.

Fletcher, Alice and F. LaFlesche
1911 The Omaha Tribe. *Annual Report of the Bureau of American Ethnology* 27 (1905–6). U.S. Government Printing Office, Washington DC.

Holder, Preston
1970 *The Hoe and the Horse on the Plains: A Study of Cultural Development Among North American Indians.* University of Nebraska Press, Lincoln.

Kent, Susan
1988 *Analyzing Activity Areas.* University of New Mexico Press, Albuquerque.

Netting, R. M., R. Wilk, and B. Arnould eds.
1982 *Households.* Academic Press, New York.

Newcomb, W. W.
1961 *The Indians of Texas: From Prehistoric to Modern Times.* University of Texas Press, Austin.

Schiffer, M. B.
1976 *Behavioral Archaeology.* Academic Press, New York.
1987 *Formation Processes of the Archaeological Record.* University of New Mexico Press, Albuquerque.

Stevenson, M. G.
  1982 Toward an Understanding of Site Abandonment Behavior: Evidence from Historic Mining Camps in Southwest Yukon. *Journal of Anthropological Archaeology* 1:237–65.
  1985 The Formation of Artifact Assemblages at Workshop/Habitation Sites: Models from Peace Point in Northern Alberta. *American Antiquity* 50:63–81.
Tomka, Steve A.
  1989 The Ethnoarchaeology of Site Abandonment in an Agro-Pastoral Context. Paper presented at the 54th Annual of the Society for American Archaeology, Atlanta.
Wedel, Mildred M.
  1972 Claude-Charles Dutisné: A Review of His 1719 Journeys. *Great Plains Journal* 6:5–25.

Wedel, Waldo
  1959 *Prehistoric Man on the Great Plains*. University of Oklahoma Press, Norman.
Weltfish, Gene
  1965 *The Lost Universe: Pawnee Life and Culture*. University of Nebraska Press, Lincoln.
Wilk, R. R. and W. L. Rathje, eds.
  1984 Archaeology of the Household: Building a Prehistory of Domestic Life. *American Behavioral Scientist* 25:611–728.
Wilson, Gilbert
  1934 The Hidatsa Earthlodge. *Anthropological Papers*, American Museum of Natural History 33(5):347–420.
Wood, W. Raymond
  1969 Two House Sites in the Central Plains: An Experiment in Archaeology. *Plains Anthropologist Memoir* 6.

PART VI

Conclusions

15
Understanding abandonment processes: summary and remaining concerns

STEVE A. TOMKA and MARC G. STEVENSON

Introduction

Whether one sees abandonment processes as transforming the material record (e.g. Schiffer 1983, 1985), or as integral components of site formation (e.g. Binford 1981), all archaeologically recovered remains have been conditioned by abandonment processes. It should not come as a surprise that, whether the examples of abandonment come from the Andean highlands, the American Southwest, or the Portuguese lowlands, the processes documented in this volume are germane to the study and interpretation of archaeological remains world wide. In fact, the cross-cultural similarities evident in numerous papers are strong indications that processes of abandonment are not culture or region specific. Rather, it appears that the contextual milieu (e.g. environmental, technological, socio-cultural factors) within which site abandonment takes place contains the factors conditioning abandonment processes.

The papers in this volume are divided into four major sections, ethnoarchaeological and archaeological case studies of regional abandonment processes, and ethnoarchaeological and archaeological case studies of within-sites abandonment processes. Ethnoarchaeological case studies of regional abandonment (i.e. Tomka; Graham; Horne; Kent; Stone) emphasize the role of actual mobility, anticipated mobility, and overall land-use pattern, as well as technological, sociocultural, and ideological factors, in occupational and locational stability, and, by implication, abandonment periodicity. Archaeological case studies of regional abandonment (i.e. Schlanger and Wilshusen; Fish and Fish; Lillios) focus on the effects of environmental and technological factors and broad sociocultural dynamics on regional occupational stability. In the case of within-site abandonment processes, the ethnoarchaeological case studies (i.e. Rothschild *et al.*; Joyce and Johannessen) deal with the complex interactions between various abandonment processes and their effects on archaeological material patterning. The archaeological case studies (i.e. Montgomery; Lightfoot; Brooks) are concerned primarily with the development and refinement of measures and criteria for the identification of abandonment processes and abandonment conditions in the archaeological record.

Overall, these papers build upon and extend our previous understanding of abandonment processes (Lange and Rydberg 1972; Schiffer 1987; Stevenson 1982). The blend of regional scale and site-specific investigations strengthens the conclusion that site abandonment processes can be understood only in their broad regional and sociocultural context. The presence of ethnoarchaeological, ethnographic, and ethnohistorical studies side by side with archaeological analyses offers yet another example of the positive complementarity of these subdisciplines of anthropological archaeology.

The papers in this volume represent theoretical and methodological contributions to the study of abandonment processes. The highly refined dendrochronological sequences developed in the American Southwest aid the investigation and identification of abandonment processes in archaeological contexts. However, the greater resolution afforded by this type of data should not be viewed as a luxury for the benefit of southwestern archaeologists alone. The finer resolution achieved through greater temporal control allows a more thorough evaluation of the fit between theory and prehistoric dynamics. Herein lies the theoretical contribution of the papers in the volume, in that only through the comparison of theoretical constructs with data can we define inconsistencies in our perceptions of how different elements of cultural systems are organized and interact to generate the archaeological patterns observed. In addition, the methodological issues raised, and analytical solutions provided, by some of the more technical papers in the volume constitute important contributions to the identification and investigation of abandonment processes in general. The refined analytical procedures and techniques discussed in some papers should be relevant to archaeologists concerned with the identification of abandonment processes worldwide.

General comments

Because previous ethnoarchaeological studies have focused on cases of planned and/or rapid site abandonment without anticipated return (Lange and Rydberg 1972) or with low probability of return (Stevenson 1982), it has been natural to view abandonment as a distinct period and final episode (i.e. permanent abandonment) in the occupation history of a site. Within the context of these studies of abandonment, the contributions to the volume shift the focus away from catastrophic and rapid abandonment and toward instances of planned abandonment with anticipated return. The decision to incorporate such a broad array of abandonment types in this volume, instead of limiting the case studies to examples of permanent abandonment argues in favor of viewing abandonment as a site formation *process* rather than as a single isolable event in the occupation history of a site.

These examples clearly demonstrate that the rapid, single-event, permanent abandonment of features or sites without future reuse or reoccupation appears to occur only under relatively unique conditions (e.g. catastrophic abandonment). Even in the case of highly mobile foragers such as the Efe (Fisher 1989), the potential exists that abandoned sites will be revisited to retrieve artifacts cached for future use. In the context of some semi-sedentary adaptations (e.g. Plains bison hunters, cf. Brooks; Graham; Horne; Tomka, all this volume; Binford 1982), some form or degree of seasonal abandonment is incorporated into land-use strategies. In these instances, the abandonment of features, structures, and sites is gradual, often spanning years prior to culminating in permanent abandonment. This gradual planned abandonment reflects the adjustments made by individual households or entire communities to fluctuations in economic, demographic, ecologic, or regional sociocultural conditions. While site abandonment under these conditions is not permanent, formation processes in the context of seasonal or extended abandonment have just as fundamental an effect on artifact assemblages as permanent abandonment.

It follows from the above that the operation of abandonment processes and their effects upon artifact assemblages and architectural features does not end with the termination of continuous occupation of a site. This lack of finality is most notable at the intra-site level where features and structures are constantly modified, rebuilt, reused, and reoccupied (e.g. Rothschild *et al.* this volume; Cameron 1991). However, it is also recognized at the regional level where sites are seasonally abandoned and reoccupied for the same or different uses (e.g. Graham; Horne), or abandoned for extended periods only to be reoccupied when circumstances permit (e.g. Tomka). Abandoned structures (cf. Joyce and Johannessen), and entire abandoned settlements (cf. Rothschild *et al.*) are periodically, if not habitually, depleted of resources to meet needs and concerns at other locations. As exemplified by a number of papers (e.g. Graham; Joyce and Johannessen; Tomka), the size and composition of the archaeological record at some sites are often conditioned by the needs of people at subsequent sites.

Overall, based on the common theme of many of the papers in the volume, we can reasonably conclude that intra-site and regional abandonments are cultural adaptive responses to sociocultural, technological, and environmental circumstances. What are the specific factors that initiate site and regional abandonment and condition the actual circumstances of abandonment? In foraging resource procurement systems abandonment is a normal and often necessary element of the land-use pattern and may be conditioned by factors related to resource structure, abundance, and degree of seasonality (Binford 1980; Heffley 1981; Kelly 1983). Given the little energy invested in the construction and maintenance of facilities and features (Kent and Vierich 1989), and the general lack of social mechanisms to maintain large aggregated populations together, residential mobility, and consequently site abandonment, is high. In semi-sedentary contexts some sites are occupied on a seasonal basis while others are occupied year-round. Their locational and occupational stability depends on both sociocultural and environmental circumstances. Site abandonment is less likely under labor-expensive adaptive or productive systems associated with fully sedentary systems (cf. Horne). While under these circumstances the abandonment of an entire site may occur less often, the differential abandonment of portions of a site is more likely (cf. Schlanger and Wilshusen; Lightfoot). The abandonment and subsequent reuse of structures may be due to limitations imposed by architectural design and materials employed (e.g. Schlanger and Wilshusen; Brooks), or household-level dynamics (e.g. Rothschild *et al.*). The abandonment of entire sites may be precipitated by system-level factors such as warfare, climatic degradation, and the failure of the existing sociocultural and perhaps even ideological mechanisms to maintain population aggregates intact (e.g. Lillios), or conversely, the presence of population aggregates capable of intensified production in regions that experienced social or environmental stress (e.g. Fish and Fish).

Continuing issues and future concerns

The papers in this volume have amply demonstrated the complexity of abandonment behaviors and the effects of abandonment processes on site contents. We have taken some important steps toward contextualizing abandonment processes and understanding some of the factors conditioning their variability. However, more basic questions remain. Are there any differences between abandonment processes noted in residentially mobile versus sedentary contexts? What are the principles underlying the operation of specific abandonment processes? What are the relationships between the conditions of abandonment (be they rapid/unplanned, or planned with anticipated return) and the causes of abandonment?

These papers highlight various formation processes responsible for conditioning artifact assemblages at the time of and following abandonment. Artifact scavenging, collecting, and recycling appear to have a strong impact at the intra-site level and in contexts where the entire settlement is not abandoned at the same time (cf. Lightfoot; Montgomery; Schlanger and Wilshusen). Although these processes may also occur among residentially mobile hunter-gatherers (e.g. following the fissioning of individual families from a camp), they appear to have a lower incidence than among sedentary aggregated populations. Curation and delayed curation appear to be significant mechanisms in site abandonments associated with short-distance moves or where site abandonment and reoccupation are significant elements of the land-use pattern. Are these differences really the product of dissimilarities in the organization of the land-use systems or are they primarily products of definition? Are the principles underlying scavenging, collecting, and curation really different? If these processes are distinct and are the products of systems level organizational differences, can they be used as diagnostics of land-use patterns? In order for each of these formation processes to be useful in archaeological contexts we need to continue defining the factors conditioning their operation.

Although the examples in this volume have begun to contextualize abandonment processes one of our challenges for the future is systematically to relate the manner in which particular resource acquisition patterns articulate with sequences of site abandonment and reoccupation. Given that abandonment is a basic element of residentially mobile land-use systems, some of the potential linkages between causes of site abandonment and material patternings are being developed in the hunter-gatherer literature dealing with mobility. Although it would be tempting to see abandonment as driven purely by ecological factors, the system does not operate in a cultural vacuum. Cultural mechanisms responsible for channeling the energy input and maintaining the structure of society also need to be considered (e.g. Stone; Horne; Fish and Fish; Lillios). This suggests that, given a particular environmental milieu, as social complexity increases the explanation of site and regional abandonment becomes more embedded in the sociocultural and even ideological matrices.

While there is a relationship between the causes of abandonment and abandonment conditions, it is important to remember that a number of causes may generate similar abandonment conditions. This is why, although the identification of the conditions of abandonment is crucial, it does not represent the explanation of the causes of abandonment. How do we proceed from the detailed material correlates reflecting abandonment processes and circumstances to the sociocultural explanatory level? To a large extent the linkages between the ultimate explanations and the material patternings noted in archaeological sites are not yet available and are in need of development.

Abandonment studies for their own sake are likely to be ultimately unrewarding and perhaps even misleading if we do not use our knowledge to address larger cultural or theoretical questions. Archaeologists should be concerned not so much with abandonment processes *per se*, but with what percentage of the behaviors associated with site abandonment contribute to the composition and relationships between material remains at specific locations. Much of what archaeologists refer to as site structure may, in fact, be the result of activities that occurred during the later stages and abandonment phases of occupation (Stevenson 1985, 1991). Moreover, these activities may be associated with behaviors that have little or nothing to do with the social and economic needs of the occupants during earlier stages of occupation. Such realizations may be potentially useful (see below).

A number of examples can serve to illustrate briefly how we might begin to put some of our knowledge of abandonment processes to work. These examples are intended not to point the way, but to suggest several of the many directions in which abandonment studies might proceed.

Among the historic Cumberland Sound Inuit of Baffin Island, Northwest Territories, Canada, differential wealth resulted in differential mobility. Not only were the poorer Inuit by definition more materially impoverished than the wealthier Inuit, but they were more socially disenfranchised. In other words, the poorer Inuit did not have the social network of relatives that the wealthier Inuit did. The socially and materially disenfranchised of Cumberland Sound were in consequence more mobile because they were constantly trying to better their material and social situations by creating and activating socioeconomic ties with related and unrelated individuals in a number of different camps.

Can we differentiate between the wealthy and the poor in terms of abandonment behavior and the archaeological record? Moreover, would it be meaningful to do so? As regards the first question, socially and materially impoverished Inuit almost always located their dwellings on the periphery of camps. Conversely, the wealthier, more residentially stable Inuit built their houses in the center of camps. Excavation of both types of features may allow us to conclude that differences in wealth condition abandonment behavior. But beyond the construction of another cautionary tale, would this be a significant conclusion?

It would, if we recognize that Central Inuit society possesses a structural dynamic, which is expressed in the kinship system, that allows Inuit social formations to fluctuate between egalitarian and hierarchical tendencies. Documentation of differential abandonment behaviors associated with each group in the historic context may allow us better to interpret prehistoric settlements with respect to these tendencies, better to understand the evolutionary trajectories and developmental cycles of Inuit groups in specific locations. Herein lies the potential contribution of our knowledge of differential status and abandonment behaviors to the social history of Central Inuit groups.

The following two examples are based on the assumptions that, among mobile hunters: (1) a large percentage of site structure may be the result of activities that occurred during late and abandonment phases of occupation; (2) these activities may be associated with behaviors quite different from those which occurred during earlier occupational periods.

Among northern foragers, resource depletion or stress is a common occurrence during late periods of occupation. In fact, it is often cited as the primary cause for moving camp. In such contexts, the kinds and/or quantities of resources harvested during earlier and later occupation periods will probably differ, with the larger, more desirable, more easily procured resources being harvested first. Studies of resource utilization, using for example faunal assemblages, may be misleading if these factors are not taken into consideration.

Resource stress in northern hunting societies can also frequently result in social tension, particularly in the domestic sphere between the sexes. In fact, resource-induced gender stress appears to be adaptive amongst northern foragers in that it promotes male mobility. Yet, since a significant percentage of site structure in such contexts may be the result of later periods of occupation, the archaeological record of such camps may inadvertently preserve artifact patterns and associations which, over the span of occupation, may be atypical of gender relations as a whole. A theory on the evolution of gender relations in hunting societies remains to be developed. However, if archaeological data are going to be used to this end, we must surely take into account the above considerations.

In summary, this volume is a significant contribution to the study of abandonment processes. It helps reshape our perspective of abandonment processes and increases our understanding of the role these processes play in conditioning the archaeological record. It is clear that future abandonment studies need to combine the study of proximate causes of abandonment with a clear and systematic understanding of the sociocultural and environmental matrices conditioning intra-site and regional abandonment.

References

Binford, L. R.
   1980 Willow Smoke and Dogs' Tails: Hunter-Gatherer Settlement and Archaeological Site Formation. *American Antiquity* 45:4–20.
   1981 Behavioral Archaeology and the "Pompeii Premise." *Journal of Anthropological Research* 37:195–208.
   1982 The Archaeology of Place. *Journal of Anthropological Archaeology* 1:5–31.
Cameron, C. M.
   1991 Structure Abandonment in Villages. In *Archaeological Method and Theory*, edited by M. B. Schiffer, Vol. III, pp. 155–94. University of Arizona Press, Tucson.
Fisher, J. W.
   1989 Links in the Lives of Hunter-Gatherers: Archaeological Implications among Efe Pygmies. Paper presented at the annual meeting of the Society for American Archaeology, Atlanta.
Heffley, S.
   1981 The Relationship Between Northern Athapaskan Settlement Patterns and Resource Distribution: An Application of Horn's Model. In

Hunter-Gatherer Foraging Strategies: Ethnographic and Archaeological Analyses, edited by B. Winterhalder and E. A. Smith, pp. 126–47. University of Chicago Press, Chicago.

Kelly, R. L.
1983 Hunter-Gatherer Mobility Strategies. *Journal of Anthropological Research* 39:277–306.

Kent, S. and H. Vierich
1989 The Myth of Ecological Determinism: Anticipated Mobility and Site Organization of Space. In *Farmers as Hunters: The implications of sedentism*, edited by S. Kent, pp. 96–133. Cambridge University Press, Cambridge.

Lange, F. W. and C. R. Rydberg
1972 Abandonment and Post-Abandonment Behavior at a Rural Central American House Site. *American Antiquity* 37:419–32.

Schiffer, M. B.
1983 Toward the Identification of Formation Processes. *American Antiquity* 48:675–706.

1985 Is There a "Pompeii Premise" in Archaeology? *Journal of Anthropological Research* 41:18–41.

1987 *Formation Processes of the Archaeological Record*. University of New Mexico Press, Albuquerque.

Stevenson, M. G.
1982 Toward an Understanding of Site Abandonment Behavior: Evidence from Historic Mining Camps in the Southwest Yukon. *Journal of Anthropological Archaeology* 1:237–65.

1985 The Formation of Artifact Assemblages at Workshop/Habitation Sites: Models from Peace Point in Northern Alberta. *American Antiquity* 50:63–81.

1991 Beyond the Formation of Hearth-Associated Artifact Assemblages. In *The Interpretation of Archaeological Spatial Patterning*, edited by E. M. Kroll and T. D. Price, pp. 269–99. Plenum Press, New York.

Index